Paul Reizin is a former TV producer and now full-time writer. He has written three novels, *Dumping Hilary?*, *Don't Try This At Home* and *Fiends Reunited*. He is married and lives in London.

D1137195

DATE
EXPECTATIONS

One Man's Voyage Through the Lonely Hearts

Paul Reizin

BANTAM BOOKS

LONDON • TORONTO • SYDNEY • AUCKLAND • JOHANNESBURG

DATE EXPECTATIONS
A BANTAM BOOK : 0 553 81638 1

9780553816389

Originally published in Great Britain by Bantam Press
a division of Transworld Publishers

PRINTING HISTORY
Bantam Press edition published 2005
Bantam edition published 2006

1 3 5 7 9 10 8 6 4 2

Set in 11.5/15pt Berling by
Falcon Oast Graphic Art Ltd.

Bantam Books are published by Transworld Publishers,
61–63 Uxbridge Road, London W5 5SA,
a division of The Random House Group Ltd,
in Australia by Random House Australia (Pty) Ltd,
20 Alfred Street, Milsons Point, Sydney, NSW 2061, Australia,
in New Zealand by Random House New Zealand Ltd,
18 Poland Road, Glenfield, Auckland 10, New Zealand
and in South Africa by Random House (Pty) Ltd,
Isle of Houghton, Corner Boundary Road & Carse O'Gowrie,
Houghton 2198, South Africa.

Printed and bound in Great Britain by
Cox & Wyman Ltd, Reading, Berkshire.

Papers used by Transworld Publishers are natural, recyclable
products made from wood grown in sustainable forests. The
manufacturing processes conform to the environmental
regulations of the country of origin.

For
R and R

Acknowledgements

Grateful thanks to my agent Clare Alexander and Doug Young at Transworld for believing there could be a book in it; to Tony Moss for improving on the original title; and of course to all the other lonely hearts encountered along the way.

Prologue

ON TUESDAY 30 APRIL 2002, I set out on my last blind date. It wasn't to Browns in St Martin's Lane that I headed. Or Café Rouge. Or any of my usual haunts. The venue on this occasion was the Royal Free Hospital in Hampstead.

Once again I was going to meet a girl. A girl to whom I'd already spoken several times, but had never seen in the flesh. I had a photo, a fuzzy image taken some while ago, which frankly raised more questions than it answered.

By now I was an expert on the etiquette and protocol of coming face to face with a stranger. I felt certain there would be no embarrassing small talk; no awkward little silences. Actually, I had a strong feeling that if all went well, I would fall for her on the spot. Nevertheless, I was more nervous this evening than on any I could remember.

She wasn't a fashionable ten minutes late. It turned out to be more like four days. Finally, shortly after eight pm, to musical accompaniment from Capital Gold – Barry White, 'You See The Trouble With Me', if I recall – Rachel Phoebe was skilfully brought into the world.

Minutes later, we looked into each other's eyes for the first time.

This book is the story of what led up to that moment.

1

I AM EARLY. I'M early for everything. It comes from a morbid fear of being late. Which itself flows from a pathological dread of being left behind.

Any further back, to the infantile trauma that may lie at the root of it all, there is only darkness.

She will be late. Women are allowed to be. Are supposed to give it a fashionable five, ten minutes before making an entrance. By the time she comes sashaying into the bar, I shall be comfortably in position, easy to identify in my midnight-blue Paul Smith suit, black roll-neck, and copy of *The God of Small Things*. She won't need to dither helplessly; she'll be able to swing right up to me, smile, deploy a slim hand for me to shake, and agree that if I am Paul, then she is Miriam. (I've thought this through, you can tell.)

But I am early.

Really horribly early. Twenty minutes, probably. With her ten-minute margin on top, we're talking half an hour of standing around getting nervous. I already feel uneasy about picking this place, the Library Bar at the Lanesborough Hotel on Hyde Park Corner. Now that I'm here, it seems far too grand, far too corporate for our purposes. I'd recently read something about the head barman being a cocktail star and the Martinis being world class. The name came right off the top of my head when she'd asked if I knew anywhere in town where we could meet.

Her voice, sexy and breathy on the telephone. I'd fallen for it instantly. Even when she revealed that she was a data analyst, I wasn't put off. I pictured glasses, creamy white blouse, layers of shiny dark hair falling against one another. I imagined her working late at the office, a pool of light cast by a desk lamp; head full of algorithms, the heart that yearned for romance . . .

'You're a boffin!' I cried, when she told me she'd studied Pure Mathematics at university.

'Not really.' A breathy resonance. Never had the words *not really* sounded more beguiling.

'Bloody hell, though. *Algebra.*' There was something powerfully attractive to me about a girl who was good at algebra. 'Do they still call it algebra?'

'I believe so.'

'We did something called vectors at school. Do they still have vectors, or have they been abolished?'

She giggled. 'My work's more statistical . . .'

'The only statistic I remember is that on average 75 per cent of all adults, broken down by age and sex, say they have difficulty getting out of bed in the morning. The remaining 25 per cent were broken down by alcohol.'

She laughed like it was the first time she'd ever heard it.

'I read something the other day,' she offered when

12

the hilarity had worn off. 'Ninety-six per cent of all documents that are filed are never looked at again.'

'Is that true?'

'It's quite sad in a way.'

'Is it? I suppose it is. Hard to feel sorry for documents, if you know what I mean.'

'All that effort. And time.'

'The futility of existence.' It was a long shot, but I thought I'd chuck it in.

'I do sometimes wonder what the point of it all is.'

'Do you? Do you really? How funny . . .'

This was marvellous. These were my sentiments exactly: what *was* the point of anything at all in the face of an uncaring cosmos? We seemed to be getting on famously, me and the mathematician. It was easily the sparkiest conversation I'd had since I finally plucked up the courage and began leaving replies for the lonely hearts whose ads I'd circled in the paper. I used to listen to their haunting voice messages on the phone before hanging up guiltily. It felt a little like eavesdropping on private pain.

'Isn't it a bit . . . desperate?' said Angela, one of my oldest friends, when I told her about Miriam.

There. Someone had uttered it. The d-word.

I'll tell you what's desperate, I replied. Desperate is leaving it to chance; desperate is continuing to drift through one's forties, hoping somehow to find a mate when one doesn't meet anyone new – never mind suitable – for months on end. Desperate is joining the book group or signing up for wine-appreciation classes – not for the Julian Barnes or the Chateau d'Yquem, but on the microscopically small off-chance of copping off with a kindred soul (Angela had done both). Desperate is hauling oneself off to yet another dinner to endure yet another bungled attempt at matchmaking. The latest had been Sally.

'You must meet Sally,' Angela had told me. 'She's an absolute riot. I'll have a dinner.'

Sally jabbered, smoked like a train and had a worrying laugh. She was a riot only in the sense that one wished to suppress her brutally with water cannon.

'So you didn't like Sally. The laugh is problematic, I agree.'

'There's no hyena in her family, is there?'

'Oh, don't be horrid. She's lovely really. Anyway, you want to be careful replying to adverts. You could meet a madwoman.'

'Really? You think so?' Men are actually rather attracted to madwomen (it's the suggestion that they could be mad in bed). However, I did agree that I needed to be careful who I dated. My conversation with Celia the social worker was a case in point.

Celia (professional, late thirties) sounded depressed. Her answer to my question, 'So what sort of people do you tend to deal with, then?' ran for a good five minutes, and left me feeling considerably glummer about life than before I'd asked it. Her reply to my next inquiry – 'What do you do for fun?' – was no more uplifting, unless you believe sewing quilts and gardening are the answer to everything. I'd fired a little Chinese philosophy back at her when she mentioned the gardening thing.

'Confucius said if you want to be happy for an hour, get drunk. If you want to be happy for a year, get married. If you want to be happy for life, get a garden.'

There was a long pause.

'Have *you* ever been married?' she asked.

'No, I haven't, not as such. Not at all, actually. Not even nearly.'

I was trying to be light and frivolous, but I had a feeling I knew what was coming next.

'I was married very young,' she said. 'Much too young. I have a daughter.'

'Really? That's . . . that must be nice for you.'

'It is, we're very close. Nerys lives with me. She's in her second year at uni now.'

'Golly.'

'Actually, I'm a little older than I put in my ad. I'm forty-four.'

My age.

'If you're a woman and you say you're in your mid forties, it puts some men off. Men who might want children.'

'I see.'

A pause. 'Do you want children, then?'

Well? Do I?

'I . . . I *suppose* so. Theoretically, I do, yes.' One of those nice quiet children. Who gets on with its Mr Men book. Who doesn't crayon all over my groovy yellow Conran sofa.

'I wish you luck with your search.'

'Thank you.'

'I'm probably too old for you.'

'Ooh, I er. It's. Well. You know.'

I pictured the gloomy garden flat (Highbury, she'd said). The stripped-pine furniture and quilts everywhere. The careworn mother. The lissom daughter wafting about. The all-pervading top note of cat pee (odd, because no cats had been mentioned).

She was right; it wasn't for me. And it had been decent of Celia to bow out.

But Miriam is mid thirties, lives in Chiswick. Likes reading, films, plays. Going out with friends. Occasional trips to the countryside. On the telephone she sounds like the bastard lovechild of Marilyn Monroe and Albert Einstein.

What's not to like?

I order a world-class vodka Martini and wait.

Mild nausea stirs in the pit of my stomach as a number of thoughts do laps round my skull: What the fuck am I doing here? I feel completely out of place in this smartypants bar. It must surely be obvious that I don't belong, despite the posh suit and the nonchalant way my newly shined shoe rests on the brass rail. The other people here, smart couples, groups of businessmen, they all look so assured, so . . . so grown-up. I bet the first encounter with their other halves wasn't like some spy drama in wartime Prague ('a tall balding man in a blue suit will be at the bar. He will be carrying a copy of *The God of Small Things*'). I bet it happened how it's supposed to: at work, at a dinner. A casual introduction from a friend of a friend. I wouldn't be at all surprised if he (the good-looking brute smoking the fat cigar) just walked up to her (the willowy blonde with the Chanel handbag) at a party and said *hello* in a certain insinuating way.

I tried it once myself. It was one of those great roiling thrashes that Angela used to throw, everyone slugging red wine out of plastic cups. The dialogue went like this:

ME: Hello.
HER: What?
ME [*bellowing above the noise*]: Hello!
HER: Oh. (*Pause.*) Hello.
ME: Do you know anyone here, then?
HER (*after a pause*): Sorry. I've just seen someone I know.

All relationships have to begin somewhere, however. Ralph, who I play tennis with, once told me how he met his partner. It wasn't in the lobby of the Danieli Hotel in Venice. Or the dining car of the Orient Express. It was the Islington branch of Marks and Spencer. He was standing at the checkout and found himself glancing into the basket of the woman in front of him. It contained, as he put it, 'a load of cakes, and sweets and crappy girly yoghurts and stuff'. There was obviously some sort of expression on his face, because when she noticed him staring at her shopping, her opening words were, 'What the fuck are *you* looking at?'

Ralph and Leanne now have two children together.

I was present when Caroline and Patrick set eyes on

17

one another for the first time. It was in the 1980s. We were all employed by the same company, though Caroline and Patrick worked in separate departments. One evening, they both appeared at the local wine bar where colleagues gathered to medicate their stress. I have never forgotten the moment when someone introduced tall, handsome Patrick to beautiful, glamorous Caroline. I swear the light in the room changed; the actual air molecules between them seemed to vibrate differently. It was like that chemistry experiment when you add thingy sulphate to whatnot carbonate and the whole shooting match goes whoosh up the test-tube because of some profound atomic rearrangement.

Patrick and Caroline have been together for fifteen years and have three children.

I used to think I knew the story of how my parents met. It was Rome, 1946. My mother, aged twenty-four, is standing outside a greengrocer's shop staring at a display of oranges. After six years of war, it's been a long time since she's seen an orange. My father, then thirty-six, comes sauntering along, stops, and offers to buy her one. They fall in love and travel to England. In the fullness of time, I am born.

I like this story, because it seems to contain a truth about the chaos and randomness of the human condition. I also like it because for some reason I think of myself as the pip in that orange. Until my late thirties I used to purvey this account to friends as an accurate summary of how I came to be here.

But it isn't true.

When I offered this version of our family history to

18

my mother some years ago, she told me that, excepting for one detail, it was completely fictitious. She couldn't imagine how I had come by the scenario. (And nor, in truth, could I. I can only conclude that I dreamt it.)

The real story is this: Rome 1946. My father is standing in a bus queue when he hears Polish being spoken. Some men are having a political discussion, and he joins in. After a few moments, a young woman in the bus queue addresses my father in Polish. She'd 'admired the way he talked' apparently, with his characteristic intelligence and passion. She invites him back to where she is lodging with her mother and two younger sisters, the youngest of whom he falls in love with. They come to England. In the fullness of time I am born.

I have wondered recently why I invented the story with the oranges. Why I liked it so much that I allowed it to go unchallenged for so long.

Was it so satisfying because it spoke of the re-demptive power of love after the horrors of war? Was it because I had orange hair as a child? Is there something life-enhancing about citrus fruit?

Is it, in fact, for all these reasons, and one more? That it's a better story than the boring old truth. A more magical one.

Like a blind date without the arrangements.

London, 1999. I am waiting to meet Miriam. I found Miriam in the Soul Mates pages of the *Guardian*. She was there in a long list of other 'Women Seeking Men'.

Attractive professional F, slim, mid thirties, WLTM sympathetic professional M with GSOH.

'Never bother with anyone who doesn't use the word attractive,' advised my friend Toby. 'Indicates low self-esteem. Probably justified.'

Toby had once 'done' the lonely hearts. Like everything else he turned his hand to, his trawl was exhaustive. Even if he hadn't discovered the love of his life, he had at least gone out with several 'bloody good sports'.

'I've been through all this malarkey,' he told me. 'It's like learning a foreign language. You just have to get hold of the phrase book. I'll be your phrase book until you get the hang of it. Use me as a resource.'

Toby speaks like this because he sees himself as a can-do sort of personality. He used to work in corporate finance until he was downsized. Now he's 'juggling'.

'If she doesn't say she's attractive, she'll be a hound. Probably have two heads. Three, quite possibly. And don't bother with anyone who claims to be *bubbly*. It means insane. Or fat. Personally, I could never go out with anyone who says *thee-etter* instead of theatre. You'll have your own prejudices, I expect.'

Toby stopped doing the lonely hearts when he started going out with the woman who lived in the flat across the road from him. One evening he watched as she tried to kill a wasp on the inside of her sitting-room window. This is just the sort of thing Toby is excellent at. When he saw she was getting nowhere, he performed a mime at his own window, offering to help.

Angela and I think he and Wasp Woman may get married.

Miriam had not only specifically employed the a-word, she'd kicked off her advert with it. Bubbly had not shown up on the roster of blacklisted vocabulary. I'm fairly certain she even pronounced theatre in a way that Toby would have approved of. After our conversation, I had a clear picture of her in my head, even down to the brown glasses she wore that I felt denoted a shy, yet sexy and playful quality behind the intelligence.

But as I wait for Miriam to arrive, I feel nervy and out of sorts. My life is full of firsts at the moment. A few weeks ago, I broke a tooth on a bread roll for the first time. Only last week, a card came through the post advising me of the passing of someone I used to know very well, 'after a brave and cheerful struggle'. Sue couldn't have been older than me.

And now my first blind date.

A woman has materialized at my side. In an instant I know that this evening is going to be a disaster. Is already a disaster.

It's Miriam – no question about that – she's mid thirties, five eight, slim build and everything, but she's definitely not the Miriam I'd been waiting for. This Miriam has one of the strangest faces I've ever come across. The phrase that arcs across my brain is *Easter Island statue*. It's a long, almost ferocious countenance that meets mine. High forehead (an estate agent might call it double-height). Thick, dark eyebrows. There are ears, really quite prominent ears, poking through straight dark hair in a most uncompromising manner. Her mouth seems awkwardly over-large; not in a sensual, vulnerable way but in an awkwardly over-large way. The eyes are brown, as advertised – yes, I'll give them that – but they lurk behind lenses that do not speak of a shy, sexy, perhaps playful intelligence. These lenses speak of an owner who is very, *very* short-sighted. All my nerves dissolve. I struggle to keep the disappointment off my face.

'Paul?'

'Miriam!'

'Sorry. Am I very late?' Only the voice, the breathy squeal, is unchanged from the mental picture, much too sweet for the solemn, not to say scary features from which it emerges. Juxtaposed against the granite-carved visage, the contrast is surreal. She sounds like she's been dubbed.

'Not at all. Would you like a drink?'

'Oh dear. I thought I was going to be terribly late. The Victoria Line . . .'

'Not at all. Don't worry about it.'

The barman shimmers up before us, eyebrows cocked. 'Good evening, madam.' It crosses my mind that perhaps he knows her. 'What would you care for this evening?'

I watch her face as she studies the drinks list, still flushed from whatever drama the Victoria Line has inflicted. *Maori warrior princess*, I'm thinking. A Maori warrior princess trapped inside the grey skirt and jacket of a London office-worker. Or Aztec fright mask. Something a bit fish-like, too. This was a face you'd see in your sleep. In a coma, quite possibly.

'Could I have a ginger beer?' she asks.

The barman doesn't flinch. Permits himself a discreet nod of the head. A weariness descends on me as I indicate that yes, I will have the same again.

'So,' she gushes. 'Here we are.'

You know how some faces look better when they're sad, or in repose – asleep even – than when they're lit by some happy emotion? I think that could be the case here. The big smile she fires up is undoubtedly sincere. Yet there is something anxiety-inducing about its uncurbed enthusiasm.

'Here we are, all right,' I echo.

Damn it. She beams at me again, like I've just dropped the bonniest bon mot she's heard in a long while. A huge face-splitting grin which doesn't suit her at all. Her eyes do something blinky behind the powerful specs. Then she sighs heavily, exhaling into my face. Her breath smells of peppermint with a hint of green olive.

'I don't really know how to do this,' she says.

It's an absurdly frank admission. By *this*, I take it she means the whole blind-date thing. The whole artifice of the occasion – or do I mean *absence* of artifice? Normally when a man and a woman talk in a bar, they haven't specifically travelled there to discover whether or not they fancy one another. It may be that they do, or do not – and they do or do not act accordingly – but nothing is unspoken about the actual encounter. Here, our meeting seems circumscribed by the invisible infra-structure of the occasion. We Both Know Why We Are

23

Here. In truth, it occurs to me, I don't know how to do *this* either.

'I think you just say the first thing that comes into your head.'

The world-class Martini has started to earn its purchase price. I can feel the cold vodka slipping into the co-pilot's seat alongside me. I am pleasantly losing sensation in that part of my brain that deals with embarrassment. If I don't fancy this woman – and I don't – there'll be no need to try and impress her. I can relax.

She sort of stares at me for a few seconds, like she's trying out a few things that might be passing through her head.

'So what do you actually do, then?' she asks.

'Sorry, I thought I'd said. I'm a producer.'

'I know you are. What I mean is, what does a producer actually *do*?'

Oh fuck. That old chestnut.

Briefly, I am tempted to give her a straight answer. The one about the producer being the bloke who brings together all the other talents and then attempts to manage them. I am tempted to quote Jackie Mason. His line about how everyone in New York says they're a producer: Here's my card, they say, I'm a producer. I'm a producer, here's my card. And that's all they produce – cards. But somehow I can't bring myself to do the accent – can't actually be bothered to try and make her laugh. I gaze for a long moment at her strange visage, each individual feature fine in itself, but all put together . . . well, for me, it just doesn't work, as we say in the TV biz. A configuration, you might say, that's been badly produced.

My heart sinks. What the fuck *am* I doing here?

But then my second Martini arrives.

'Did you get many replies to your ad?' I inquire, changing the subject. *Attractive*, she'd written. Strictly speaking, she wasn't *un*attractive. Just weird looking. *Well* weird.

'About thirty,' she replies.

'Really?' So many? 'So how many chaps have you seen?'

'None. One. Well, you actually.' Heavy sigh. 'You're the first.'

And then she blushes.

Oh great. Oh, just fucking great. Two blind-date virgins.

If anything was ever pointless, this surely was it.

I must be a fast learner. It's only my first blind date, but already I've absorbed Lesson One.

LESSON ONE:
The telephone is like radio.
The pictures are better.

As Miriam tells me about the building work she's having done at her flat in Chiswick – and I chuckle knowingly about the perfidy of the men in white vans – I marvel at the contrast between the mental picture I had developed based on her voice alone and the remarkable female actuality that sits before me now.

We've found ourselves a quiet pair of armchairs opposite a pillar. She's gobbling the world-class complimentary nuts – I am fascinated at the way they vanish between her powerful jaws – and relating a fairly dull tale about a trip to a specialist bathroom-tile outlet with her friend Jonathan. The point of the story seems to be that if you have a small bathroom, you can make it feel bigger by using really big tiles – or is it really small ones? Anyhow Jonathan, who had recently renovated his own bathroom, had firm and specific views on the topic. However, once they reached the outlet, which for some reason was located in Croydon, and with Jonathan's help she had selected some very expensive limestone tiles, there followed a major disagreement between Jonathan and an employee of the outlet over their suitability for a confined space.

'Jonathan got terribly heated, because he studied the subject.'

'Bathroom tiles?'

'Art and design. At one point he started talking to this man in Italian.'

'Excitable, is he?'

'I think the tile man took against him when he started on about Renaissance architecture. In Croydon. On a Saturday afternoon. It was all rather embarrassing.'

Miriam mashes several cashews into her open maw with the palm of her hand. As she continues with the story, I allow my eyes to sink beneath the surface of my Martini, and summon to mind the woman that I'd *imagined* behind this voice. Oddly, that woman didn't have ears. Well, she did, but they weren't so defiantly in your face as these were. That woman's brown eyes contained a shy intelligence rather than a goggling myopia. That other woman's lips, though full and sensuous, did not look like they could take a hard-boiled egg in one. Sideways. That woman, in a nutshell, resembled Sandra Bullock. Or Renée Zellweger at a pinch. If this one resembles any sort of movie star, it's Harpo Marx.

'I think Jonathan was still upset by the argument, because that's when he went through the red light and the policeman pulled him over.'

Was it true, as the old proverb has it, that men fall in love through their eyes, women through their ears?

'He just totally lost it. Not with the policeman, with the steering wheel. He was slapping it and swearing. He actually went purple with anger.'

Other people's lives. They're so peculiar, aren't they? Not *odd* peculiar necessarily . . . *peculiar* peculiar. There's something of other people's farts about other people's lives. Something a bit warm and disgusting about the dreadful little details. The aesthete male friend. The cosy car trip to Croydon. What was he doing helping Miriam buy bathroom tiles in the first place? Who *was* Jonathan? An ex, maybe? And why such a hair-trigger? Was he one of those talented youths who have grown old and angry at the widening gap between their beautiful dreams and mundane reality? Was he perhaps on powerful medication? Why was I being told all this? What, above all, did any of it have to do with me?

'He was in quite a lot of pain. And it actually turned out he'd dislocated his finger when he bashed the wheel. We had to wait three hours in casualty.'

I laugh. Serve the pretentious little fucker right, is what I am thinking.

'I suppose it is quite funny really.'

She sighs. Peers at me through the queasy aquarium lenses.

'I mustn't keep going on about myself. What about you?'

I have a sudden vision of what's lurking in my fridge. Cold roast chicken and coleslaw. That's what I'd rather be doing right now. I'd rather be at home, eating cold roast chicken and coleslaw. And chips. The plate on my knee, watching – what am I missing for this? – the documentary on Channel Four about plane crashes. If you survive the impact, you have ninety seconds to escape the flames, it said in the TV preview.

'What about me?'

She thinks about it for a moment. 'When did you lose all your hair, for example?'

'I haven't lost *all* my hair,' I retort. 'There's still quite a lot left, actually.'

I'm pretending to be hurt by the clumsy phrase for ironic purposes. Underneath, however, I really am a bit hurt.

'You didn't mention it on the phone.'

'Didn't I?'

'You said six foot two, blue suit and—'

'*The God of Small Things*. Perhaps I thought it might have—'

'. . . it wouldn't have put me off.'

I was going to say it might have put *people* off.

'So when *did* it go?' she persists.

'It didn't just *go*, as you put it. There was no one moment. It happened imperceptibly slowly over the last twenty years.' Anyway, when did you wake up and discover you had a face like a haddock?

She sits staring at me. Perhaps my last reply came out a bit more sharply than I'd intended. In a consciously warmer tone I say, 'You know, I never think about it until someone reminds me. Is it a problem?'

'Oh no. Not at all. My dad was as bald as a coot – I loved him to bits,' she adds quickly.

The waiter approaches.

You should never drink more than two Martinis. It's more or less an internationally accepted principle. By rights, fish-face and I should shake hands, call it a goalless draw, and retire to our respective suburbs. But somehow this doesn't feel quite the right moment to conclude the proceedings.

'Well, I will if you will,' I find myself saying.

When did I first feel myself growing old?

I believe it was the night a couple of years ago when I was lying in bed unable to sleep because of a loud party going on in the flat upstairs. And by loud, I mean loud.

There had been no neighbourly word of warning. It actually began *after* I had retired for the evening. I lay listening in disbelief as what sounded like a dozen or so

29

people set about enjoying themselves with a breath-taking disregard for anyone in the flat below, viz, me. By three in the morning, in the way of evil parties, it had shrunk to the hard core. It was possible to make out individual voices, cackling and bellowing to be heard above the insanely loud music. I never previously had any feelings towards the lyrics of the tune 'Hi Ho Silver Lining', but after four plays in a row with full accompaniment, it seemed to me as loathsome as a Nazi marching song. By four, Marvyn Gaye's 'Sexual Healing' was booming through an otherwise quiet apartment. By five, all was silent.

I know what you're thinking. And at any time, of course, I could have picked up the phone and complained to my neighbours about their appalling racket. They might even have turned it down, who knows?

But here was the point: if I had, I would have crossed the line. I would automatically have become *one of those people who complain about loud parties*. The same sort of people who wear grey anoraks, visit garden centres, and worry that the country is being overrun by asylum-seekers. Who enjoy Andrew Lloyd Webber musicals, read *Reader's Digest* and believe in 'moderation in all things'. People who have never heard of Blake's observation that the road of excess leads to the palace of wisdom. In short, the enemy. If I'd made that call, I would have swapped sides; I'd have signed up with the forces of the embittered middle-aged against the spirit and exuberance of youth. Never mind that the revellers in question weren't much younger than me; psychologically, I would have grown carpet slippers and a button-up cardy and turned into Victor Meldrew.

So I didn't. I stewed alone in the darkness instead, dreaming of a thousand revenges to wreak on my selfish-bastard neighbours. And in the act of struggling to stay on the youthful side of the divide, I felt myself growing old.

I guess if one is going to grow old, it helps to have someone to grow old *with*. Angela and Toby and I have had plenty of wine-fuelled evenings debating this subject. Angela says she wants to turn into a mad old spinster who spits in the street and wears a lot of purple (except I don't believe her). Toby says it's a fact that men in couples live longer than single men, although single women tend to outlive married women. Keeping a pet improves longevity too, apparently. Warm blood is important here; dogs and cats are excellent, terrapins and goldfish less effective.

I doubt somehow that I shall be growing old with Miriam.

For some reason I am telling her why the third Martini is known as the Mona Lisa: it's because after three, you find you can't get this stupid smile off your face.

There is a long pause. I have the horrible feeling that I will actually have to explain the joke, when she says something fascinating about the Mona Lisa. She'd come across it in *Scientific American*: an explanation for why the woman's smile in the painting is so elusive. If you stare directly at her mouth, she says, her smile seems to disappear. But if you focus on the background, or a detail of her costume, it returns. The reason, she explains, is that human peripheral vision is more attuned to spatial qualities than central vision. In other words, the *smiliness* of the Mona Lisa's smile is better registered in a sidelong glance than full on.

Interesting, I reckon, that she should choose to tell a story about a woman's mouth. It occurs to me that perhaps some men might find Miriam's sexy and alluring, those big lips at the entrance to powerful jaws. Her ears, too; in truth they're perfectly pleasant ears, it's only their angle of rotation with respect to the vertical that is controversial – and again, maybe there are those who would see a charming vulnerability about them. Even her eyes contain nothing to give one nightmares, I realize, when she briefly removes her bottle-bottom specs. And now that her nose is no longer overshadowed by the optical apparatus, I notice that it's an ideal lady nose. Not so small as to be unviable. Not so large as to cause hilarity or despair.

The rest of her, in the grey business suit and pale blouse – something small and gold hanging against the marble skin of her throat – the rest of her seems well enough proportioned. OK, the legs that emerge from the skirt and lie at an angle against one another, perhaps they're a little thicker than one would prefer in an ideal world. But then I'm not exactly George Clooney myself.

'So tell me everything about you, then,' she says.

Sorry, but fuck me if a small thrill, emanating some- where in the small of my back, doesn't choose that moment to travel through my body.

'Everything would take too long. I could do a précis.'

She smiles. And for a shocking moment a kind of alien glamour cloaks her like a mist.

'Go on then.'

Something's happened. The unfortunate creature of ten minutes ago seems to have been replaced by a much more dazzling invention. The room too feels different. Like it's realigned itself somehow. Rather than the two of us folded into our self-enclosed huddle, now it feels as if our lines of force have exploded outwards, touching all the other people in the bar like those bolts of lightning in the final scene of *Raiders of the Lost Ark*, except no one here is screaming in agony as they shrivel to dust.

It's probably all to do with vectors.

'Do you think you could ask me questions?' I request weakly.

'Where were you born?' She doesn't even pause to think about it.

'London,' I snap right back. I name the year. 'Went to school in H——'

'Sorry. When did you say?'

'What?' *Oh fuck.*

'You're . . . how old?'

'Me?'

Do I dream it, or does she reach for a world-class nut, balance it on a thumbnail, flip it into the air like tossing a coin, and catch it expertly between her impressive mandibles?

'If I heard you correctly . . .'

Gulp. 'Yes . . .'

'You're forty-five.'

Sinking feeling. 'Forty-four.'

'Your birthday's coming up.'

'June.'

A deadly pause. Her eyes have stopped swivelling. Now they're locked on to a spot in the centre of my forehead, the most favourable locus for an assassin's bullet, I can't help thinking. An enigmatic smile roams the continent of her chops. Even if I looked sideways, it would still fill my vision.

'You were forty-two when we talked on the phone.'

'Really? Are you sure?'

'I remember these things.'

'You're a mathematician. There is another explanation, of course.'

'Yes?'

'That we've been sitting in this bar for two years.'

'Is that what it feels like?' An almond tumbles through space in slow motion. And then it is gone.

'Not at all. Listen. Do you think it's a dreadful lie?'

'Was it a lie?'

'More of a fib. A mis-statement.'

'Two years in forty-four. Within a margin of error of 5 per cent. I *suppose* that's acceptable.' Behind their grimy windows, the brown eyes twinkle. 'So are you really a producer, then?'

'Miriam.' I Miriam her for dramatic effect. 'Miriam. I'm sorry to say . . .' Heavy sigh. 'I really am.'

Not good. Getting caught in a lie on your maiden blind date. But what's that line in *The Tailor of Panama*?

Never tell the truth. It's the surest way of being found out.

Why did I lie? Why did I bother to lop a piddling two years from my forty-four? I guess the logic was this: forty-four is inescapably *mid forties*. We're talking trips to garden centres, complaining about the neighbours' noisy parties, the glass half empty. By contrast, forty-two is early forties, still connected to late thirties, and by association mid thirties. Still 'young' if not actually, technically, young. Anyhow, my friend Toby told me that everyone lies in the lonely hearts.

'Size ten always means size twelve. Size twelve means overweight. And if she says she's Rubenesque, don't offer her a lift home if you're worried about your suspension.'

According to him, my lie wasn't even a proper lie, more a kind of 'rounding down' of the figures.

'You'd be amazed how brazen they are. Mid thirties turns out to be forty. Late thirties can mean up to fifty. Oh, and they all say they like occasional trips to the country, which is so much bullshit. They say it to make themselves sound healthy.'

But Miriam isn't forty. Not unless she's aged exceptionally well. Her skin has that moist, springy quality. And I was wrong about the legs, incidentally. Now that I study them really closely – it's OK, I'm not staring, I had a good look when she got up to visit the ladies' – I see they're not thick. Not at all. They're not *thin*, I'm not saying that. There's just something pleasing about the way they strike the ground. It's by no means an ethereal glide; but nor is it a juddering stomp. It actually seems about equal – her weight under gravity bearing down against the return pressure of the spinning earth's centrifugal force (I think that's the arrangement, isn't it?). She's neither splintering the floorboards or floating off towards the light fittings. As she threads her way back across the carpet towards me, I find myself admiring the way she.

How she.

The fact that her.

Golly. These Martinis *are* strong. Definitely mustn't have another one.

I glance at my watch. Fuck, it's ten pm. How did it get so late already?

She drops into her seat, flings a curtain of brown hair behind one ear and detonates a bunker-busting smile across the nuts at me. I notice she's reapplied the lippy and given herself a fresh blast of fragrance.

'This is *fun*,' she declares.

Perhaps I'm wearing a bit of a stupid expression because she adds, 'Don't you think?'

'No, it is. I'm having a lovely time.'

I am, actually. What started out as a disastrous evening has changed its character completely. Fish-face has morphed into an exotic creature; I have a sudden vivid fantasy of the two of us falling on to a bed together. I'm holding on to her ears as we subside into the sheets. The huge lips peel back when the moment arrives . . .

'Do you know the bee joke?' I find myself asking her.

She shakes her head.

36

'It's a very curious joke, this. It doesn't technically have a punchline. And the world is divided into two classes of people: those who find it funny and those who do not.'

'Oh dear. Which will I be, do you think?'

'No way of knowing. Could go either way. You want to hear it?'

She nods. If a distant alarm bell is ringing in my head, I do not hear it.

'There's these two blokes, right. And one says to the other, What have you been up to, then? And the other replies, Me? Oh, nothing much. Well, actually, since you ask, I've been breeding bees . . .'

I am telling Miriam the bee joke. This must mean I am trying to seduce her. I'm fairly certain that I've told the bee joke to every woman I've slept with in the last twenty years at some point during the early stage of our courtship. It is for me, I've come to realize, a trigger joke: the urge to relate it is triggered by desire. Of course it's not that the bee joke is so funny that any woman who hears it will laugh like a drain and then struggle frantically from her underwear. Far from it. At least half those who hear the bee joke remain puzzled as to why it is considered a joke at all. In a sense that is the bee joke's enigmatic – even erotic – charm: will she, or won't she?

I suppose I must have been to bed with some women who didn't find the bee joke amusing, but I can't remember their names just at the moment.

It takes about two or three minutes; there are some nice little absurdities and amusing repetitions along the way, and Miriam is smiling appreciatively, wanting to find it funny. Close to the end, however, the waiter returns. Doesn't the silly fool realize I'm in the middle of a story? Before I know what's happened, I've performed the international hand signal for *Same again, matey, and you can bring the little lady some more nuts while you're about it*. I move towards the big finish. Or the bit where there should be a proper punchline, if that is your way of thinking. I swallow hard and deliver the killer words.

The smile freezes on her face. A sort of gurgling sound emerges from her throat.

'Is that it?'

'Yup. That's the bee joke.' That's the bee joke, all right.

Her disappointment is a little heartbreaking to witness. 'Oh. Well, I did enjoy the way you told it . . .'

'It's the ending, isn't it?'

'I'm sorry.'

'Don't be. There are three billion people on the planet who wouldn't find that joke funny.' On the other hand, there are three billion who would wet themselves.

'Do you know any others?'

'What, funny ones?' Loads. But none that possess the bee joke's unique quality. 'I used to think that I was a dog once. I did, honestly. Then I went to see a psychiatrist and he cured me. I'm quite all right now. Really, I am. Go on, feel my nose . . .'

Maybe she's a dog-lover. Maybe it's the laughter of relief. Maybe – the thought crosses my mind – she's laughing at me rather than with me. Anyhow, Miriam appears to find this sweet old gag indecently amusing. It's really quite a strange sight, the solemn icon that is her face, split asunder by mirth. I have another powerful surge of desire for the peculiar creature.

What was that quote? The one by Isaac Singer that I scribbled into my notebook the moment my eye fell across it. 'The pleasure he might receive from this woman's body would never be as strong as his lust for it.'

It had troubled me at the time. How could you ever know a thing like that? In comparing physical pleasure and lust, were you comparing like with like? Could the two concepts be measured sensibly in the same currency? If they could, did one lust unit equal one pleasure unit, or were we talking of an exchange rate? Say, ten units of lust to one unit of pleasure. And if they couldn't be directly compared, then were they at least related through some formula? Pleasure equals lust multiplied by anticipation divided by the square root of your collar size.

Perhaps it was too early in our relationship to bring this topic up with Miriam, although as a scientist, I would expect her to have definite views.

This woman's body. The phrase echoes through my head like a mantra. Would she mind if I held her ears during sex, I wonder? There is something powerfully insistent about the thought, and it might be a good idea to keep those jaws where you could see them.

Hmm.

I decide to move the conversation on to a philosophical plane.

* * *

The fourth Martini is definitely a bad mistake. Not that the third was any sort of great idea, clearly.

The fourth may be critically impairing my ability to communicate some important thoughts on the subject of love and happiness, although you wouldn't know it from Miriam's expression. As I expound my theory about modern man's absurdly high expectations in these areas, the Easter Island statue is as serious as I've known it.

'I mean, in the great scheme of things, does it honestly matter whether I find the right person to be happy with? Or whether you do? Whether any of us do.' I throw my arms open to include the population of the Library Bar in this. The fat fucker with the big cigar looks unfeasibly pleased with life, unfortunately. 'How could it possibly matter? There are so many bloody people everywhere. So many *lives*. Did you know there are more people alive today than have ever died? How can they all expect to find love? It's mad, isn't it? I mean, what's so special about any of us that we deserve happiness? In the olden days, they wouldn't have felt entitled to a happy life, would they? They would have been grateful to have food on their shoes. On their plate, I mean. Shoes on their feet. Merely to avoid pain would have been sufficient. And in a hundred years we're all dead, anyway. Sooner, probably. And, by the way, what *is* happiness? *A dog sunning itself on a rock.* I read that somewhere. Rather good, don't you think? Dog doesn't need another dog to do that.'

My theory is a version of the argument I advanced the other evening round at Angela's. As I made my case, Angela nodded and went hmm. She tends to agree with the last thing she's heard. Toby said I was talking bollocks.

'Just because according to you the universe is a cold and indifferent place doesn't mean I shouldn't have a good time,' he countered. 'In fact, it's a bloody good reason why I should.'

Angela nodded vigorously. 'Yeah,' she interpolated.

'The way I see it, smile and the world smiles with you,' he added gravely.

Miriam asks, 'Wouldn't you like to settle down one day? Have children, if that happened? It doesn't sound so unreasonable.'

Those dread words, *settling down*. There was a time when I couldn't hear them without a bell tolling. Settling was what happened to breakfast cereals during transit. Or old buildings. In Turgenev's *Fathers and Sons*, the hot-headed hero Bazarov has been to visit his parents in the country. As they wave him off at the garden gate, he thinks of them – heartbreaking image – as two old funguses grown round the bottom of a tree.

I peer into Miriam's face. 'Why? Would you?'

'With the right person . . .'

'But that's my *point*!'

Am I shouting? Someone at the next table has looked round. The fat fucker. 'That's my point,' I hiss. 'There is this expectation that there *is* a right person. Somewhere Out There.'

'I do believe that. Yes.'

'Where were *you* born, then?' I don't know why I ask.

'Lima.'

'What, Lima, Chile?'

'Peru.'

'Of course. Yeah, Peru.'

'I'm quarter Peruvian, quarter Egyptian, quarter Irish, quarter English.'

'Fucking hell. I mean, blimey. I mean, that's quite some pedigree. Heritage, I mean.'

'My father was a diplomat. We travelled a lot when I was young. I grew up in Totteridge, though.'

Miriam's transformation is complete. She seems to me to be the most glamorous woman I have seen in ages; albeit a specialist, austere glamour as challenging as it is alluring. The Totteridge detail notwithstanding.

'Tell me everything about you, then,' I demand. About all your unsuitable boyfriends, not too many, I hope. 'Did you go out with whatshisface? Mr Arsehole from the tile shop?'

'Jonathan?'

'By arsehole I mean nice chap, of course.'

'Jonathan's been a good friend to me.'

'Why do you put it like that?' Has he perhaps been consoling you in some misery that I should know about? Is he even now planning to move from good friend to . . . something friendlier?

'It's so hard to know what people are really like, isn't it?'

'There was a famous shrink. Not Freud or Jung. One of the others. After a lifetime in clinical practice, he said that at the end of the day his patients remained as strange to him as the birds in his garden. Isn't that beautiful?'

She looks at me like she doesn't know what I'm talking about. I lurch off in search of the gents'.

This was too good to be true. My first blind date and I had hit gold. OK, we didn't have much in common, perhaps; and she hadn't laughed at the bee joke, which didn't augur particularly well. But she seemed to be enjoying my company and her looks were *spectacularly* . . . spectacular. What would it be like to wake up next to that face? Would her exoticism of background translate into a sexual exoticism? Would it be like going to bed with four different women?

Would she mind if I held her ears?

I must be more pissed than I realize. Because when I emerge from the toilets, I can't find the Library Bar. Whichever way I turn, somehow I always end up in the hotel reception area. This happens several times and begins to become embarrassing. When I eventually locate it – in a place so obvious, I can't understand how I could have missed it – I can't see Miriam. Where we were sitting, the two chairs opposite the pillar don't seem to be there. I wander around for a few minutes – the bar is confusingly bigger than it appeared – then I finally catch sight of the fat fucker with the cigar. Nearby, *The God of Small Things* is lying next to my empty Martini glass, but there is no sign of Miriam.

She's probably gone to the ladies', I decide.

I wait.

I order another drink while I wait.

Ladies often take a long time in the ladies', don't they?

She does not reappear.

She never reappears.

Eventually the f.f. with the c. and the willowy blonde totter off into the evening. The waiter brings me a world-class bill on a silver tray.

Had Miriam and I actually said goodnight, and my brain, super-saturated with Martini, simply failed to retain the memory? It can be the only explanation.

I don't recall getting home. Of the rest of the evening, there is only darkness.

2

'YOU DIDN'T TELL HER the bee joke, did you?'

Angela is suitably amused by my dating disaster.

'Might have.'

'He tells that joke to every woman he fancies.'

Toby shakes his head. 'Bad call. Women don't want jokes. They want charm.'

'If only I could have twatted a wasp for her with a rolled-up *Telegraph* . . .' My sarcasm is lost on him.

This is the official post-mortem. We're halfway through a bottle of something firm and fruity with notes of gooseberry, leaf mould and bus tickets that Angela had been recommended at her wine-tasting group. I have not yet announced to my old friends the two further important lessons I have learned in the blind-dating game:

LESSON TWO:
If you're going to lie,
be professional about it.

LESSON THREE:
*Never drink more than
two Martinis. Or stick to
soft drinks, like house white.*

Morticia, my ex-girlfriend, was scathing on this last point, I remember.

Actually, she's not really called Morticia. It's Beverly. Morticia is just my pet name for her.

'You were dribbling drunk when you made your pass at me,' she once declared. 'It was appalling.'

'It worked though, eh?' I believe I may have winked.

She sniffed. 'I only let you in because I thought if I left you in the street you'd be run over.'

'I don't remember much being wrong in the bedroom department.' Now I definitely did wink.

'Oh, *please.*'

Morticia has no sense of humour. It was exchanged at an early stage for a set of curves that would cause – forget heart failure in a moose – we're talking myocardial infarction in a dugong.

'Anyhow,' I continued, 'when I topped up your glass, I don't remember you saying, *Oh no, I couldn't possibly.*'

She sniffed, a little louder than the previous sniff, and regarded me sourly. Mummy isn't angry, just very disappointed, sort of thing.

'Besides,' I added, pressing the point home, 'what scene of seduction isn't accompanied by a bottle of something cold and dry sitting in a nearby ice bucket?' To say nothing of the river of cocktails that may have gone before.

Morticia's expression morphed into one of universal despair. The one she deploys when seized by the indifference of an uncaring cosmos; or the news that the plumber had been caught in very bad traffic on the North Circular and he was looking at tomorrow now, or possibly never.

In the present case, I took it to mean *Men have always let me down, and you were no exception.*

Morticia and I had somehow battled through eighteen months together before finally twigging that we weren't so much from different planets as different galaxies. These days, we continued to deplore one another fondly and met periodically for dinner to prod the bruise, as it were, and observe that it no longer hurt.

'You don't need to be dating strangers out of the newspaper,' says Angela, adding further purple fluid to my glass. 'You should meet my friend Rochelle.'

Toby and I exchange glances. 'What's she like?' I inquire cautiously.

'Oh, she's lovely,' she replies, like I should have known. 'She's just really, you know . . . *nice*.' She pulls one of those smiley, shivery faces that people do in the context of fluffy bunnies, cooing babies and the like.

'Nice,' I say dryly.

'Sweet,' she ripostes. 'Lovely,' she adds for clarification.

'What does she do?' I ask, heart sinking.

Angela names a particularly awful TV series of the moment, a great free-range turkey of a show that's both a critical and ratings catastrophe. 'She's the producer,' she declares proudly.

I am not snobbish about this. In my so-called career, I too have produced some pretty deplorable programmes. I know the effort that goes into making a dud is no less than that needed to create a hit. They all seem like good ideas at the time.

'What does she look like?'

'Honey blonde. You like blondes. My height. Perfect heart-shaped face. You'd love her. She makes her own jewellery.'

A bell is ringing. 'Makes her own jewellery?'

'She used to have a stall.'

'Does she clank?'

'Don't be horrid.'

'Does she in fact wear so much metal about her person that she clanks?'

It's coming back to me. A guest at one of Angela's dinner parties. A pudgy blonde woman with short arms who couldn't move without setting off a whole sequence of clanks, clatters and clangs. When she walked through a room, it sounded like a prisoner dragging his chains. When she laughed, it was like emptying a suitcase of old cutlery into a skip.

'She's very talented.'

'I've met her. To be honest, she isn't my type.' Though I could see she would have a definite scrap value.

'It's all about the first fifteen seconds,' says Toby. 'Two people meet – boom. There's this massive two-way information superhighway where both parties hoover up masses of non-verbal material about the other. Fifteen seconds later – boom – it's all over. It's been proved scientifically.' He does that thing with his lips that means, *That's the way the world is, matey, better get used to it*. 'You never get a second chance to make a first impression.'

'That's beautiful,' I remark. 'I'm going to write that down.'

'I didn't know about *you* after fifteen seconds,' says Angela.

'What? You and me? We've never been out, have we?'

I am jesting. We did go out. A long time ago when the world was young, as I like to put it. In a more innocent age, when you could get four sherbet dibdabs for a penny and mobile phones were the size of a house brick.

'It took weeks,' she explains to Toby. 'Months for him to wear me down.'

'You would have known at an unconscious level after fifteen seconds,' he maintains.

'He mounted a campaign. It was like a medieval siege.'

'I don't recall having to use catapults. Or slow starvation.'

'Basically,' says Toby, 'if you don't like what you're seeing after fifteen seconds, you should eject.'

'Actually Rochelle's going out with someone,' says Angela, without any apparent shame.

Perhaps because I have known her for so long, I am not surprised by this statement. 'Sorry, *why* did you think I should meet this woman who's going out with someone?' I inquire kindly.

'Oh, she's not in love or anything.'

I *think* I understand the logic. If I were to make a big play for Rochelle, if I were to breeze enough desire, charisma and charm in her direction, she might be moved to ditch her colourless suitor and, assuming he didn't launch any counter-campaign, I should then be well placed to claim the ferrous TV producer for my own.

Toby and I exchange another look. I have a feeling he may have been at the same dinner party.

'Bad thing, too much jewellery,' he says. 'I caught the strap of my Rolex in a girl's earring once. One of those spidery, dangly jobs. Made a bit of a hash of getting it out. Girl panicked. Relationship never really recovered. Anyhow,' he adds over our laughter, 'are we just going to sit here yacking, or is someone going to dial out for some grub?'

Toby gives me a lift home. He pilots us through the dark north London suburbs with the same no-nonsense approach he brings to everything in his life.

Despite my disaster at the Library Bar, he maintains that the lonely hearts remain 'a highly effective way of increasing one's throughput of eligible females'.

'Throughput.'

'I don't regret doing it for a moment.'

'Even though Wasp Woman was in the house across the road all the time?'

'The more women you meet, the readier you'll be to accept the right one when she comes along. It's a receptivity thing.'

In the wake of several glasses of Angela's house purple, this sounds oddly like wisdom.

After a bit I ask, 'Would you go south of the river? To meet someone?'

Toby shoots me a sceptical look. 'Where are we talking?'

'Dulwich.'

He sighs, pivoting the car into West End Lane with the heel of his hand like a minicab driver.

'What does she do?'

'Actress.'

'What else?'

'Interested in psychotherapy. Plays tennis. Makes collages.' I feel my friend wince. 'Writes poetry,' I add weakly.

It was what she'd put in her advert.

He guns the car towards the turning for the Finchley Road. 'Doesn't sound too good. I may as well be frank.'

'Actress, though,' I plead.

Something about the way he drops into second for the junction tells me all I need to know about Toby's views on the subject of women – even actresses – who do collages and write poetry.

'Actress,' I reiterate. With the unspoken assumption that she won't look like the back of the 134 (unless she specializes in character parts. Unless her last role was Tremendously Ugly Woman at Post Office Counter.). 'Actresses are vain, glamorous and sexy.' I'm hoping.

'You've spoken to her?'

'She sounded perfectly normal. Well, I say that.

Actually, she did sound a bit weird. But weird's good. Weird's interesting, isn't it? You want a bit of mystery. A bit of enigma. Life being struggle, and all that.'

'Weird, in my experience,' says Toby wearily, 'is just weird.'

I find it hard to agree with this last sentiment. Everyone I have ever been out with, it seems to me, has been a little bit . . . *different*, shall we say, somewhere along the line.

'Normal's so . . . normal, isn't it?'

'I like normal,' states Toby.

'What about Tamara? You can't claim Tamara was normal.'

Toby had gone out with Tamara for ages and she was madder than a cut snake, as he regularly used to tell me.

'I'm not saying there isn't a place in life for really top-drawer nookie. But in the end, one seeks stability. Stability, clarity and purpose.' Toby is the only person I know who still uses the word *nookie* un-ironically.

'Not collage and poetry, then. And an interest in psychotherapy.'

We pull up outside my building. 'What sort of acting does she do?' he asks. 'Stage, film, TV?'

'Experimental, I think she said.'

He looks at me like I'd just announced I was suffering from an incurable disease.

'Call her again. Ask her to name her favourite actress. It's a trick question. The answer is always someone they think they look like. If she says Juliette Binoche, you're laughing.'

52

'If it's Mollie Sugden, I hang up, right?'

'Good luck,' he says gravely. He even proffers me a hand.

His words echo in my head as I drive towards Dulwich.

Weird, in my experience, is just weird.

It was true, she had sounded weird. For a start, there were the three messages on my answering machine in reply to the one I'd left for her on the *Guardian*'s Soul Mates voicemail system.

First message. In a deepish voice; educated, with a low rasp to it.

Hello Paul. This is Annie. From the Guardian. *I guess you're not at home. (Long pause.) OK. Well. There's no reason why you should be. You could be doing anything. How would I know? (Nervous chuckle.) OK. Well. Perhaps you'll give me a call when you get in. (Another pause.) OK. Well. Bye then.*

Second message:

Paul, Annie again. From the Guardian. *You're still out. I don't believe I left you a number. For you to call me. (Long pause – then she reads the number very slowly, as though dictating it to a child.) OK. Well. Give me a call when you get this. Where are you, by the way? (Nervous laugh.) You don't have to answer that. OK. Well. Bye then.*

Third message:

*I'm actually going to bed in around twenty
minutes, so don't call me this evening, please.
(Long pause.) This is Annie, by the way. From the*
Guardian. *Also, I should have said, someone else
might answer the phone. Two other people. One's
called Denise and the other's a man. I think his
name's Clive. He hasn't been here long, though he's
got a dog. (Long pause.) OK. Well. Goodnight
then.*

I had just returned home. I was just playing through
the tape for a second time when the phone rang. It was
Annie. From the *Guardian*.

'Hi,' I replied breezily, though really I was a bit
spooked. It was quarter to midnight. Polite society had
stopped making phone calls some while ago.

'You've been out a long time.'

'Have I?'

A lengthy pause followed. Finally she said, 'We
speak at last.'

I was tired and slightly pissed. 'Indeed. Indeed we
do.' Best I could manage.

'Do you want to say where you've been?'

'Er. Dinner, actually. With some pals from the BBC.'

'Ah,' she exclaimed. 'I've got a bone to pick with the
BBC.'

'Really? What have they done now?'

'I'll tell you about it some time.'

'Was it to do with the snooker? People are incensed

54

when they muck about with the snooker. They get more complaints to do with mucking about with the snooker than anything else.'

Another pause followed. 'So what do you do, then?' It wasn't the snooker, apparently.

'Me? I produce factual entertainment.'

With a heavy heart – it was late, I could feel sleep circling over my head – I gave her my tired old line. About factual entertainment being a genre that's not factual enough to be called documentary, nor entertaining enough to be, er, entertainment.

She was not especially amused. In fact I received the distinct impression that she hadn't understood.

'Did you respond to any other adverts?' she asked.

'Yes. One or two.'

'Have you met anyone?'

'I did, actually. Yes.'

'What was she like?'

'What the bloody hell has it got to do with you?'

I didn't say this. It was what I was thinking. Instead I replied, 'It was a perfectly pleasant evening. Yeah.' I didn't mention the Zambesi of vodka Martinis. Nor the waking up the following morning fully clothed. 'So have you had many replies?' I inquired.

'I had a really long conversation with a man who gave his mobile telephone number. And then when I asked if he wanted to meet, the line went funny. I think he hung up.'

'Oh dear.'

'When I called him back, there was a woman's voice. "The number you have dialled is unavailable."'

'The posh woman who lives in the phone.'

'What?'

'Oh, nothing.'

'The woman who lives in a phone?'

'It was a joke. Forget it.'

There was a long pause while she considered this idea. Then, 'So would you like to meet some time?'

'Sure.' Anything. Just let me go to bed.

She explained she lived in Dulwich. Perhaps, she suggested, we might meet in her favourite café. They did a very good inexpensive lunch.

'Would I have seen you in anything?' I asked, when the arrangements had been completed.

She mentioned a show with an absurdist title. Something like *Purple Cheesecake Revolution*. Or it could have been *Orange Fandango Brazil Nut*. 'We took it to the Edinburgh Festival,' she said. Either way, I hadn't heard of it.

'How will I recognize you?' she asked.

'Well, I'm six foot two . . .' Hmm. Perhaps not the blue suit on this occasion. 'I'll be carrying a book. *The God of Small Things*. Do you know it?'

There was a pause. 'What colour hair have you got?'

Ah. How to put this?

'Brown. It's a sort of reddy brown, I suppose. But I might actually be wearing a baseball cap. Black with a red letter A on the front. For the Atlanta Braves.'

'I can't tell you what I'll be wearing. It'll be whatever I decide to put on that morning.'

'It doesn't matter. I'm sure we shall discover one another.'

A long and pregnant pause followed. Did that last statement sound like I think it sounded? Why had I phrased it like that? Did it contain the suggestion that our clothes were immaterial; that our bodies would inevitably discover one another (with a curiosity, an intensity and ultimately a passion that no amount of mundane arrangements could submerge)?

'See you next Tuesday, then,' she said. And she rang off before I could say another word.

There's an actor who lives a few streets from me. One of those distinguished silver-haired characters you'd instantly recognize from a thousand TV dramas even if you couldn't immediately summon his name to mind. He's not in demand these days, but in the past I can imagine him playing the sympathetic family lawyer who can get tough when the occasion demands it. Or the upstanding businessman suddenly staring at marital and financial collapse. At a pinch, the senior police commander juggling conflicting demands on his hard-pressed force in a modern society.

Every few days, I clock this stalwart of the airwaves and the West End stage on his way to or from the High Street, toting his wicker shopping basket. I confess that as we draw closer, I play a cruel little game with him. It goes like this: at first, I utterly ignore him. I look ahead, I look up, I look down, I look across the road, I look at my watch, I look anywhere but directly at him. It's only as we are almost level, only at the point when we are about to pass one another and it's very nearly too late

. . . only then do I finally fire my gaze straight into his pink, pleading face.

What I receive in return is a wonder to behold. This former icon of the British drama establishment actually *flowers* with pleasure. His anxious eyes seem to glitter at the recognition in mine; something happens to the set of his head on his shoulders. It's as if his whole persona is saying, *Oh, you've noticed me. Oh, thank you. Thank you.* As if this grand old chap doesn't exist until someone looks at him.

It's what actors are like, I guess. They have a need to call our eyes upon them. And unless someone's looking, in their own eyes somehow they feel they don't count.

I suppose I imagine that Annie from Dulwich has some of this same neediness. She'd described herself as tall and slim, late thirties. The interest in psychotherapy, I have decided, denotes a sinuous, inquiring spirit. The reference to tennis, a sure sign of fitness and vigour. Collage . . . hmm; actually, I've always had a fairly dim view of collage, it being neither big or clever in my opinion to scissor out bits of magazines and glue them down with feathers and other old crap from the bottom of one's handbag. Still, along with the poetry – hmm, poetry – it's all adding up to a healthy, self-aware, creative individual who it's surely worth crossing the river to clap eyes upon. In the picture of her I have in my head, she resembles the young Vanessa Redgrave as Isadora Duncan. Coltish, with plenty of elbows and knees and faraway looks. Mercurial, a little bonkers even, but hey. Who is Toby to say that weird is just weird?

But it isn't leafy Dulwich. By the time I consult the *A–Z* again for details of the final approach, it's clear that my destination is more like Peckham. Or to give it the benefit of the doubt, the nameless sprawl that lies between the two south London 'villages'. I pull up opposite a shopping parade: there's a launderette, a newsagent, an off-licence (window covered in wire mesh), minicab office, pizza-delivery outlet complete with fleet of padlocked mopeds, betting shop, mini-market, and on the corner, as promised, George's. Not the delightful little bistro I had hoped for with imaginative soups, *moules* this and *coq au* that chalked on the blackboard. From the look of the bashed-up tables and chairs inside, the tomato-shaped ketchup dispensers and the notice in the window, wittily penned on a paper plate, announcing details of the 'Workers Breakfast', the venue for our encounter is a greasy spoon.

I am only ten minutes early. It occurs to me I could wait in the car. I could even hide behind the sun-dried copy of the *Big Issue* that I keep on the rear shelf and view my lunch date at a distance. If she turns out to be a gargoyle, the faint perfume of burnt rubber need be my only calling card.

But it would be bad faith, I decide. Besides, a great big fry-up could be the answer to the sense of alienation and unease I develop whenever I find myself heading south off the Elephant and Castle roundabout. The Germans probably have one of their horrid long words for it. *Sudbrukenpanik*. Literally 'south-of-the-river panic'.

For a café around lunchtime, George's is curiously

empty. Indeed, I appear to be the only customer. The sad-eyed Greek-looking bloke in the grease-spattered cardy who brings me a cup of tea I take to be the eponymous proprietor.

'I'm waiting for someone to join me,' I mention by way of encouragement.

He nods. Or shrugs, it's hard to tell. It's rather as if he doesn't give a shit.

I study the various food options in the padded plastic menu. 'Little Bit of Everything Omelette' sounds intriguing, and I am tempted to inquire as to the specific contents of 'George's Special Mixed Grill'. I realize I'm actually feeling rather nervous about this. Perhaps an evening rendezvous, with the opportunity for an ice-breaking glass of wine or two, might have been a smarter plan. On the other hand, my previous alcohol-assisted encounter could not be thought of as a resounding triumph.

Outside, everyday life goes on. Vehicles pass. Young mothers push prams. As I sit marooned in the silent, deserted café, citizens are engaged in forward motion, children are growing up. Once again, the phrase *What the fuck am I doing here?* does laps round my head. Time seems to have slowed to a crawl. I have a premonition that the Annie who lured me to this unpopular eating station will not turn out to be the ethereal beauty of my imaginings.

I spot her coming from a long way off. So far off indeed that it wouldn't be too late to scatter a few coins on the table, leg it to the car and vanish into the south London traffic.

But I am paralysed. Here – I see it clearly – is my fate.

And like your shadow rising to meet you at evening, as Eliot put it in his poem, there's really no avoiding the bugger.

'I always have the bubble and squeak. Bubble and squeak please, George. With plenty of onions, the way I like it. And a glass of tap water.' From the depths of a shapeless shoulder-bag the colour of dried mud, she brings up a battered leather pouch. 'You don't mind, do you?'

I shake my head, a little stupefied. On the out-spread inner flap, nibbled fingers begin to fashion a cigarette.

George isn't going to write anything down, he's going to attempt this from memory alone. As his gaze shifts on to mine, do I detect a note of amusement behind the soulful brown eyes? A faint twist to the lips that wasn't there a minute ago? Bubble and squeak *the way she likes it*. I wonder how many times George has played maître d' to Annie and her unsuspecting victims from the *Guardian*.

'Mushroom omelette,' I croak. 'And a Diet Coke.'

She parks the rollie in the corner of her mouth and fires up with an impressively battle-scarred Zippo lighter. There is the usual conflagration of extraneous Rizla and loose tobacco strands. Over her shoulder, a digital clock above the kitchen door reads 1:05.

'You made it, then,' she says.

'Oh, yes,' I reply, barely keeping the bitterness out of my voice. Oh yes, I made it all right. There were only about a hundred thousand other things I could have been doing, but instead I chose to slog halfway across London, to a disused café in Peckham for a lunch date with . . . with a mad old hippie.

Mad Old Hippie. There is really no getting round it. Everything about her screams MOH. The rat's nest of grey hair streaked with henna. The ancient denim jacket. The dreadful cheesecloth shirt. The sad woven top, the exact hue of cold porridge. The chipped chunk of pottery strung round her neck. The ankle-length linen skirt that somehow highlights the insect bites on her ankles.

The – gulp – sandals.

The faint, unmistakable, odour of feet.

I nod towards my copy of *The God of Small Things* lying on the table between us. 'Didn't really need to bring the book, did I?'

Large grey eyes hold mine as she contemplates this statement.

After a bit, she asks, 'Have you ever read anything by Jung?'

'Never,' I declare firmly. I am tempted to add that I'd read somewhere he was a Nazi sympathizer. Wearily I inquire, 'Are you a Jungian, then?'

Actually, I wouldn't care if she turned out to be a fucking Martian, I am so narked at the misrepresentation. Why didn't she say she was a mad old hippie? It's true that she's tall. Almost imposingly so. And OK, even if she isn't slim – it's hard to tell under all the hippie clobber – then at least she isn't fat. But late thirties? Late *nineteen* thirties, maybe.

The truth: she's probably around forty-four. My age.

'Am I a Jungian?' She smiles to herself and blasts off a jet of fag smoke. 'You know, I'm not really into labels,' she replies, making me want to slap her.

'So your interest in psychotherapy. What form does it take?'

She begins rooting in the bag again. I catch sight of a wad of old newspaper clippings secured with rubber bands, the skeleton left behind by a bunch of grapes, and a very battered A4 notebook. She comes up empty handed.

'Sorry. I thought I had something with me. Do you ever do that?'

It isn't rhetorical. She appears to want an answer. 'Yeah. It's been known.'

'It was my poem. I wrote this poem. Not a long poem. I read it to Pierre and he liked it. So I showed it to a few people and they liked it. And then I sent it to a man I know in book publishing. He never mentioned anything about it, so I thought he was considering it for publication. And a long time went by, and he still didn't mention it – and then I found out he'd left the firm. I couldn't find out where he'd gone. They wouldn't tell me. Also, they denied ever receiving it. And then later they said they had *no record* of ever receiving it, which isn't the same thing. And about a year after this, this was two Christmases ago, I was watching the BBC, one of the films they put on over Christmas, and there was my poem. At first, I was completely gobsmacked to hear it. And then I began to get angry because of all the money.'

A sinking feeling grows within me.

'Your poem. It was in a film?' She nods gravely. 'Someone . . . someone reads it out, do they?'

'Tom Hanks. No, the other one. Tom Cruise. The one who was married to what's her name? Elizabeth Thingy.'

It's worse than I thought.

She's not just a mad old hippie. She's a deluded mad old hippie. Where do I even begin?

Listen, you silly bint. There isn't a way in the world your crazed jottings would ever find themselves in a Hollywood movie. This bloke you know in 'book publishing', he's read your poem and been so blown away by its genius, has he, that he's chucked his job, flown to LA, and flogged it to . . . who exactly? 'Hey, I've found this great poem, it's just perfect for the new Tom Hanks vehicle.' Hasn't it occurred to you that the producers of this picture could probably afford to hire their own people to write any poems they might need? Why would they steal one from a shambolic old trout such as yourself? And also, the time-frame's all wrong. There would need to be much longer than a year between writing your crappy poem and it appearing in a TV showing of this film. How dare you advertise yourself in the Guardian, *anyway?*

'I rang the BBC. They told me my call had been noted.'

'They do get a lot of . . .' Cranks. 'Calls.'

'Is there anyone you could speak to?'

'At the BBC? I don't think so.'

'This man I sent it to in book publishing . . . no one knows where he's gone. Or they're not telling. It's cost me thousands. Maybe more.'

And then the terrible thing.

She smiles.

The bared teeth, now I notice them properly, have a rearward slope; they point back down her throat. If I were a dentist I could probably give you the precise location of the grey dead-looking one in the upper left quadrant. If I were a dentist, I should be tempted to administer myself a powerful anaesthetic.

'It's careless of the BBC, don't you think? Not checking up on who's written what?' I can only shrug. 'You work there,' she says. 'What if you wrote something and somebody stole it and it got read out on ITV?'

I feel a dangerous combination of lethargy, irritation and helplessness settle upon me, the same sensation I have often experienced in meetings with television executives, or when about to go down with a dose of flu. The most annoying part of her statement are the words *you work there*.

Yes, I have worked at the BBC for the last four years, hopping from contract to contract to produce this or another harmless piece of disposable television. For the last six weeks, however, I have not worked there or anywhere else, for the simple reason that the man who hires me has left the Corporation. I have lost my Baron at the big table, as I liked to think of him. The bones that were once cast down to me ('You don't fancy making a hidden camera show with Dale Winton, do you? Actually, it's just a pilot at this stage . . .'), these bones are cast down no longer. Like the axe that has lost its handle and has not yet received a new one, the question can be fairly asked: in what sense can I still call myself a producer? I have lost my job and it's true, I shall *probably* get another one, but no one is beating a path to my door, I notice. I have the uneasy feeling that, in my reply to Annie's advert, the claim that I 'work in TV' – along with the two years I shaved off my age – was a little misleading.

Being currently at liberty is one of the reasons I am free to make lunch appointments with mad old hippies on the other side of the capital city.

'I don't think it quite works like that,' I tell her.

The clock on the wall reads 1:08.

There is no way out, I realize. I'm as trapped as a lobster in a pot. Something about those backward-sloping teeth reinforces the idea of no escape. There's nothing for it but grimly to endure. All things must pass, I tell myself. And this too will end.

'So you play a bit of tennis, then?' I inquire, just as she forks an indecent amount of bubble and squeak into her mouth.

She nods her head. Chews. Wipes away a leak of grease from the corner of her lips. She's spilt some down the cold-porridge flaxen chemise too, I notice. My eye catches on the chunk of pottery. It really is the most charmless piece, being little more than a triangle of clay with some sort of dimple pressed into it. There seems no more reason to hang it round your neck than hurl it to the bottom of the garden.

'You're probably very good,' she says finally.

'Not at all. My game's rather erratic. I'm capable of playing some good shots, but there are way too many unforced errors.'

It is, I am aware, an over-elaborate answer. A simple shrug would have done as well. Or a thunderous raspberry.

'Do you serve over-arm?'

'Er. Yeah. I do, actually.'

'I don't.' She says it like it's something to be proud of. I am assailed by another sinking feeling. 'Really I need to get a new bat. It's wooden. It used to live in one of those squeezy things. What are they called?'

Heavy sigh. 'A racket press.'

'Pierre must have damaged it somehow. If we have a game, perhaps you've got a spare one I could borrow.'

I ignore the suggestion. There will be no games. No loans of sports equipment. 'When was the last time you played?' I ask. To the nearest decade will be fine. And why, by the way, did you add tennis to the list of your interests?

Annie tucks a stray sprout of hair behind an ear and regards me squarely through startled grey eyes. 'School, probably. What's it called where you use those shuffle-cock things?'

1:19.

Time seems to be moving more slowly here in south London. Somewhere in a dead file in my imagination, I realize, there must be a scene where the coltish actress and I embark upon a set of tennis; some sort of intense if playful exchange, her whippy cross-court backhand returns, my own ungettable down-the-line winners; the two of us standing at the net afterwards, a little red-faced and panting, but happy.

Technically, I may have just lost the will to live. 'Backgammon,' I reply in a daze.

'How's your omelette?' she asks.

'Fine, yeah. How's your . . . yours?' It seems I cannot bring myself to mouth the words *bubble and squeak*.

'Good. Not enough onion, though. There's never enough onion for me.'

A long silence follows, punctuated only by the sound of metal against china and the creak of jaws. For a few moments, I lose myself in an abstract composition of egg, mushroom and burnt bits. When I glance up, I find her looking at me.

'Would you like to read my poem, then?'

A number of possible replies present themselves for consideration:

1. No.
2. No. I probably shouldn't. In case I steal from it unconsciously.
3. No. Furthermore, I've just realized I've got to leave right now. Sorry.
4. No. Fuck off with your poem. Where's the weird but creative performing artist I crossed London to meet? What have you done with her?

5. No. In fact, if your poem – if *all* your poems –
   were on fire, I wouldn't piss on it. On them.

'Yeah. Sure,' I say.
'I think there's a copy at the flat. Did you drive? We
could go back in the car together.'

Somehow, it's still only 1:19.

If I were more of a hysterical type, I could be
seriously panicking by now. I have seen inside her
handbag; I definitely do not want to see inside her flat.
I decide to steer the conversation back to psychotherapy. It's a topic I have developed a growing interest
in, having recently moved towards what is depressingly
called 'mid-life'. More and more frequently, I wake
with the question framed upon my lips, 'What is the
bloody point?'

I have a friend of a particularly mordant cast of
mind who always answers queries of this nature by
commenting, 'Ah, well that's it, you see. There *is* no
point.' He sometimes adds, 'No one said life would be
fair. Or even interesting.' Bob is from the north of
England; I recall he once advised me, 'It's all about
fucks, not books, lad', a line which sounds better in a
Yorkshire accent.

Bob's is clearly a coherent world-view, and one with
which I have a degree of sympathy. But if even a bleak
bastard like Bob had found someone he wanted to
share his days with – the long-suffering Cecile – I
couldn't help wondering why I hadn't.

Arnie, the manager of my favourite Italian restaurant in Crouch End, has a particularly direct way of couching this issue.

'Hello, Mr Paul,' he says cheerily. 'You married yet?'

Arnie, who comes from somewhere near Venice, is a fan of the holy estate. Marriage – and babies – is plainly the best thing that ever happened to him, and I know it's only because he wants the best for me that he always brings it up. Even my mother (who also only wants the best for me) knows better than to ask every time we meet.

'No, Arnie. Not yet. Yeah, table for three, please.'

'You should be married, Mr Paul.' Sometimes he adds, 'A man should be married at your age.' He might even squeeze Toby's arm, or put a hand on Angela's shoulder, and finish off with, 'Why can't you find him a nice girl, eh?'

They laugh. 'Yeah, right. If only,' I reply. 'Bottle of house red and a bottle of fizzy water, please.'

But Arnie was right. Why wasn't I married? Or even *nearly* married. I thought it mightn't be a bad idea to lie on someone's couch and allow them to poke around in my Unconscious for clues. I even went as far as to visit a fairly eminent shrink in Belsize Park for an initial series of consultations. A pair of beady black eyes regarded me from a thicket of beard as I trotted out as much of my life story as I could pack into fifty minutes. Towards the end of our second appointment, he observed that none of my significant relationships had lasted much beyond two years. On this basis, that I didn't seem able to commit to a long-term project, he declined to accept me as a client. My only regret is that before leaving I didn't have the presence of mind to say, 'That's OK. You were fired anyway.'

'You're like me,' is Angela's view of my single status. 'You just haven't met the right person yet.'

I am suspicious of the 'right person' explanation. If there is one special someone out there for me, how can I possibly hope to find her? There are six billion souls on the planet. What if mine lives in County Sligo? Or on the Kamchatka peninsula? Even if she's only one stop away on the Northern Line, how are we ever to contrive an encounter?

No, the truth must be that there is a right *type* of person. And there are hundreds, probably thousands, maybe tens of thousands of women I could happily make a go of it with. This is both good news (I'll find someone; so will Angela) and a little sad (what happens to the other 9,999? Would I have been better off with one of them? This may be a guy thing.).

Toby believes it's about biology and timing. 'The fact that you're asking the question is suggestive,' he told me when we discussed it. 'You're ready to meet someone.'

'So we're just monkeys, are we?' Their horrid red bottoms glowing like traffic lights when hormone levels reach criticality.

'When you're ready, almost anyone will do. Boom, end of story. If you're actually compatible, all the better.'

'So, for you, any woman with a wasp that needed squashing? Boom.'

'If you're up for it, boom. Yeah.'

Morticia's take is typically withering: 'You've got a perfectly cosy little world of bars and friends and restaurants,' she drawled one evening over dinner. 'You're much too old and crabby to make room in your life for children. And a wife would only get on your nerves.'

This dismal scenario, I could see, did contain a grain of truth.

Children.

It was indeed hard to picture children in my comfortably minimalist bachelor apartment. Children, with their snotty noses, awful eating habits and terrible taste in brightly coloured plastic (to say nothing of the double-incontinence, emotional lability and crippling life-long expenditure). Even visiting examples of the species managed to create remarkable amounts of chaos given very little to work with. A bowl of fruit or a Sunday newspaper could be returned to its constituent atoms in moments. I felt a little old and crabby merely thinking about it.

But you can go round in circles talking to your friends about this stuff. Better maybe to pay a complete stranger. Lie on his couch, drop a long pole into the muddy pond, give it a good stir and see what comes up.

'So, psychotherapy,' I say to Annie. 'Is it a theoretical interest, or is there a practical aspect?' Are you seeing a shrink, is the question I'm too polite to ask. 'Who are you into?'

Her stare is quite disconcerting. The big grey eyes

really ought to blink more often. Out of consideration for others, if nothing else.

I continue, 'I mean there are Freudian therapists, Jungian therapists, Transpersonal, Reichian, Kleinian therapists. Some are into Adler, some into Winnicott. There are so many different schools.'

'I'm into Katz,' she declares.

I might have known it would be an obscure one. 'What sort of thing do they go in for?' I sigh.

Annie pushes her empty plate to one side. Begins to roll another cigarette.

'They're good listeners,' she says. 'You can tell them all your problems and they don't judge you.'

'Essential, I would have thought.' Part of the job description, really. Although if you told your shrink you wanted to sleep with ocelots, he'd be bound to form some kind of view of you. (Lady ocelots, I'm talking here.)

'They exude a great sense of wisdom.'

Ah yes. That old chestnut. The bloke with the beard in Belsize Park used to nod and hmm and stroke his beard and generally convey the impression that he'd got it all pretty sorted out. 'But they're not supposed to give you straight advice, are they? They're meant to lead you to discover the answer for yourself, like a good maths teacher.'

She looks at me like I'm a bit backward.

'Pierre tells me what to do. In his way.'

'Pierre's your therapist?'

'Yeah.' She giggles girlishly (not a pretty sight). 'One of them.'

'Really? How many have you got?'

'You'll probably think this is awful.' Another sickening girly grin. 'Seven,' she says.

'*Seven!?*'

She sighs. 'There was only one to begin with. Then I got a second. That was Pierre. He was sort of passed on to me by a friend. Then . . . well, I think they become addictive after a while.'

'What sort of thing do you talk about? I mean, how deep can you go?' Fuck me. Seven therapists. She's battier than I thought.

'With Pierre, anything. It's because he's older.'

'Seen it all.'

She laughs. 'Yeah.'

'Hard to shock.'

'Definitely.'

'Do you tell him your dreams?'

'All the time.'

'Does he offer interpretations? Or does he just sit there and say, Well, what do *you* think the purple giraffe in the helicopter means, then?'

Another odd look. As if she's not sure whether I'm taking the piss. 'I read my poetry to Pierre sometimes. He's the only one who seems to understand it.'

Uh-oh. I am anxious not to revisit the poetry thing. 'If it's not a rude question,' I ask, 'how much do you pay him?'

'Sorry?'

'Per session.'

'Pierre?'

'Is he local? Or do you have to travel a long way?'

'Is he *local?*' Annie looks a bit confused. 'Pierre lives with me.'

I am taken aback by this statement. 'He *lives* with you?'

'I live with all of them.'

I open my mouth, but nothing much in the way of actual dialogue comes out. Maybe a sort of croaking noise.

'They're company for each other.'

No. Still nothing.

'People think if you've got that many, they must smell. But they don't at all. They're very clean.'

Now I don't even try to speak. I just stare.

'Actually, Lola gets a bit moody. Sometimes she does a little protest poo in the bath.'

A coin – something bigger than a penny, a quid maybe – finally drops.

'You're not talking about psychotherapists, are you?'

Not Katz.

Cats.

Annie tells her problems to her cats. The one named Pierre even has to listen to her dreams and her fucking poetry. Is it any wonder he vandalized her tennis racket? If I were Pierre, I'd be right up there alongside Lola, laying whopping great cables in the bath on a nightly basis.

'It's nice that you're so interested,' she says. 'A lot of people are hostile towards animals.'

I wave my hand dismissively, not because I am not one

of those people, but because I am too cross and weirded out to speak. I have somehow become alienated from my own life. Only a matter of weeks ago, it seems to me, I was a fully functioning north London TV producer with a job to go to, bars, friends, restaurants, etc. Now I find myself lost in some Beckettian landscape, lunching with a madwoman who owns seven cats.

LESSON FOUR:
Ask in advance about cats. Excessive
numbers are a negative indicator. Dogs
too, probably. Livestock generally, I imagine.

'Am I what you expected, then?'

Her question takes me by surprise.

'Not exactly.' I don't wish to expand on this statement, so I add, 'It's not very busy in here, is it?'

'You're not exactly what I expected.'

'Really?'

'You said you had reddy-brown hair.'

'What there is,' I say with what I hope is a flinty look in my eyes, 'is reddy-brown.'

'I like bald men,' she says with a sickening gleam. 'My last boyfriend was bald. Actually, he wasn't completely bald, he had one of those ponytails. He grew it because without it he thought he looked like every other bald bloke. I told him he was wrong. I said it made him look like a bald bloke with a little grey ponytail.'

I have a vivid fantasy where, when she says *bald* again, I drive a fork through her eyeball.

'What happened to him, then?'

'He went back to Spain.'

Excellent move. 'I see.'

'He used to say that having no hair meant the sun warmed his thoughts better.'

'Did he really?' Did this bald twat have any other brilliant philosophical insights, I wonder?

'He was Spanish.'

'What was he doing with a raddled old bag like you?'

No. Much as I'd like to, I don't say it. I say, 'Well, shall we get the bill then?'

She looks alarmed. 'Don't you want sweet?'

'Er. No, not really. I couldn't.'

'George does a great sticky toffee pudding. Best in Dulwich.'

'This isn't really quite Dulwich, is it?' I suggest. It's fucking Peckham, you lying trout.

'You won't get a better sticky toffee pudding any-where,' she maintains. 'Sticky toffee pudding please, George.'

I wait for it, but there is no additional guidance about the desired stickiness or toffeeness of her dessert selection. Would it be rude to walk out now, I wonder? Probably, but I can't. A creeping malaise has settled over me like a shroud. I am paralysed by the scale of the mistake I have made. Annie isn't a near-miss, a case of someone who's 'a nice enough person, just not for me'. It's not even that I might begin to see her hidden allure after four Martinis.

Four hundred wouldn't be enough.

Call me narrow-minded, but I never want to go out with someone who has a therapeutic relationship with her (seven) cats. Another important lesson suggests itself to me.

LESSON FIVE:
*If she sounds weird, she probably
is weird. Weird isn't automatically a
bad thing, but just so you know.*

There's no one to blame for this but myself. Her gauche, manipulative manner – borrowing tennis rackets, cadging lifts, getting me involved in her absurd drama over the stolen poem, trapping me here while she orders pudding – I should have picked up on it from the three messages she left on my answering machine and from our phone call itself.

LESSON SIX:
*Listen more carefully.
The clues are there.*

'You keep looking at my pendant. Do you like it?'

Had I really been staring? If I had, it was only at the awfulness of the thing. A dun-coloured slab, the exact colour of dun (whatever dun may be) with the impress of somebody's thumb in it.

'Is that a thumbprint?'

'The sculptor's. An old man in Diego's village makes them. He says they bring the wearer luck.'

'And has it?'

'Well.' Annie does something girlish with a straggle of hair. 'I've met you, haven't I?'

In war movies, that noise on the submarine deck when enemy warships are spotted on the horizon. A loud *whoop-whoop-whoop*, accompanied by the rumble of boots on metal and imprecations from a senior officer to 'Dive, dive, dive.' These, roughly speaking, are the sound effects playing in my head.

A huge portion of sticky toffee pudding is brought on. Or it may be that stuff they use to fill holes in cars, it's hard to tell. Annie sets about it with a sickening enthusiasm. The last piece of dialogue hangs in the air like the threat of storms.

It's 1:35.

We are still the only customers in the café. When does this place ever get busy, I wonder? It can hardly be a favourite with the pre-theatre crowd. A suspicion grows that it's all an elaborate stage-set. That any moment, the walls will fly apart, a studio audience will be revealed baying with laughter at the latest hidden-camera reality-TV show: *When Lonely Hearts Go Wrong*. Hey, that's not a half-bad idea, it occurs to me. *Lonely Hearts From Hell*. I might rattle out a couple of pages by way of a treatment and see if I can get anyone to bite.

Outside, traffic continues to flow. Citizens pass on foot. All the reassuring signs of normal life are in place. Two policemen saunter by, that special copper-saunter they're taught at coppering college, slow and approachable, so small children feel able to run up and say, ' 'Scuse me mister, two men are robbing the Post Office.' They'd save me from the mad old hippie, surely. If I dashed up and explained everything, wouldn't they give her a blast of pepper spray and drive her back to her menagerie with a sharp word in her ear about telling porkies in a national newspaper? 'It's not nice, Annie. Wasting an unemployed TV producer's time. Let's not be hearing from you again.'

Perhaps I've died. Perhaps my car struck another vehicle on my way to meet her and I was killed instantly, and this is purgatory. Punishment for all the bad shows I've made in my time.

(Actually, scrub that. I'm going straight to hell for the Dale Winton pilot *alone*.)

Then I have a rather brilliant thought. If I can contrive for my mobile phone to ring, I can be urgently 'called away'. A crucial decision needs to be made in the world of factual entertainment, sort of thing. It's been nice to meet you, sorry our date's lasted less than an hour, but that's showbiz. There's a menu on my Nokia 3310 where you can rehearse all the phone's on-board ring tones. All I've got to do is somehow discreetly tee it up, then hit the big button when I'm ready.

As Annie works her way through the sticky toffee pudding, every now and again flicking a glance in my direction and smiling oddly, I slip my fingers into the right-hand pocket of my jacket. The little silver fellow's lying there all snug in the dark, but the buttons are impossible to make sense of unseen. My left hand starts to fiddle idly with *The God of Small Things* as she masticates.

'Good, is it?' I inquire.

'Mmm.'

'Looks quite . . . sticky.'

'Is. Yeah.'

I make a bit of a show of casually sliding the book over the table edge to find the point where it tips over; I toy with it there for a few moments in an irritating fashion – and then allow it to fall.

As I lean down to reach beneath the table, my right hand deftly whips out the Nokia. Quelling the urge to gag – the aroma of feet is much more pronounced at this level – my right thumb goes into action.

Keypad locked. *Shit.*

Press Unlock and then ∗. *Fuck.*

Keypad Active. Followed by an animated tick symbol. *Come on, come on. Yes!*

Menu. *At last.* I thumb through the options:

Phone Book. *No.*

Messages. *No.*

Chat. *Fuck off.*

Call Register. *Ditto.*

Tones. *Ditto.*

Settings. *Fuck. Gone past it.* Thumb back to

Tones. *Select.*

Ringing Tone. *Select.*

Ring Ring. *That's my boy.*

Pausing only to clock a big yellowing toenail poking through a sandal and a constellation of insect bites about her ankles, I emerge into the light.

The weapon is primed.

My thumb is cocked.

I believe a small cruel smile plays on my lips. Rather like an actor's as he's about to de-trouser the firearm and speak the line, 'Sorry, Toots. But you're not going anywhere.'

Annie wipes a smear of toffee from her lips with the back of her hand. 'A cup of tea to finish, and then you can take us home,' she says.

'Sure.'

I am feeling almost giddy with relief. At the moment of my choosing, I can abort this hideous encounter with the twitch of a digit. Now that I feel in control again, I am calmer. I might even spin this out for a few more minutes, enjoying the moment, sort of thing.

What shall I tell her? Sorry, I've just heard my flat's on fire. There's a last-minute legal problem with a programme I made. That was the Director General; I'm needed urgently back at the ranch.

'So what are their names, then?'

'The cats?'

I nod. I'm toying with her. 'I know about Pierre and the one that craps in the bath.'

'Lola. She doesn't do it very often.'

'No. I don't expect she does.' If Lola lived under my roof, just once would be enough.

'There's Oscar. And Zappa. And Busby. And . . . why do you want to know?'

I don't want to know, you silly cow. I'm just passing the time. 'No reason, really.'

'Do you have animals? Actually, you can't really *have* animals, can you? It's not like you own them or anything.'

'Isn't it?' I should have thought that was the exact arrangement. 'I bet they don't pay their own vet's bills.'

'They would if they could.'

'If they earned money.'

She laughs. 'Yeah. That's funny. If they went out to work.'

I feel the moment drawing near. 'What are the last two called?'

Annie gazes at me for a couple of seconds. 'Snuffy and Badger.'

Those must have been the words I was waiting for. I press the button.

Nothing happens.

'Guess why he's called Badger.'

I press again.

'Sorry?'

Nothing. Not a peep.

'Can you guess why Badger's called Badger?'

I feel mild panic building in my breast. My thumb is stabbing at the Nokia.

'Er. No.'

'Oh, come on. You must do.'

The fucking phone is fucking mute.

'What?'

'Can't you guess why he's called Badger?'

I am fucked. Fucked by a phone.

'Is something the matter?'

'Nothing. It's . . . it's nothing.'

'Shall I tell you?'

Heavy sigh. The heaviest yet. A sigh amongst sighs. 'Go on then.'

'It's because he looks like a badger.'

'Really?'

'Yeah. He's got a snouty little face and white markings. When we get to the flat, I'll have to introduce you very slowly to Badger, to give him a chance to get used to you. He doesn't really like new people. Specially men.'

The clock on the wall reads 1:42. This has been the longest forty-two minutes of my life, and I speak as someone who once tried to read *The Magus*.

Annie puts three spoonfuls of sugar in her tea and stirs for what feels like an age. I continue to watch in silence as she begins to fashion another roll-up.

Hell, as Sartre said so correctly in my opinion, is other people.

I am gripped by the paralysis of the inevitable. It seems to be a generally accepted fact, a given, that we are going back to her flat. How this has arisen, I no longer know, but I can picture the scene when we get there: the hippie slum with cat hairs. The drifts of old newspapers and disused poetry lying around everywhere. Fleas the size of ping-pong balls swinging off the light fittings.

She'll show me her collage. We haven't even touched on the collage, but somewhere, I just know it, there'll be a canvas covered with old crap that's indistinguishable from the heap of other old crap it's being assembled from. There will be feathers, bus tickets, eyes removed from doll heads.

Her bed – oh, God save me – her bed will be a mattress on the floor covered in a jumble of shawls and cushions and discarded clothing. (Why am I visualizing her bed?)

There'll be a used frying pan on the stove containing cold remains of scrambled egg.

A bottle with a melted candle jammed into it.

A twist of cat shit in the bath.

My world is reduced to two opposed certainties.

There is no way on earth I am going back to her flat.

There is no way I can think of to avoid it.

Somehow I can't bring myself to make the easy speech, 'Actually, I don't think I can come back this afternoon. There are a few things I need to do. Maybe another time.'

How hard would it be to declare, 'You know something? I really need to get home. There's an important document I need to read ahead of a meeting tomorrow. I'll call you. We'll have that game of tennis.'

Or even, 'I am such a dummy! I completely forgot. I have a dental appointment this afternoon. You'll have to excuse me.'

I think the reason I cannot bear to make any of these speeches is that I am afraid of the expression that will appear on her face. The scene is quite tragic enough already; I am unwilling to take responsibility for further disappointment.

We pay the bill.

We are standing up to leave.

This is the moment: I have to speak now, or it's proceed directly to cat-poo central.

And then she says, 'I'll just nip to the loo.'

The loo?

I didn't even know there was a loo. If I'd known there was a loo, I would have gone there to frig the mobile. Perhaps it isn't an official loo – there are certainly no signs on view – perhaps Annie has a special arrangement with George. Once a week she brings him a customer, he lets her use the loo. They go back to her flat . . . they are never seen again.

As she vanishes behind the counter, she turns and flashes me the terrible smile, the one with the teeth pointing the wrong way. In an instant, I know what I have to do.

I wait a beat. And then another beat. And then I start walking towards the door. George's eyebrows form themselves into question marks.

I hold up an index finger. 'I've just got to do the thing,' I explain.

After the frying and the fag smoke, the fresh air is like a slap round the face. I walk briskly to the car – don't run, I tell myself, don't look back, don't jump up and down cheering – I feel like an escaping POW in a black and white war film.

The key wobbles wildly as I try to engage it in the lock.

I tumble in and start the engine. I'm sure there is plenty of room between me and the bus behind as I pull out, but he hoots anyway.

'Oh. My. God.' It feels good to be free.

'Jesus. Fucking. Christ.' I often talk to myself when I'm alone in the car. (It comes from being an only child.)

'*Aaaaaaaaaaaaaaahhhhhh.*'

Only as I cross Waterloo Bridge do I realize that I've left the handbrake on.

3

'I TELL YOU, SHE was the stuff of nightmares.'

The guests at Angela's dinner party are gratifyingly entertained by my encounter with Annie.

'I can't believe you just ran away,' says our hostess. 'What must she have felt like when she came back and you weren't there?'

I shake my head sadly. 'It was her or me.'

'I'd have done the same,' says Toby. 'Only I'd have done it after five minutes. There's nothing worse in my book than an old trout acting the coquette.'

There are howls of protest. Even Wasp Woman gives him a playful slap across the arm.

This is Wasp Woman's first public outing, the first time she's been exposed to Toby's friends en masse, and she's holding up rather well. Jennifer is what Angela and I would call a Proper Person. By which we mean a mature, fully functioning adult, as opposed to a basket-case or a half-wit. The fact that she works within the National Health Service as an administrator makes her all the more worthy of the PP label, as do the sexy rim-less glasses and the responsible attitude towards alcohol (i.e. not knocking it back something chronic). Even more persuasive is her friendly, level tone, all of which is in complete contrast to Toby's ex, Tamara, who by now would have got pissed, taken offence at something and burst into tears.

Angela has used the occasion to invite along a young man she has hopes for. Scott, however, is not quite a Proper Person. He is a squat, somewhat swarthy character whom Angela introduced to us as a fire-eater. 'But he doesn't do fire-eating any more,' she explained. 'He's trying to get into telly.'

Scott smiled one of those winning wide-mouthed grins. 'I do a bit of juggling, too,' he said in an un-compromising Australian accent. 'Bit of unicycle. Bit of comedy. Your basic all-round bloody entertainer.'

It was obvious Angela fancied him. From the way her head flopped sideways towards him and from his easy, breezy manner around her, I took it that tonight would be the night. I felt a tiny bit depressed at the thought of the short-arsed, barrel-chested Aussie jiggling around on top of my old friend.

'Would she have failed the hacksaw test, mate?' he asks. 'Would you have rather sawn your own arm off with a hacksaw the next morning than woken her up?'

'I'd have sawn my own head off . . .'

Morticia, who is here with her very irritating boyfriend Malcolm, rolls her eyes: at Scott, at me, at the banality of the conversation, it's not clear.

'If you spoke to this pathetic creature on the phone beforehand, why did you agree to go out with her?' she inquires.

'You're right, of course. I was finessed into it,

somehow. She's one of those women – those people – who make all sorts of assumptions, whole *hierarchies* of assumptions that you can only undermine by having the energy to pick your way back to the initial assumption and exposing it. I got caught in her web of unexamined assumptions. Does that make sense?'

Scott says, 'So when are you seeing her again, mate?' which makes me like him a bit more.

Malcolm now demonstrates why he is so very irritating. 'Bit desperate, isn't it? Having to find women in the papers?'

Morticia and Malcolm are Proper People. Morticia might even be a VPP. They met at a weekend training seminar.

'Is it?' I reply. 'Where did you find Beverly, then?'

'Weekend training seminar,' he says with a bit of a smirk.

'Who crept into whose room?' asks Angela.

'I believe she crept into mine . . .'

There are cheers and whoops. Morticia can't decide whether to be lightly amused or mortified at the revelation.

'I did ring up and invite her,' he protests.

'What was his chat-up line?' I ask. I hope it was something really duff.

Morticia's hand flies to her lips. She has to suppress a rare burst of hilarity. 'He asked if I wanted to pop over and watch the Formula One from Monza.'

Something about the way she says Monza makes everyone round the table howl, even Jennifer, who doesn't know her. Malcolm is suitably embarrassed and I warm slightly to the dull stick.

'Did you tell the mad hippie the bee joke?' asks Angela.

'No I bloody didn't.'

'What's the bee joke?' asks Jennifer.

'The bee joke,' I explain, 'is a unique joke that leaves half the world cold, but the other half find hilarious. I myself belong in the latter camp, but there's never any telling which way it will go.'

'He tells it to women he fancies,' says Angela.

'Oh, God. That awful joke about the beehives. The one that's not even a joke.' This is Morticia. She has made this statement to remind the table that I once desired her.

'It's quite true, you weren't amused.' I neglect to add that in the whole of our eighteen months together, I probably told Morticia one to two jokes per week, a total – not including off-the-cuff humorous remarks – of 100, let's say. She laughed – as distinct from smiling thinly – at no more than four. If I remember, I'll put them in an appendix at the end.

'Go on then,' says Malcolm. 'Let's hear it.'

'I couldn't possibly.'

'I know it, mate,' says Scott. 'Is the punchline . . . ?' He leans in very close and whispers in my ear.

'That's the one,' I confirm.

'No, you're right,' he tells Morticia. 'It's about as funny as a fire in an orphanage.'

'Did she phone you afterwards?' asks Angela.

'The mad hippie? No, she didn't.'

Odd, that. I was reasonably certain that she'd pursue me to the ends of the earth, that she'd become one of those people you can never quite escape. Possibly, to the man she knew in the publishing trade, she was such an individual and he had used the opportunity to remove her from his life when he'd changed jobs. Mind you, Angela's dinner party is taking place only a week after my Flight From Peckham. Each time the phone rings nowadays, a riptide of unease goes through my guts as I pick up the receiver.

My hope is that she's lost my number. Or that Pierre has shat on it.

The Flight From Peckham. I think I shall always remember the wondrous sense of release I felt as I made my escape through the south London sprawl. Something uncomfortably creepy about the fact that we were the only people in that strange, brooding café. If this were a magical-realist novel, I would force myself to return to the scene several weeks later only to discover . . . no café. On the corner where I expected to see George's, there would be a butcher's. Or a locksmith's. 'There was a pub here once called the *King George*,' an old-timer would tell me. 'A bomb fell on it in the Blitz. No one was killed except a homeless woman called Annie who used to kip behind the bar. They found her shoes two streets away.'

Perhaps I should have phoned her. Made up some load of bollocks about why I'd vanished: I'd seen someone, a rival who wanted me dead; I went to fetch the car, then I lost my way back; I entered a hypnogogic fugue state (it's a thing I do) and the next thing I knew,

I was at home watching *Countdown*. Someone as hopeless as Annie would surely have excused hopelessness in another.

But I knew the truth, I thought.

Men had done it to her before. Diego, the bald twat with the ponytail who'd fucked off back to Spain. The bloke with the poem who'd left no forwarding address. Even the caller on the mobile phone who'd hung up when she'd suggested a date.

Men ran from her. .

Only Katz stayed loyal. Only Katz went *mmm* and listened to her troubles.

The next afternoon I call Angela to thank her for a nice evening.

'Was it all right?'

'Perfect. Loads of wine. Old mates. Some new ones. It was richly enjoyable.'

There is a pause. 'You didn't say anything about the food.'

'Top scoff. Absolutely full marks in the grub department. No complaints whatsoever.'

'You don't think people minded that the fish pie had no crust on it?'

'Not at all. I'd say it was a talking point.'

'I didn't realize the recipe carried on over the page.'

'You said. Everyone had seconds.'

'They weren't just being polite?'

'Look, never mind about any of that. What happened with himself?'

'Who, himself?'

'Who? The *fire-eater*. Did you? Have you?'

From the other end, a heavy sigh. Then in a squeal she says, 'We did it on the carpet!'

'Blood. Dee. Hell.'

'I know!'

'At your age!'

'Not bad, eh?'

'And?'

'Are we going out? I don't know, really. But I'll tell you what. He's . . . he was awfully passionate.'

'I probably don't need to hear this bit.'

Manic giggle. 'He was fan-*tastic*.'

'Oh, please.'

'I came about six times.'

'He did say he was an all-round family entertainer.'

'I can barely walk.'

'That is definitely too much information.'

'What do you think of him?'

'Seemed very pleasant, yeah.' Fucking cocky stud bastard.

'Do you think other people liked him?'

'I'm sure they did. He was very . . . very likeable.'

'He's only thirty-two.'

'Jesus.'

'I know.'

'He seems terribly into me.'

'Clearly.'

'What do you think? Can I ring him?'

'He hasn't called?'

'Not since he left.'

'About an hour ago, right?'

'Do you think he liked me? I mean from the body language, could you tell if he liked me?'

'I would have thought it was pretty clear, wouldn't you? From the ruined carpet alone . . .'

'But he won't think that I'm easy, or anything? Men think these things, don't they?'

'I think he'll be feeling pretty pleased with life, that's what he'll be feeling.'

'Toby and Wasp Woman are going away for the weekend. Do you think I should get Scott to come away with me?'

'Could be a bit soon.'

'I loved the story about the mad hippie. You ought to meet my friend Rochelle. She's lovely.'

'She clanks. We've been through this.'

'I told you you'd only meet madwomen in the newspapers.'

'I'm refining my technique. It won't happen again.'

'Just you be careful, my lad.'

'You too.'

After we hang up, I realize I feel faintly depressed. Six times?

Fucking cocky stud bastard. It must be all that sunshine and seafood.

Attractive professional F, mid 30s,
seeks sophisticated, professional M,
35–45, for nights out, maybe more.
Looks immaterial. SOH essential.

It had been this advert that made me decide to refine my technique. As I drew a big red circle round it, I felt she could have been talking about me.

Sophisticated. I do sophistication. I can loll against a bar in a smart suit and say something that sounds intelligent. I can mix an excellent vodka Martini. I read novels in translation; I see movies with subtitles. Yes. In short, I've got sophistication coming out of my arsehole.

Professional. It is not unprofessional to be between contracts.

35–45. No argument here. I won't even need to tactically enhance my age profile.

Looks immaterial. I always remember something my northern friend Bob said about a handsome if dull colleague of ours. 'The trouble with being a good-looking bastard like Nick is that he's never had to bother developing a personality.' I relate to this statement strongly.

SOH essential. Not a problem. If nothing else comes to mind, I shall tell her what I just read in the paper. The last words of the famous Mexican revolutionary Pancho Villa. As he lay dying in the arms of his campadres, this inspirational figure is reported to have said, 'Tell them I said something.' Or maybe those of the American Civil War general as he looked towards the enemy lines: 'Don't worry, they couldn't hit an elephant from that dist—'

Nights out. I have been on more nights out than you can shake a stick at. Everywhere from Walthamstow dogs (ironically) to TV awards dinners (I'm always on that loud table by the toilets). My preferred format for a night out is strong drinks followed by dinner at the favourite Chinese restaurant in Soho (although women are usually dismayed by the restaurant's powerful lighting and Third World toilet arrangements).

Maybe more. Yup. I'd be up for that. Definitely.

It was when I called Julia's message line – Julia! – and listened to the soft, sexy voice that verged on the posh, the easy intelligent manner as she spoke about what she was like ('eclectic, broad-minded'), what she enjoyed ('books, films, all the usual pursuits'), and what she wanted in a man ('an intellectual equal who can make me laugh') – it was then that I realized that I couldn't just say the first thing that came into my head by way of a reply.

I needed a script.

A couple of hours of trying things out on the laptop, and I had one.

Julia. Hi. My name's Paul.
See, we're on first-name terms already.
I'm six foot two.
True.
Forty-two.
I know, I know . . .
I live in north London and work in TV.
Just let me run with this for a bit.
For fun, I do a lot of the usual urban stuff.
Sooo sophisticated . . .
I read a lot, play tennis; go to the theatre, cinema, bars, restaurants. And every now and again I go off and get lost in the countryside.

Your average well-rounded Londoner, in other words. Note that I didn't say 'lose myself' in the countryside, which would have made me sound like some sort of fucking poet.

I'm bright. And funny. Bright enough not to attempt to prove it here.

Bit too clever-clever? Hmm. Don't know.

I guess I'd like to find someone who's capable of being serious and, like me, equally capable of being very frivolous.

One does like a bit of both, I find.

Anyhow – I won't go on. If you like what you've heard, give me a call.

The script seemed admirably succinct. I practised reading it out, slipping in a few ums and ers and pauses along the way, so it didn't sound like I was reading it out.

I called Julia's message line and, after negotiating a passage through the star keys and hash keys, succeeded in recording a decent 'take', as we say in the broadcasting trade.

Then I waited.

She rang that evening.

'You sounded nice,' she said by way of a curtain-raiser.

'I am. I am nice. Very nice. Ask anyone.'

She laughed. She actually fucking laughed. I felt like that product that does exactly what it says on the tin.

'You sound nice too,' I added hopefully.

'I'm *quite* nice,' she allowed.

'Good,' I replied. 'No point being too nice. People think you're soft in the head if you're too nice.'

'One needs to be just nice enough.'

'Exactly!'

'Not in a cynical way . . .'

'In a *nice* way.'

'Precisely.'

This was marvellous. Less than a minute had passed, and already we were bantering like some quick-fire double-act.

Then she said, 'Two nice people like us should probably meet, wouldn't you say?'

'Definitely. Be foolish not to.'

'One evening, after work?'

'Perfect. Where's good for you?'

'My office is off Longacre.'

'How about Browns? Do you know it?'

'That very *crowded* place on St Martin's Lane? With the fiery torches?'

'That's the one.'

'How will I recognize you?'

'I'll be wearing my black leather jacket, probably. Black roll-neck. And black trousers, I should think.'

'Very much in black, then. What colour is your hair?'

'Er. About that . . .'

'Yes?'

How to phrase this. 'Listen, Julia. I should probably

tell you. I, er.' Deep breath. 'I don't have as much hair as I once used to.'

And then another small miracle. She laughed again.

'I wouldn't worry about that.'

'You don't mind?'

'You've got *some* hair?'

'Oh yeah. Quite a bit really. It's just that it doesn't entirely go all the way across the top.'

'Sounds very contemporary. I look forward to our meeting.'

'Just a sec. How will I recognize you?'

'I'm five nine. Chestnut hair. Tawny coat.'

There was a pause. 'Shouldn't we have some more conversation now? About books and films and holidays and what have you?'

'We can do all that in Browns, can't we?'

After we hung up, I punched the air. This was a ragingly promising beginning, but I had to check myself against over-enthusiasm. Julia had *sounded* sexy and funny and smart over the phone . . . but the very first lesson I'd learned in the lonely hearts business cautioned against making assumptions at this stage. You get a picture of someone in your head, and in walks Frankenstein's mother.

We'd certainly clicked easily enough on the verbal channel. Nevertheless, by agreeing to curtail further discussion until we met, I'd denied myself vital raw material that could have yielded further clues about her. Perhaps there was one very big fact that she wanted to keep up her sleeve until we met. That she weighed seventeen stone. Or would be wearing an electronic tag.

I didn't even know what she did for a living. She could be an unemployed TV producer for all I knew.

(She did sound nice though, didn't she?)

Browns at six-thirty on a Wednesday evening is, as she predicted, crowded.

I find myself a position at the bar from where I can monitor the door, order a glass of house white and begin to get nervous. The place is swarming with young women. And awash with hair. What colour *is* chestnut, exactly? Is it like those shiny conkers I used to collect in my childhood? Come to that, what's tawny? There are tawny owls. And I've heard of tawny port. We're talking very specific shades of brown, aren't we? This is a use of language that denotes a sharp eye for detail, I conclude. I would probably have said brown. Brown coat, brown hair. Leaving aside the hi-blondes and the jet-brunettes, most of the hair here is firmly in the brown section of the spectrum. Perhaps it'll be easier for her to clock me. There aren't many blokes of six foot two dressed entirely in black, sporting not as much hair as they used to.

I've got to be sophisticated and funny, I remind myself. Oh yeah, and professional.

But I spot her the moment she steps through the entrance. (So *that's* tawny; I might have been tempted to describe it as monkey-sick.) The hair, however, is unmistakably chestnut, a deep, complex, lustrous brown that makes me want to put my face in it, even from this distance.

And now she's moving towards me, a slow smile on her lips and a sleepy look in her eyes. Toby was right. Less than fifteen seconds have elapsed – it can only be two or three – we haven't even spoken yet, but it's happened.

Boom. I feel like a weekend fisherman who's landed the prize barracuda.

She's a knockout.

'Paul?'

'Julia.'

She offers me a bunch of fingers. They feel warm and vaguely moist. As though she's recently applied cream.

'You found it then,' I say stupidly.

'It wasn't difficult,' she replies pleasantly. 'It was right here, where it's always been.'

Posh. Not super-posh, but definitely classy. One of those long pale faces that speaks of the English countryside; war memorials and cricket pavilions; idyllic summers with loads of brothers and Labradors. Earrings hang either side of it.

'Drink?' I croak.

'Do you think we should stay here? Only it is a bit . . . you know.'

I knew. A bit too office crowd. 'Let's leave.'

'Finish your wine first.'

There is an ease about the way she speaks to me that I find tremendously attractive. Her lips are not generous, I note, but they have been delicately drawn and are by no means . . . er, mean. Small fine teeth fill her mouth. So small and fine indeed, that I wonder whether she has been supplied with more than the usual number (I am not a dentist, I should make it clear). Brown eyes glitter at me as I drain my glass.

Fuck. Have you ever done that one where you somehow miss your mouth and your drink pours down your chin and then on to your shirt, with some ending up on your shoes, even?

'Bloody hell. How did I do that? Sorry.' She must think I'm a complete pilchard.

'I know somewhere we could go, if you like.' She is sweetly ignoring my distress over the wine spillage.

'Sure. Wherever.'

She turns, allowing me to wipe the worst of the deluge off my chops as I follow. Her hair, I notice, is really a wonder. It flares and gleams as it catches the light, sliding against itself in layers, just like in a shampoo ad. We hit the street, falling into a companionable stride as we make our way in the direction of Trafalgar Square, her heels clop-clopping agreeably alongside me.

'So what bit of TV do you work in?' she asks.

'I produce factual entertainment at the BBC, I'm afraid. How about you?'

'We do PR.'

Excellent. A media whore, like myself. 'Got any interesting clients?'

She shoots me a look. 'All exceptionally dull. Without exception.'

At the side of the Coliseum, we turn into a dark narrow alley that's strewn with litter and smells strongly of wee-wee. I briefly entertain the fantasy: this is a trap. Any second, masked men will spring from the shadows; the last thing I feel will be a gloved hand across my mouth, and the hypodermic needle slipping into my thigh. Forty-eight hours later, I'll wake up on a rubbish tip, missing a kidney.

But she's ringing a bell by a brass plate on the wall.

'It's a little place I know.'

'Sweet, isn't it?'

It is sweet. Low lamplight illuminates a warren of intimate wood-panelled rooms. From the crumpled bohemian look of the clientele, this is a gathering place for lawyers, architects and critics rather than music promoters, video directors and web designers. We settle on to two chairs either side of a tiny table. I order another glass of wine; she, to my disappointment, asks for mineral water.

'Do you not . . . ?'

'I do,' she replies. And leaves it at that. The tawny coat has been discarded in favour of some sort of modern-woman trouser suit. She's slim. And fills those trousers pretty damn effectively, I note. Above, there's a lemon-yellow blouse with an unbuttoned, mannishly high collar. Above that, two brown eyes sit in a sleepy expression on her face and contemplate me with pleasant amusement.

Don't fuck this up, I'm thinking. Be sophisticated. Give her some SOH.

'So do you come here often?'

I can't believe I said it. But miraculously, she does

not shudder or in any other way recoil from the horrible cliché.

'I bring clients here sometimes. It's cosy and quiet. You can hear what the other person's saying.'

'Oh Christ, I know. It's an age thing. Eyesight, hearing. It all goes downhill after . . . after a certain age.'

Julia looks a little surprised that I should be bringing this up, but I plough on. 'I had to have lunch with a psychic once. She claimed to be in touch with Kenny Everett on a psychical plane. I took her to Kensington Place. The noise level was louder than a road drill. If it were a factory, they'd have to provide ear-defenders. I couldn't hear a bloody word. Was a total waste of time.'

Julia doesn't look all that impressed by my sparkling anecdote.

'Kenny Everett is the DJ who died of AIDS,' I throw in for clarification. 'They reckon he caught it off the same bloke who gave it to Freddie Mercury.'

This extra bit of background hasn't helped.

'Julia!'

'James!'

Julia has leapt to her feet to greet a tanned, handsome, floppy-haired character who has wriggled out of the woodwork from somewhere. They do the kissy-kissy thing – she holds on to his arms during the embrace – then they natter with obvious enthusiasm about where they last saw one another. Was it Jack's birthday party? No, it was Bruce's wedding. No, it wasn't; it was poor Philippa's funeral. When Bruce made that awful speech and Alex had a row with the vicar in the churchyard. They stand there, smiling at each other, slightly breathless. *Introduce me*, I'm screaming silently. *Only I'm finding it increasingly hard to maintain this pleasantly disinterested expression.*

Now he's saying, 'I'm going to stay with Louis in LA for a bit. But after I come back. Definitely. I'd love that.'

The kissy-kissy thing again. Twice. I mean *both* cheeks, for God's sake. He grants me a sort of semi-nod when he finally fucks off.

'Sorry,' she says when she sits down. 'That was so rude. I should have introduced you.'

Well, why didn't you then? 'Who was that?' I ask as lightly as I can.

'James? Oh, I've known James for donkey's years.' As if that explained anything. Her eyes are shining, I notice. They're certainly more alight than when I was relating my fascinating tale about Freddie and Kenny.

'I recently met an old school friend who I haven't seen for thirty years.'

She stares at me, a little distracted. She pulls that pleasant face girls pull when they're not actually listening.

'Funny. He was a bit of an oddball then. And he's still a bit of an oddball. I guess people don't change that much.'

A pause while she considers this dazzling insight into the human condition. 'Did you recognize him?' she asks finally.

'It was amazing. He looked exactly the same.' Apart from the short trousers and the cap and the Cycling Proficiency Test badge.

My hand reflexively strokes my hairline. I decide not to tell her how, midway through the second pint, he sniggered; then couldn't stop sniggering; then was seized by irreversible hilarity; then literally cried with laughter; then, finally, still spluttering with mirth, managed to cough up, 'So what happened to the barnet, mate?'

Suddenly, I think I twig why Julia didn't introduce me to her floppy-haired friend. I do it myself, from time to time, so I can't really blame her.

She'd forgotten my name.

The drowsy, distant expression is back. I feel like a fly on the other side of a window, buzzing soundlessly against the glass.

'Why did you put an ad in the paper?' I hear myself ask. 'Don't you get to meet tons of people through your job?'

'Clients,' she replies with depthless sadness. 'And marketing and publicity people.'

'Ah.'

She nods a solemn nod. She may be a posh girl slumming it in medialand, but I still can't fathom it. Women like her are asked out three times a day, aren't they?

'Anyway,' she says with a small smile, 'what about you? You've told me hardly anything about your life.' She picks up her glass of mineral water and prepares to be enthralled.

OK. Here we go. Sophistication. Humour. Wit. Charm. Professionalism.

'I. Er. It's. What about it?'

'Well.' She tries to think of something she might like to know. 'What are you producing at the moment?'

'Actually, I'm sort of between engagements right now,' I admit.

'Like an actor. Resting.'

'I've been trying to write a novel.'

'You are lucky. To have the time,' she says, though she doesn't look like she necessarily means it.

A silence falls between us. I can feel her slipping away. I need to do something to kick this encounter up a gear, to recapture that flirty optimistic rapport we had on the phone. I want to tell her, Look, I'm not really like this. I'm quite amusing and cheerful normally. If we could just go back to my flat, put some music on, and do in a bottle of wine or two, I'm sure I could be a little more scintillating.

She seems perfectly polite, and just friendly enough ... but I'm getting no real chemistry. What would a master seducer do at this point, I wonder?

'Do you know the bee joke?' I ask.

She looks a little startled. 'The *bee* joke?'

'It's a joke I know. Lots of people don't find it at all funny.'

'Is it very *long*?'

'Not at all. Couple of minutes, I'd say.' And by the way, do you perhaps have something better to do?

'I don't think I do know it.'

'OK. There's these two blokes, right. And one says to the other, What have you been up to, then? And the

108

other replies, Me? Oh, nothing much. Well, actually, since you ask, I've been breeding bees. Really? Yes, he says. I've been breeding bees; I've actually managed to breed a bee this big.' With my hands, I indicate an insect measuring around ten inches long. 'Good God, says the man. I know, says the other. A bee this big . . .?' The thing with the hands again. 'How many have you got? Well, he says. Let's see, I've probably got ten thousand of them . . .'

Is she amused? It's hard to say. In any case, I have no alternative but to carry on. I don't overly drag it out, but neither do I rush it. The bee joke, I think you'll find, has its own natural pace and rhythm, and in this, as in all the best comedy, timing is.

Everything.

I have reached the line before the punchline. She is actually smiling now, sensing the approaching denouement, waiting for the big finish.

My heart is thumping as I deliver the coup de gag.

I have to admit, I've done it better. But it doesn't matter. I am rewarded with a genuine, full-throated chuckle. Her shoulders shake, her pupils flash, sparkling water glints from the tips of her eye teeth.

'That's quite funny,' she says, clearly surprised.

'I'm so glad you think so.'

'I know someone who'd adore that joke. Do you know the Colony Room?'

'You mean . . . as in, The Colony Room?' As in the notorious Soho watering hole made famous by Francis

Bacon and Jeffrey Bernard and all those giant pissheads of yesteryear?

'Do you fancy a visit? We might find Alex in there.'

Alex isn't here. In fact, Alex hasn't been seen all week. But I am sitting in the Colony Room, the legendary sixties members club where artists used to rub shoulders with burglars and barrow boys (and where appropriate, take them back to their studios). It's all quite agreeably scruffy, with some rather good art hanging on the walls. Damien Hirst and Keith Allen are standing near the bar, barking at each other.

Literally barking.

Barking as in woof-woof.

'Absinthe,' says the barman knowingly. (This, it should be noted, took place in the days when the bad boy of Brit Art drank alcohol.)

'Not Good Boy Choc Drops, then.'

He laughs. But my bon mot is wasted as Julia, sitting in the corner, hasn't heard it. Apart from the hound-impressionists, we appear to be the only people in.

I deliver our drinks – wine, still mineral water again – and struggle to come up with anything that might set this date alight. Her very choice of beverage is deeply suggestive to me of how un-sparkling, how un-intoxicating she must be finding this encounter. Me, I could sit here all evening watching that hair sliding around, the sleepy smile drifting about the delicate features. I am falling for her; I am falling for her deep sense of calm and entitlement (this could be a posh-girl thing), to say nothing of the exciting way she occupies her trouser suit.

Confession: I have never been terribly expert at this seduction business. My 'technique', insofar as you can dignify it with that name, has not significantly evolved from my days as a student, when the aim would be to get both parties as incapable as possible and hope for the best.

'The thing about women,' Toby once told me, 'is they want to be wanted. It's as simple as that. They find our desire for them seductive in itself.'

'Even if the bloke's got three heads, say?'

'The most gorgeous pieces of totty are quite often found with the ugliest of men.' *Totty* is another one of those words only Toby still employs without heavy quotation marks around it. 'Explanation: dedication. If you push on a closed door long and hard enough, it will open to you.'

'The door is flattered and charmed by the effort one is going to? The strength and duration of the pushing is, of itself, flattering and charming? Just to be clear.'

'Women,' he commented, 'respect our need for them.'

'They wouldn't find it irritating. All that grunting and shoving?'

'This is central. Women are Not Like Us.'

Angela, who was present at this discussion, nodded in agreement. And then voiced the opposite view. 'But you've got to *like* the chap. What if it was some horrible great brute . . .' – and here she made a face to frighten children with, her mouth going one way, eyes

111

swivelling, shoulders hunched, a Quasimodo sort of effect. She produced a drooling sound effect to accompany it.

Toby pounced. 'This is exactly my point. Eventually, you would be *moved* by the monster's desire for you.'

Oddly, I found myself agreeing with Toby. Some arrangement of this sort must have been at work in the case of . . . I shall call him X: a former colleague of mine who, whilst not the hideous apparition brought to life above, was a character of few obvious qualities. Possessing neither wit, nor looks, nor intelligence, it seemed obvious to me that X was a dud. A soft-boiled egg. In that memorable phrase, a shot lettuce. His was clearly a ridiculous existence, and while I stepped back from recommending that he throw himself off a convenient high building, I couldn't for the life of me see what the point of the bloke was.

And yet. Heavy sigh.

And yet, women thought he was, if not the bee's knees, then maybe some other part of the bee. The bee's shinbone. Or the bee's ankles. Several really quite attractive colleagues of ours – there was W, who reminded me of a sexy duck; Y, who was as tall and skinny as a model; beautiful Z, who cried in the pub when he left her for A – all these lovely young women allowed themselves to be invaded by X.

X, for Christ's sake!

X, whose name would make your heart sink if you learned you were to be stuck next to him at dinner (it would, I promise you).

X, whose one exceptional quality was plainly that of persistence.

Night after night he could be observed in the favoured post-work hostelry, leering across the top of his glass into his target's chest area, smiling wolfishly and muttering . . . well, God only knows what. Nothing he ever said to me came close to what you or I would call charming or interesting. Clichéd drivel, I should have said, were the *mots justes* here. His victims, meanwhile, seemed . . . perhaps the best word is *hypnotized*. Bemused, their eyes would shine a little wider, their lips might part slightly as X droned onwards. Spatially, I noticed how he would often trap them against a wall or a pillar, somehow interposing his body between them and any direct route of escape. Every fibre of his musculature – if that is the word for what must have been a fairly flabby physique – every atom of his being said *I want you*.

And it worked. He must have worn them down. Sheer *application* seemed to do the trick because, sure enough, weeks later it would become apparent that X and Y were finally an item. The look of mild confusion on the sexy duck's face had become one of satisfied complacency. Released from her position up against the pillar, she seemed infuriatingly content to paddle alongside this fool. And he – and this was the real killer – he didn't even have the brains to gloat. To realize what a catch he'd made.

The silly fucker thought he actually deserved her.

I ask you: how annoying is *that*?

(God, I am bitter, aren't I?)

* * *

I can't help thinking that matters would be greatly improved if Julia and I could just do things the other way round. Instead of all this halting, silly conversation leading to the goal of falling into bed together, surely if we just fell into bed together, it would pave the way to a proper conversation. I, for one, would certainly feel more relaxed about life.

Probably a long time must have passed with no one saying anything at all, because now she pipes up, 'So you're not actually working at the moment?'

I'm sure she didn't intend it to come out like a slap in the face, but I feel a little stung. 'Not at the moment, no.'

'The novel you're writing, though. That must be exciting.'

Is she taking the piss? Everyone I know who's ever been unemployed has begun writing a novel. Or at the very least trotted along to Rymans for a packet of printer paper and some of those nice Japanese pens.

'When I say I'm writing a novel, it would probably be more accurate to say I'm toying with a few ideas.'

Actually, it would be more accurate to say I've begun writing the same story five or six times. It's about a young man who works in TV who one day finds himself with no job and no girlfriend. Beyond that, I've no idea what happens to him. I've also taken the opportunity to 'refresh' my CV, condensing it to a single page, altering the typeface to something more contemporary, and – gulp – removing my date of birth. I haven't gone so far as to actually send it to anyone.

'How lovely,' she says dreamily. 'To have the time to write.'

'It is quite nice, yeah.' So long as you can stand the silence. And the shortage of gossip. 'Your own boss, sort of thing. No dickheads or wankers to answer to.' No actual income to speak of either.

She smiles. 'They can be a problem, can't they?'

'Tell me about it!'

Why have I become some sort of barrow boy in Julia's presence, I wonder? I think it *is* a posh-girl thing. Probably I am a little fascinated by this world of Sarahs and Emmas and Fionas that I have never been a part of. It's telling that I have never gone out with anyone you'd call posh. Classy, yes. Beautiful, sexy, unique, distinctive, lots of other words like those . . . yes, yes and yes again. But posh, never.

I guess Morticia was the closest to posh, and she isn't properly posh. You can have any number of Prada handbags; you can buy an ottoman and bury it under a ton of Christie's catalogues and issues of *Country Life*, but you'll always be Beverly from Southgate, won't you?

I remember the first time I tried to get off with a posh girl. She was called Poppy. In all of my eighteen years, I had never come across anyone of that name outside a children's story book. What she was doing at Manchester University in the mid-Seventies was a mystery. Also slumming it, I guess. She was one of those wispy willowy girls who seem to travel about in their personal bubble. She only had to open her mouth for me to picture the wisteria-clad pile in the home counties, the snoring Labrador in front of the Aga, the handsome, sporting brothers. The fact that she liked smoking dope and listening to Pink Floyd's *Atom Heart Mother* made her all the more attractive to me, and to the other males in our little drug-taking circle.

When I managed to get her alone, I did everything in my power to impress her. I told her how much I was into R D Laing ('mad is only a label that society sticks on people who won't conform'). I raved about a clearly cultish novel that I'd just read, *V* by Thomas Pynchon. I allowed her to look at my Salvador Dali poster. And at some point during side two of Carole King's *Tapestry*, I think I tried to kiss her. (All right, I know I did.)

Perhaps I'd missed a step in the process leading up to that moment, because the outcome was not a success. Indeed, she acted as if nothing had happened, removing my hand from her hip in a businesslike manner, standing, yawning, and commenting that she had better call it a night because she had to be up early for a midday lecture on Chaucer.

'Thanks for the smoke,' she said at the door, well-brought-up to the end.

Of course, Poppy could be a grandmother by now. But here am I in another decade – another *century*, practically – with another posh girl, once again struggling to make an impact in the face of all that breeding, that lineage, that . . . er, poshness.

116

And now another floppy-haired character has popped up out of nowhere. He looks a bit more raddled than the last one, his tanned face being a little pock-marked, and there being something ancient behind his eyes. Nothing wrong in the follicular department, however. The bloke's got fucking curtains of it sprouting all over his head.

He and Julia are driven to do the kissy-kissy thing again.

'Perkin, this is Paul.' She *remembered*.

'Hi,' I say lamely. After a pause, I add, 'Did you say Perkin?'

With infinite boredom the young man explains. 'My distant ancestor was Perkin Warbeck.'

'I think we did him in History,' I reply. Some sort of shit-stirrer, wasn't he? Led a revolt against taxes. Or hedges, or some such.

'You would have done,' asserts the present Perkin. Then to Julia he says, 'Are you going to Oliver's fortieth? I could run you up there if you are.'

'That's sweet of you.'

They stand staring at each other for a few seconds. Then Perkin says, 'So how do you know the great Julia, then?'

'Well,' I begin. The *great* Julia? 'It's. Well. The thing is. Julia and I. It's. Actually.'

'Actually Paul works at the BBC,' she says brightly.

'Ah,' says Perkin, significantly. 'The BBC.'

I am about to explain that since my boss left six weeks ago and my contract ran out and my electronic pass expired, I haven't worked there or anywhere else.

117

But Perkin continues, 'Who's that newsreader who's always wrinkling her nose?'

'Sorry?'

'Bloody attractive girl, but she always wrinkles up her nose when she smiles.'

'I, er.'

'Ask her to stop it, would you?'

'It's actually not something I'd normally get involved in, to be honest.'

Perkin seems disappointed. 'Shame. Makes her look pre-sexual. Somebody ought to say something.' Then to Julia he adds, 'I just ran into Logan.' He mentions a venue I don't catch.

'Was he asking after me?' she inquires.

'Yes and no,' he replies and they both laugh.

When Perkin fucks off – I mean when Perkin bids us goodnight – Julia says, 'That was Perkin.'

'And how do you know the great Perkin, then?' I inquire. Were you once lovers, perhaps?

'Golly. Good question.' Then after a pause, 'Should we go somewhere a bit more comfortable?'

It was rhetorical, the one about being more comfortable. Because moments later we are on the march through Soho again, her heels banging on the paving stones as we zigzag our way through its alleys and thoroughfares, the chestnut hair swinging about in the neon lights, a very determined expression parked on Julia's countenance.

'This is somewhere else you know, is it? Where we're going to?' I pant alongside.

118

She does not hear me. Or if she does, she declines to reply.

Moments later, she practically hauls me through a gate in some railings and down a flight of steps.

'Very cutting edge,' she mutters. 'Hardly anyone knows about it.'

A stab on a bell and we are admitted to a velvety gloom, pin-pricked by hundreds of tiny spots of light. It's the level of illumination they bathe those jumpy little night creatures in at the zoo. As my eyes adjust, sofas and armchairs, a bar, the outlines of several dozen handsomely bored people resolve into the shadows.

'Julia,' someone growls.

'Bryan!'

An older man in a beautiful suit, single rays of halogen pinging off his dark floppy hair, embraces my companion. As they part, I realize there is something terribly familiar about his long, narrow face.

'Was that . . . was that Bryan Ferry?' I hiss as we glide across the carpet.

She shoots me an old-fashioned look. Or she could have been peering over my shoulder, it's kind of hard to tell in this light.

We perch at the bar. 'Cosmopolitan,' she commands. The barman doesn't wait to discover what I would like in the way of a drink before he goes about his business.

'Quite dark in here,' I comment, to get the chit-chat re-started.

Julia is distracted. She's fumbling around in her handbag and comes up with a cigarette.

'I didn't think you—'

'I don't.'

To be honest, I'm beginning to feel like a bit of spare part here. Away off in the shadows, surrounded by a group of other shadows ... is that Madonna? Or merely someone who looks very like her?

'This Oliver friend of yours. Who's forty. Would I know him?'

She turns to look at me. An indefinable expression travels across her face. Some nameless pain, or a touch of wind, it's impossible to guess.

'Paul. Listen, I—'

A figure has hoved up beside us in the gloom. A tall, dreamy-looking chap with the floppiest hair I have ever seen on a human male. The sheer extravagant *weight* of the stuff is an affront. So too is its luxuriant thickness. The obscene abundant growth of it and the effortless way it seems so securely anchored to his skull makes me feel a little unwell. The plain fact is, if this fucker's hair were any floppier, his head would fall off.

Not that I'm envious, or anything.

There is no friendly kissy-kissy this time.

'Logan, this is Paul.'

He nods at me, sending great swathes of plumage crashing about, whole banks of it set on the slide. It seems to take about five minutes to come to rest.

Julia says, 'Do you think you can give us a moment?'

For one horrible second, I think I am being asked to go and make myself scarce. But it's they who take themselves off, floating away to a nearby sofa for what is plainly a heart-to-heart.

Instantly, I see it all too clearly. Julia and this Logan bloke – maybe it began as a hair thing – they were once an item, and are no longer. This is that immediate period following the break-up where one party or the other attempts to make sense of what has happened, or mounts a bid for reconciliation, or hurls a glass of red wine over a perfectly good piece of John Smedley knitwear.

Their body language is gruesomely fascinating. Both are kind of jack-knifed into the sofa, their heads and their feet almost touching, their sexual organs as far away from each other's as practicably possible in the space allowed. Her wrists are doing a lot of gesticulating. They semaphore a commentary containing insistence, frustration, and a little helplessness in the mix as well. He's staring at her dreamily, nodding now and then, and possibly (maybe it's my imagination) stifling the odd yawn.

I realize:

1. I have lost the will to live.
2. I am starving. We have not eaten.
3. There is nothing immediately edible in my fridge apart from a jar of pickled cucumbers, a tube of tomato paste and two elderly eggs. (Hmm, Mediterranean cucumber omelette, perhaps?)
4. I have missed a documentary about giant squid. Apparently they have overtaken humans in terms of bio-mass. This means giant squid now occupy more room on earth than mankind, although not yet on the Northern Line.

121

What the fuck am I doing here?

The ex-lovers' conclave lasts about half an hour. I reckon most blokes in my position would have stormed off in a huff, but something keeps me rooted to my bar stool, and not just the thrill of being in London's hottest undiscovered night spot; not even when Alan Yentob comes in, still yacking on his mobile phone. At one point, about halfway through, Julia turns towards me and raises a speculative thumb – I thumbs-up her in reply. I guess I'm intrigued to see how this turns out.

Finally, the two of them rise from their sofa. They stand closer to one another than friends would, but still do not embrace. He sort of tilts his jaw, as though readying it for a snogette, but she turns away sharply, and in seconds has returned to her vacated place alongside me.

'Sorry.'

'Not at all.'

'*Really?*'

'Forget it.'

'You must think I'm awful.'

'Very far from it. That chap was a . . . a previous, I take it.'

'Golly. Was it that obvious?'

I pull a face. The one that says, *Yup, there's not much you can hide from a trained observer of human nature such as myself.*

'When did it finish?' I ask quietly.

She sighs heavily. As she fumbles for a cigarette, her face begins to wobble out of control.

'Exes, eh?' I jump in to cover her embarrassment. 'They'll fucking do you up, every time.'

How is it that I have once again become some kind of gangland personage? I feel like I'm channelling one of the Kray twins.

A fat tear carves a shiny track down her cheekbone as she sets fire to her Marlboro Lite.

'Listen. Julia. I didn't mean to—'

She waves a dismissive hand. 'I'm sorry. I'm not really ready to do this.'

And then it all comes spilling out. About her and Logan. How they'd been going out, on and off, for four years. How at first it was very much the big romance, how she'd actually allowed herself to think he could be The One. How they'd lived together for a while, and everything was fine, and they'd even discussed the 'M' word (most probably after a rousing fuck, I imagine, though I keep this thought to myself). But Logan is an artist, a painter actually, and he isn't very good at the old bourgeois lifestyle. In particular, he seemed to resent the idea of being a kept man, being as how his daubings weren't exactly flying off the gallery walls (I paraphrase). Things began to get a bit sticky between them so they decided it might be better for everyone if he moved out of her comfortable flat in Clapham and found some shit-hole of his own for a bit. After he did, the relationship improved hugely, his mood bucked up, his work became 'freer', and the two little bunnies were all happy again for a while. But then – well, wouldn't you know it? – Leonardo meets someone. A woman, to be exact. She says he's welcome to turn the top floor of her house into a studio stroke bedroom, and before long he's living up there and working up there, and not long afterwards, by the sound of it, his tubes of acrylic aren't the only things being squeezed on a regular basis, the dirty fucking dog (once again, I paraphrase). Anyway, this arrangement doesn't last, Logan being Logan, and soon he's bunking up with some fellow called Louis (the same Louis that James was going to visit in LA, I wondered, but didn't press the point). And then he starts shagging Louis's sister, which doesn't endear him to Louis, nor to Louis's sister's boyfriend, who attacks him with a table lamp, and one night he even pitches up on her (Julia's) doorstep, and they end up in bed together. And, well, frankly Paul, what can she tell me? He's just *impossible* . . .

A pause to consider her last remark. 'Lovely hair, though,' I quip.

A small miracle follows. The look of anguish that has accompanied this tale dissolves into laughter. Full-throated, genuine laughter. Better than for the bee joke, even. It seizes her for a full thirty seconds or so, all manner of cathartic stuff seeming to pass in its tide (acceptance, retrenchment, renewal and what have you). Rarely, if ever, have I said quite such the right thing at the right moment. And because I have magically turned pain into pleasure and now feel that anything is possible, when she stops laughing and is just sitting there looking at me with her head on one side, I have an idea.

'Paul—' she begins.

I cut her short. I lean over and kiss her.

Perhaps I missed a step in the process leading up to this moment, because the outcome is not a success. Indeed, she acts as if nothing at all has happened, rearranging her hair somewhat and commenting that it has been a lovely evening, she's enjoyed it, and is sorry if she has bored me. We must do it again some time.

'Don't tell me. You have to be up early for a midday lecture on Chaucer.'

I don't say it, but it's what I'm thinking.

4

'YOU THINK SHE USED you as a stalking horse for this Logan chap?'

Toby's question is a surgical strike upon an area of doubt in my mind.

'What? To make him mad with jealousy? Hmm. Could be.'

'Did you kiss her?' asks Angela.

'*No!*' I reply, outraged at the suggestion. Toby and I look at one another. One of those *tsk, women* looks. 'Anyway,' I come back on the attack. 'Never mind about me. What about you and shagger-boy?'

Angela affects not to know who I am talking about. Once again, we are arranged around her sitting room debriefing one another about the latest twists and turns in our romantic careers.

'The unicyclist. Juggler. Mr bloody Six Times a Night.'

'Scott? He's gone skiing.' Then she pulls a face. A look of mock-agony. '*He hasn't rung me,*' she wails. 'Don't you think he should have rung me? I've tried to ring *him.*'

'What do you mean, you've tried?' I inquire.

'The thing is, I don't really know where he's staying,' she replies.

I see it all too clearly. Mr Six Times a Night is never going to return from his 'skiing trip'. He's about to join the long list of Angela suitors whom we've shaken hands with and said *Good to meet you* to. Whom we've sat next to at dinner and made polite conversation with. Whom we've affected to like (some of whom we actually did like). One more among the many miscellaneous blokes who've blazed brightly for a few weeks or months and then – *pfff* – vanished like the smoke from the snuffed candle after the last minicab has departed.

In the meanwhile, I have struggled to draw any lessons at all from my date with Julia. Beyond our dazzling debut on the phone, we didn't seem to have made any deeper connection. The evening felt like stepping through a door into another world – her world – of private drinking clubs and increasingly floppy-haired young men. If I had to reach some sort of conclusion, it would be that I failed to sparkle – and she failed to fancy me.

It can happen, I guess.

But why did I fail to sparkle? If I'd acted as charming and amusing and – fuck, yes – as sophisticated as I'd been billed; if I hadn't told that cretinous story about Kenny Everett catching AIDS off the same person who gave it to Freddie Mercury; if I hadn't spilled wine down my face; if I generally hadn't been on the back foot throughout . . . would things have turned out any different?

Sparkling is a curious one, isn't it? You cannot

sparkle in a vacuum, I find. Some women inspire one to sparkle, and others – even those you *wish* you could sparkle for – they somehow fail to activate the relevant mechanisms in the brain that are responsible for sparkling. Somewhere, probably an inch and a half above the roof of your mouth, there's a vulgar little nodule that's been there for millions of years which, if fired up the right way, turns you into Pierce Brosnan, but if denied the correct inputs, leaves you burbling crap and decanting Sauvignon on to your boots.

And the kiss? There was a time when I might have replayed the scene endlessly in my head, mentally howling with mortification every time I leaned across and put my lips against hers. Oddly, although I did not admit it to Angela, I did not wake the next morning cringing with embarrassment at the memory. I guess it's a sign that I'm older now. My view is: hey, it was just a kiss.

I feel curiously indifferent about the whole encounter.

LESSON SEVEN:
Fuck it. If it doesn't work,
it doesn't work. Move on.
Next, sort of thing.

'So what about you and Wasp Woman?' asks Angela.

'Oh, we're fine,' Toby replies.

I feign a look of mild interest. But I know – because Toby has specifically told me not to tell Angela – that he is going to propose to her.

'Fuck. King. Hell,' I believe was my exact response when he vouchsafed this news. 'You don't hang around, do you?'

Toby looked rather pleased with himself. 'No sense delaying once you've got all your little ducks lined up in a row.'

This was a piece of business wisdom, I gathered. 'Well, congratulations.'

'Too soon,' he cautioned. 'Haven't actually popped the question yet.'

'How are you going to . . .' Break it to her. '. . . go about it?'

'Posh restie – River Room at the Savoy, probably – atmosphere of mystery and romance, timeless Father Thames flowing past the net curtains. At a suitable point – after the main course and before the pud, I'm guessing – I whip out the padded blue box, sink on to one knee and make the speech. Would you do me the greatest honour, sort of thing, girls love all that bollocks. Then she says yes, presumably. Turns on the water-works. I, meanwhile, hope to Christ I can get up again in a dignified fashion.'

'You're actually – really – going to get down on one knee?' Toby is built for comfort rather than speed, as they say.

'Definitely. Just like knights of old in armour bold.'

'In the Savoy?'

'There isn't a woman in the world whose heart wouldn't melt at a piece of theatre like that.'

'You said, she says yes *presumably*.'

'Yes, she does. Presumably.'

'You don't know for sure?'

'Well, I haven't asked her. It would spoil the moment.'

'I don't think I could bear the uncertainty. I mean – what if? – I'm sure it won't happen. But what if she says no?'

Toby did something businesslike with his lips. The sort of expression the lizard-faced factory owner pulls before deciding to close the plant with the loss of twelve hundred jobs, all production transferred to Korea. Then he regarded me in what appeared to be a new light.

'Funnily enough,' he replied, 'that is the one outcome I hadn't considered.'

I understood why Toby didn't want Angela to know about his marriage plans; I would feel the same. Angela would over-emote. She would become so excited about the whole project that the actual proposal could end up feeling like an anticlimax. Also, inevitably, burdened with such a bit of high-grade gossip, she would be forced to share it with everyone she knew; somehow Wasp Woman would discover her boyfriend was going to ask her to marry him before he'd even sauntered along to Asprey-Garrard and bought the second-cheapest ring.

Now Angela is saying, 'You know, you should meet my friend . . .'

'Oh God, not her again. The incredible clanking woman.'

'No. Not Rochelle, actually.' Angela pretends to be offended. 'There's a woman in my reading group.'

Toby and I exchange deadpan glances. I think it was the phrase *reading group*.

'Go on,' I say wearily.

'Not if you're going to take that attitude.'

'Please. I have no attitude. What's her name?'

'Sylvia.'

'*Sylvia!*'

'What's wrong with that?'

'No one's called Sylvia any more. How old is this creature?'

'You are *so* rude. She's around our age.'

Ah.

'Well, what about her? I presume she doesn't clank or laugh like a donkey . . .'

'She's a very sweet woman. Far too good for you, actually.'

'What does she do?'

'Nothing. She's retired.'

'*Retired?* You want to fix me up with a *pensioner?*'

'She's *not* a pensioner. She had her own business.'

'Know what I'd do if I were you?' says Toby. 'I'd advertise. Instead of running after all these loops, I'd run an ad myself.'

I am struck by the simple brilliance of this idea. 'Fuck. Why didn't I think of that? The loops can run after me.'

'When you advertise, you reverse the psychology. Suddenly, you're inside the tent pissing out.'

'Instead of being the fish, I become the fisherman.'

'*They* nibble on *your* hook.'

'I don't know why I didn't think of it.'

'OK, here's how it works. You run an ad. You get, say, twenty replies. Ten you can reject straight away. Too old, obvious nutters, whatever. The other ten you call up, chat to on the phone. *Hello. How are you? Tell me all about your boring job at Camden Council, blah blah blah.* Five turn out to be duds, right? Leaving five you're prepared to date. You book them in; if you're lucky, there'll be one you'll want to see again.'

Angela is appalled by the cold calculus of romance. 'That is so horrid,' she protests.

'Way it is, I'm afraid. You can double them up to save time. See one at six o'clock, the next at eight.'

'How would you feel if you were one of the women who didn't even get a call back? Or what if you had the phone call, and then he didn't want to meet you?'

Toby shrugs. 'You'd get over it, probably.'

'I am very excited about this,' I admit.

'What will you put in your ad then?' says Angela. 'Bald, unemployed TV producer, the wrong side of forty . . .' She starts giggling at her own wickedness. 'Bald, unemployed TV producer, wrong side of forty, superficial, unable to commit – dislikes cats! – drinks too much. Seeks gorgeous young Barbie doll to shag. Must not be irritating in any way. Or clutter up his flat. Or generally make difficult demands. Must be prepared to only ever go to one particular Chinese restaurant in Soho and eat raw chicken.'

'Mmm. *She* sounds nice,' I respond. 'Do you know her?'

*   *   *

I wasn't always an unemployed TV producer.

When I left university, I had a job writing advertising copy. I became quite interested in how words could say one thing and mean quite another. *A Slagdons Lawnmower will give you a lifetime of smooth, trouble-free service*. It meant it will work until it breaks down; the lifetime is the lawnmower's, not yours. My best line was for a range of fire surrounds. *Come Over To Our Place*.

Mostly, however, the work sickened me. I wasn't required to dream up garlands of praise for cigarettes or nasty new drugs, though our little firm would have killed for a tobacco account or the chance to push some really unpleasant pharmaceuticals. No, it was more the everyday nature of our client's products that so sent a chill through my soul.

Carpeting. Stretch covers. Light bulbs. Industrial gates and doors (including barriers).

People needed carpeting, of course (*Sink your toes into rich pile luxury*) and maybe it was a good idea for there to be several brands to choose between (*Select from our unrivalled range of colourways*). But why did I have to give a fuck whose carpet they bought? Or lightbulb? Or industrial door?

I think it was the stress of learning more than I ever wished to know about the light-bulb market – and no, it really isn't fascinating once you delve into it – that made me phone in sick one Monday morning, and then, as it were, grow sicker.

However, I did learn something about the power of

133

words in print. In particular, in ads where there was a coupon to clip or a number to telephone, I learned about a publishing technique called a 'split run'. In half the copies of the periodical in question, the text of an advert would be altered by a single word, with a significant difference in the numbers of people who responded to each version.

No one ever gave me a list of the most influential words to use, although *free* and *new* were generally thought to be pretty hot.

Now, all these years later, I have to advertise myself.

A quick survey of the marketplace – the Men Seeking Women column of the *Guardian* – indicates a variety of approaches to the ad's vital first few words, the ones they set in bold type to catch the eye.

There's the terminally frank. **Bored in Peterborough**.
The feminine. **Caring and romantic**. (It has its place, no doubt.)
The one that raises more questions than it answers. **Sincere Doctor**.
The racy. **Hi Girls!**
The saucy. **Hello Gorgeous!**
The literary. **Pierre Seeks Natasha**.
The opera-loving. **Aria Out There?**
The too clever by half. **We Can't Go On Not Meeting Like This**.
The drunk. **Laid Back Liverpudlian**.
The alcoholic. **Celtic Spirit**.
The positive (but actually rather depressing). **Not Drowning But Waving**.

The spiritual. **God Moves In Mysterious Ways**.

The indescribably boring. **Seeing Is Believing**.

The post-modern. **How Do People Write These Things?**

The unwise. **Funky Fat Frog**. (He's seeking a princess, but I fear the damage is done.)

And the plain foolish. **Born 1943**.

After no more than a couple of hours playing around with ideas, I come up with the following:

Intelligent witty man. Tall, professional, 42. Seeks the woman missing from his life.

In cold print on my laptop, my ad strikes me as admirably free of cheap puns; businesslike yet endlessly romantic, with all its talk of missing women. Use of the word *life*, too, I feel, conveys a seriousness of intent. This advertiser, one understands, is not seeking a woman for a short, meaningless affair – although he's not ruling one out, clearly. Nor has he said anything about the sort of woman he wants. He has offered no strictures in regard to age or shape or professional qualifications. What a truly open, non-superficial person he must be. He seems to be looking for a central figure. He didn't say *a* woman. He said *the* woman. Maybe – gulp – for life.

The other great virtue of the ad is that it's essentially true. Apart from the forty-two thing. And the professional thing, though that is surely a temporary blip. My hope is that it's just intriguing enough to make them reach for the phone and listen to my voice message.

Short, but not too short, shall be my watchword here. And sweet, but not too sweet. I decide to adapt the script I wrote to Julia:

> *Hi. My name's Paul. I shall keep this fairly crisp: I'm six foot two, I live in north London and I work in television. For fun, I do a lot of the usual urban stuff. I read a lot. Play tennis. Go to the theatre, cinema, bars and restaurants. And every now and again I go off and get lost in the countryside.*
> [Pause for sincerity.]
> *I guess I'm looking for someone clever, funny and slim. I think those are the essentials, really. Tall might be good. Jewish might be good; I'm Jewish myself, but utterly non-religious. Actually, I think it's terribly difficult to legislate for this stuff. I just think you know it when you see it. I probably want someone who – like me – is capable of being serious . . . and equally capable of being very frivolous.*
> *Look, I won't go on. If none of this has put you off, then do please give me a call.*

Twenty years in the broadcasting business has, I hope, furnished me with the ability to deliver a script as though it were coming off the top of my head. It's largely a matter of varying one's tone and pace, inserting small hesitancies, and not placing the emphasis on all *the* wrong words.

136

I read it aloud about a dozen times, so I'm familiar enough with the text that it falls into a natural rhythm. Then I dial the number and record a 'take' on to the Soul Mates telephony.

Then I wait a couple of weeks for my ad to appear.

There is now, I realize, a ten-step process between me and the woman missing from my life. Ten hurdles we have to clear before we get to the point where we can remove one another's clothes in a serious or frivolous fashion, however it is that the mood takes us.

1. She must buy the *Guardian*.
2. Her eye must fall upon my advert.
3. She must think *hmm*, and want to know more.
4. She must dial my voice message.
5. She must be pleased by what she hears.
6. She must be pleased enough to leave a reply (and a phone number).
7. I must like what I hear.
8. I must be moved to call her up.
9. This phone conversation must lead to a date.
10. The date must be a success.

The process involves a systematic series of cut-outs, instantly aborting the mission should a failure occur at any stage in the sequence. Looked at in this fashion, the possibilities of success do seem somewhat remote, but no more so perhaps than the chances of any two people meeting and deciding they wish to be serious and frivolous together.

In the meanwhile, Angela informs me that Scott has returned from his trip, but is proving elusive. From being all over her, he's now finding it hard to make time in his busy schedule of juggling and fire-eating to pencil in an appointment. I fear the worst and begin selling shares in him.

I tell her, 'To be honest, I thought he was a bit . . . you know.'

'What, you know?'

'A bit frivolous.' My word of the month, plainly. 'I don't think he took you seriously enough.'

'Oh.' I've deliberately referred to him in the past tense. She sounds disappointed.

'If he was a girl, you'd call him a flibbertigibbet.'

'What does that mean?'

'Fun. Very jolly and everything, but fundamentally unreliable. Don't set your heart on it, in other words.'

'Do you think if I went round to his flat . . . ?'

I have no desire to see my old friend standing on a pavement staring at an upstairs window in Earls Court.

'I would tend to draw a line underneath him,' I suggest softly.

'It's so hard,' she says with a sigh. She sounds like *she knows*. 'You know, when you really fancy someone.'

I feel the little spurt of rage and jealousy. Is it really possible? *Six* times in one night?

'He had the most amazing body.'

'What could you talk about afterwards, though?' He wasn't exactly Spinoza, was he?

'He was quite funny about his childhood.'

'Mucking around with wombats and whatever.'

'Are you *sure* if I didn't go round to his flat . . . ?'

Angela isn't the only one having trouble with their romance. To my unforgivable glee, I notice that Malcolm and Morticia seem to have hit – if not the rocks – then choppy water. It's her birthday party. The flat in Marylebone throngs with people I came to know quite well when we were going out, and now only need to meet once a year. For a reason that I never understood, she always invites 'Mummy and Daddy' to her birthdays. Mummy is a soft-faced kindly soul who stares with something like disbelief at the posh accoutrements her daughter has surrounded herself with. For some reason she is extravagantly happy to see me.

'How *are* you?' she asks, sounding like she actually wants to know. '*So* nice that you and Beverly have remained friends.'

Daddy, by contrast, is a gimlet-eyed old bastard in a tweed jacket and regimental-effect tie who at one point in his career was a driving instructor. I can't help feeling that years of being thrown about by dangerously bad motorists go a long way to explaining his famously bad temper. He stands, red-faced, listening to one of Morticia's duller friends, and looks ready to explode.

I've sensed right away there's a *froideur* between the birthday girl and her beau. The way she ordered him to deal with my jacket and find me a drink, the lumpen manner in which he plodded off to do as he was told, spoke to me of a wall about to receive writing upon it.

He is smoking rather hard, I'd say, and one eye seems to be blinking rather more than the other. She, meanwhile, is a picture of icy calm: I know that look, and he is right to be rattled.

As I'm snaffling up some of the remaining quails' eggs, Malcolm sidles alongside and launches into conversation.

'You bought her a book, I see,' says the condemned man.

'I did. The new Ian McEwan. You can rarely go wrong with the new Ian McEwan, I always say.'

For some reason, Malcolm is someone who inspires me to talk crap at him. Don't ask me why. Maybe I don't consider him to be someone worth thinking up proper dialogue for.

'What did you get her?' I ask.

'A necklace, a silk scarf, a CD – well, a double-CD actually – tickets for the ballet. A sort of wallety-purse thing. Underwear. Dinner at the Caprice. Oh, and I had her tennis racket re-strung.'

'Fuck me, she's got you well trained.' *Underwear*.

Malcolm does not brighten. 'Actually, she's in a bit of a mood.'

'Really? I hadn't noticed.'

'She's been in a bit of a mood for weeks, as a matter of fact.' There is a long pause. 'When you were . . . when you were *together*, did you find that she could be moody?'

I begin to feel rather sorry for the daft young chump. How to put this? 'Beverly is . . .' The moody cow's moody cow. The moody cow against whom all other moody cows can be judged. Against whom all other moody cows are just having an off day. '. . . She is prone to moods, yes. I'd try not to let it bother you.'

At the other side of the room, the subject of our discussion is listening, apparently rapt, to what is no doubt another balls-aching anecdote from her pointless friend Freddie.

'Freddie is an absolute joy,' she once told me in all seriousness. (Freddie, so far as I could tell, was an overweight insurance agent who, like Morticia, had reinvented himself, in his case as a would-be foppish wag. To my mind, it didn't come off, and there are few things more tedious in this world than failed foppish wags.)

She looks fabulous, however, in her slinky figure-hugging green velvet birthday number, and of course she knows it. Freddie's goggle-eyes are running up and down her curves as he prattles on and flaps his wrists about.

'How's good old Freddie?' I ask with a sudden surge of joy. It is Malcolm, not I, who now has to find a special place in his life for Freddie and the rest of Morticia's terrible friends.

Malcolm is gazing at Freddie with ill-disguised distaste. 'Good old Freddie,' he parrots.

'Quite a character,' I chip in evilly.

'Priceless,' he adds. Quoting, I feel sure.

I allow a second to pass. Then another. Then I add, 'Of course, there are those who think he's a fat fucking twat.'

Malcolm turns his puzzled expression on to mine. He can't tell if I'm kidding.

He laughs. 'Yeah. He is a bit, isn't he?'

I think to myself: I give it a month at the outside.

The one other event of any note that happens while I wait for my ad to appear is that I go on a date.

It is a bit of recidivism. I answer someone else's advert. I guess I still hanker for the romance of the unknown. The thrilling little moment – the same moment where every relationship has to begin – when two total strangers set eyes upon each other for the first time and have the same thought: Shit, I'm missing *Frasier* for *this*?

All that need be said here is that her name is Wendy. We meet at Browns. And if she's thirty-eight, I'm McCauley Culkin.

Her best line: 'Do you have a pension?'

My best line: 'It was nice meeting you. We must do it again some time.'

And then it is Saturday. In the Soul Mates section in the *Guardian*, buried amid announcements from **Lonely in Lancashire** and **Hot To Trot** and **Passionate Environmentalist**, is my message in a bottle.

It is nearly six in the evening before I receive my first reply on the newspaper's voicemail system. Something horribly familiar about the deepish voice. Educated, with a low rasp to it.

Hello Paul. My name's Annie. OK. Well. I guess I should start by telling you about myself. I'm tall, I'm an actress . . .

Well, how about that? The mad old hippie.

But the next day there are six replies.

Six!

Six actual live women who want to meet me. Six breathing, viable females who have read my words, listened to my voice and now wish to move forward to the next phase. I am so thrilled I call Toby to tell him. I think I catch him in bed with Wasp Woman. (You can always tell, can't you?)

'Be very picky,' he warns me. 'There are a lot of lying scumbags out there.'

'Have you asked her yet?' I whisper.

'Yeah, you too, mate. Bye.'

I play my messages over again.

1. **Vivien**. Works for a charity. Says she's 'attractive without being a beauty'. Sportingly confesses to being 'a few years older than you'. Hmm.
2. **Sophie**. Thirty-seven. Says she's sitting at home 'a bit drunk with a friend'. Works in computing. 'Am I clever?' There is a pause while the friend thinks about it. 'All right, am I funny?' I note she doesn't ask about slim.
3. **Beth**. Says she's led an 'unconventional' life. Currently shares a flat with her twin brother – how weird is that? – and organizes exhibitions. Doesn't mention her age, but says she's a size fourteen (that's not petite, is it?).
4. **Jo**. Therapist, writer and teacher. Calls herself

'slim, with exceptionally long legs'. I scribble fat exclamation marks into my notes alongside her name until she says she likes tall men 'with all their own hair and teeth'.

5. **Patricia**. Thirty-five. Works in 'mental health'. Says she's 'Italian looking', which I take to mean dark-haired and bug-eyed with a big conk.

6. **Alice**. Mid thirties. Has done 'all sorts'. Currently a stand-up comic. There is an energy and intelligence to her words that makes me underline her number three times.

A stand-up comic! A woman who *tells jokes*. Instantly I can tell she's clever and funny, but will I fancy her? This time I resolve to listen especially hard for clues. There must be subtle ways one can hear if someone's, say, dangerously overweight (timbers groaning?), some note or catch in the voice that might betray a face only a mother could love.

Alice, though. It's one of those names, isn't it? A name to whisper softly across a pillow. Have you ever met a fat Alice? Or an Alice who looked like the back of a 134? Not to be confused with *Auntie* Alice or *Allison*, which are entirely different concepts, of course. No, to me Alice speaks of summer zephyrs, of butterflies on the wing. I have a good feeling about Alice.

It's a feeling that in no way dissipates when we speak on the phone. She has a refreshing matter-of-fact quality about her that I find highly promising.

'Do you play any sort of sport at all?' I ask at a suitable point in the conversation. 'For relaxation purposes. After the stress of performing, as it were.'

'I don't *play* anything,' she replies. 'I run. It's bloody boring, but it's what I do. I can't get interested in chasing balls.'

'Isn't jogging supposed to be very bad on the knees?'

'I don't jog. I run. I go very fast.'

This is excellent news. Alice is clearly not one of those red-faced women one sees wobbling painfully through the park; she's the other sort, the sort who streak by in tight Spandex, leaving vortices of dust and barking dogs in their wake.

I cheer inwardly. And I believe I have discovered an important diagnostic tool in the inexact science of blind dating.

LESSON EIGHT:
Ask her about sport. If she groans,
you might want to consider hanging up.

We agree to meet at a bar in Camden. She's on stage later that evening. 'I might even let you watch the act,' she says.

'I'd love to,' I reply.

'You haven't heard it yet.'

This is true.

'So what do you look like?' she inquires. 'Other than being six foot two.'

I fill in the missing details. 'Oh. And. I, er, don't have as much hair as I once used to.'

She is unfazed. 'You and half the males in Camden.'

'I'll be wearing a black leather jacket. Black trousers. Black shirt, probably. Black shoes.'

'You and *all* the males in Camden.'

'I'm looking forward to meeting you, Alice.' I Alice her for extra up-front intimacy.

'Yeah. You too, Paul.'

She Paul-ed me. Things could not look better. And, as card players put it, I have an ace in the hole.

I shall tell her the bee joke. She may not laugh, but there's no denying its specialist interest.

Here's a novelty. She's there before I am. Perched on a stool in front of a pint, nattering to the bloke behind the bar.

I like her immediately. Flinty blue eyes sparkle at mine when we shake hands. She's got that spiky blond highlighted hair that says *attitude*. The set to her jaw speaks of someone who doesn't take too much crap. A battered trench coat over a lean-looking frame adds to my impression of a Woman Who Doesn't Overly Worry What Others Think.

She's good-looking, but not in an obvious way. I take this to be a good thing after the Easter Island Statue, the Mad Old Hippie and the Beautiful Dreamy One Who Was Fundamentally Unavailable (I have decided).

Alice is real. And, dare I say it, apparently normal. This seems like an obvious improvement in the state of affairs, and a tribute to the new strategy of advertising myself rather than jumping through other people's hoops.

'So how many women answered your advert?' she inquires in a friendly enough fashion, although there's a challenging note in her expression that I find rather exciting.

'Fourteen up to now. You're the only one I've met, though.' Which isn't to say that I won't be giving some of the others a call. 'How many did you reply to?'

Her pint pauses midway to her lips. This was clearly an excellent riposte, giving as good as I get, sort of thing.

'Three,' she replies. 'I met one last night.'

'What was he like?'

She takes a good long pull on her lager and sets down the glass.

'Truth?'

'Why not?'

Poker-faced, she gazes at me while she forms the thumb, index and remaining digits of her right hand into a particular configuration. For a moment I think she's about to demonstrate some particular piece of guitar fingering, the opening, say, of 'Stairway To Heaven'. But then she starts shaking it around in a vulgar, and to my way of thinking much too frenzied a fashion.

'Ah.'

'You did ask.'

'I did, didn't I? What was wrong with him, then?'

'Well he was a tosser, wasn't he?'

'Yes. I gathered that. I just wondered what variety of tosser.'

'Oh, you want the nasty little *details.*' She's smiling at me; it's one of those strange, regretful, almost bitter smiles; as though she sucked on a lemon shortly before embarking upon it.

'Men are always so fascinated by other men's failings,' she announces.

'They are, aren't they,' I concede. (Well it's true. They are.) 'Whereas women are one great big happy, wholesome, mutually supportive sisterhood.'

It was meant to sound warmly satirical, but I think it might have come out a bit sharply. She blinks, shrugs, and begins tinkering with the precise position of her beer glass on its little cardboard mat.

'So what exactly do you *do* at the BBC, Paul?' she asks after a bit. Her chin, I can't help noticing, has lifted from its last position by about ten degrees with respect to the vertical.

I don't particularly like the stress she laid on the word *do*, just then. But I give her my line about factual entertainment. I leave out the stuff about being unemployed and writing a novel.

She snorts.

'What did you do before you were a comic?' I inquire. 'I mean, how does one get into it? The comedy business, as it were.'

One wall of her trench coat has fallen away, revealing a leg clad in blue denim; it's a shapely leg that widens pleasingly as it meets the edge of the bar stool. The leg ends in some kind of desert boot which oscillates about her ankle like a radar.

'I've been everything,' she reveals. 'Teacher. Care

148

assistant. Journalist. You name it. Occupational therapist.'

'I guess it's all good material to draw on for the act.'

Her jaw ratchets up another couple of degrees.

Was it the way I said *the act*? Is *the act* one of those phrases that performers are allowed to use but in the mouths of non-performers sound presumptuous, gauche, or even offensive?

I hear myself saying, 'I bet people are always telling you jokes.'

A soft smile appears fleetingly below the hard blue eyes. 'Only men.'

I can't help myself. 'Do you know the bee joke, at all?'

Now the jaw moves through ten degrees with respect to the *horizontal*. Geometrically, this is a much more encouraging signal.

'There's these two blokes . . .' I begin.

Because she's a professional, I give it everything I've got. She listens with interest, dropping in a couple of bitter-lemony smiles, nodding, generally going with it. Towards the end, her foot even stops swaying and she forgets to play with her beer glass.

I deliver the punchline.

There is a very long pause. She nods once more.

'That,' she says, her face like a tombstone, 'is actually *very* funny.'

Encouraged, I do a couple more I like. The one about the man who goes to the doctor to receive the results of the tests.

' "Give it to me straight, doc," he says. "How long have I got?" Doctor reads through the results. He says, "Ten." Bloke says, "*Ten*? What do you mean, *ten*? Ten what? Ten days? Ten weeks?" Doctor says, "Nine." '

Alice nods. She's plainly heard it.

'You've heard it.'

'I've heard them all, mostly.'

I try again. 'Bloke goes to the doctor. Says he thinks he's a dog–'

'–ever since he was a puppy.'

Shit. 'OK. This woman decides to have a facelift–'

'–and the man says, "I was behind you in the queue at McDonald's." '

Fuck. She *has* heard them all. 'OK. Man and a woman are playing golf–'

'The woman says, "Sorry, love, I've got the painters in, but you can root me up the shitter if you want." '

The next few words die on my lips. 'Sorry?'

'It wasn't the one about the man and the woman playing golf for fifty pounds a hole?'

'No, it wasn't actually.'

She shrugs. 'I haven't offended you, have I? You look a bit shocked.'

'Not at all.'

'I know lots of worse ones than that. How do you know when your sister's having a period?'

'I. Er . . .'

'Your dad's cock tastes like shit.'

Now I *am* a bit shocked. The graphic imagery in the denouement to the golfing story was intriguing for the laissez-faire attitude of the woman quoted, not to mention the specific vocabulary employed. But the latter is probably the most unpleasant joke I have ever heard, and I speak as someone who went to school with small boys.

Still, there is something about a woman talking dirty, isn't there?

With a big smile on my face I say, 'That. Is. Disgusting.' I hope she understands I am amused ironically, through sociological interest in the horrifying nature of the material, and for no other reason.

'I'm glad you enjoyed it.'

She drains the rest of her pint.

'Would you like another?' I ask.

'Definitely,' she responds.

'Don't you find drink blunts your . . . your performance?' She's on in about two hours.

The chin ascends twelve and a half degrees on the vertical axis.

'Not at all. How about yourself?' She wriggles out of her trench coat, allowing it to collapse down the sides of the stool.

She's in jeans and some sort of close-fitting zip-up jumper with a high neck. Free of the Columbo outfit, I become aware of her wiry body as it cranes around trying to attract the barman's attention. In a small gap above the top of her waistband, a vertebra pokes out painfully. Jammed into her nearside back pocket are several folded pages of A4, crammed with tiny blue handwriting. Her act, at a guess.

I suddenly become aware of her vulnerability. I have an urge to walk in and begin again. It's not that we've got off on the wrong foot, exactly; more that she feels a little prickly to me and there are probably ways I could play this better.

'Do you find you get nervous?' I ask sympathetically. 'Before a show.'

She looks at me like I'm stupid or something. I have the feeling she's trying (and failing) to think up some cutting riposte. Then she calls across the bar, 'Oi! Who do you have to sleep with to get a drink round here?'

After a couple of fresh pints have been safely delivered – I decide to eschew wine for fear of ridicule – she says, 'So tell me about you, then. What made you put an ad in the *Guardian*?'

'I guess I wanted to meet a *Guardian* reader.'

The sucked-lemon smile. 'What happened to your last relationship?'

I don't really want to get into all that, so I reply, 'I seem to have had quite a few relationships where we get about two years down the road, and then the road runs out. If that doesn't sound too glib.'

'It does.'

'You're unfamiliar with the scenario?'

'Would you say you are a commitment-o-phobe?'

'Not at all. I should have thought two years is a major slice of anyone's life. Particularly in one's *fertile* years, if I can put it like that.'

'Put it however you want. But you're the one who ends it, right?'

'Not always.'

Actually, thinking about it, this was precisely the way most of my two-year stretches had come to a conclusion. It wasn't that the road ran out. Rather, it was I who deliberately steered across the central reservation into the path of oncoming traffic. Which isn't to say that one or two of my travelling companions hadn't provided some grievous provocation.

Now she asks, 'Have you ever had a same-sex relationship?'

'What, with a man?'

'No, with a giraffe. Of course, with a man.'

'No.'

'I thought not. Men like you don't. Women do, though. Most of my women friends have dabbled.'

'Batted for the other side.'

'Experimented with their sexuality. They're not as shit-scared of the idea as men are. Men are terrified they might find out they like it.'

'It isn't that men usually know if they fancy other men?'

'*Fancy*. Fancy's such a male word, isn't it?'

'Plenty of women talk about *fancying* men.'

'Yes, but it doesn't mean the same thing when a woman says it.'

We seem to be having some sort of *argument* here. Alice's knuckles, I notice, are rather white when she reaches for her pint. I wonder what I have done to upset her. How to bring the conversation to a warmer pitch?

(She's right about men and women, though. Many of my women friends have some 'dabbling' in their pasts. It was usually at university, and by and large they didn't seem to mind talking about it. None of my male friends have. Or if they have, they haven't coughed up yet.)

'What happened to your last relationship?' I ask as gently as possible.

Mentally, I brace myself for a tide of invective. But Alice looks like all the fight has gone out of her. A slight woman sits on a bar stool, swinging a desert boot.

'Was he another performer?' I probe after a bit of a lull.

She nods. 'Another comic.'

'That must be hard,' I suggest. 'People always think two comics living together ought to be hilarious. All those jokes flying around over breakfast. It's probably not like that, is it?'

She takes a long, deep swallow, and carefully sets her pint glass back on its beer mat. 'Ray was a total cunt.'

She deploys the word with profound relish. Plenty of *kkk* on the opening syllable and loads of *tttt* on the finish.

'Was he?' I reply rather weakly.

'He nicked my best gags. He stole my albums. He flooded the bathroom. He slept with my best friend. And didn't even have the decency to dump me to my face.'

I shake my head. Words fail me, sort of thing.

'He left a note on the ironing board.'

'Despicable.'

'Cunt is the word.'

I feel a terrible temptation to hoot with laughter. I think it may have been the detail about flooding the bathroom. Plumbing-related incidents – so long as they happen to other people – always fill me with a despair bordering on hilarity.

'How long had you been–?'

'Too bloody long.'

'I'm sorry.'

'I'm not.'

'Would you like another–?'

'Definitely.'

For a thin creature, she can certainly hold her Kronenbourg 1664. After several pints of the gassy yellow fluid, I am feeling distinctly woozy, but Alice appears unaffected. It seems like the moment to try another joke on her.

'You know the one about the three old ladies in the home?'

The flinty blue eyes regard me with mild interest.

'These three old ladies are sitting round in the day room discussing their Alzheimer's, right? First one says, "Last night, I had it really bad. I woke up to go to the toilet, but by the time I got there, I couldn't remember whether I wanted to go Number One or Number Two."'

As Alice has not already contributed the punchline, I assume she hasn't heard this particular anecdote.

'Second old lady says, "Oh, that's nothing. Listen. Last night I woke up, desperate for something from the kitchen. But by the time I got to the fridge, I couldn't remember whether I was hungry or thirsty."'

The suggestion of a genuine – non-lemony – smile has broken out on the face of the stand-up comic.

'The third old lady shakes her head. "You two sound like you got it real bad, no question. Me, thank God, touch wood . . ."' And here I rap on the bar twice. ' ". . . touch wood, I'm not so sick." '

I leave a pause. Then in the persona of the third old lady, I look round and cry, 'Come in.'

The little miracle. She laughs. A small moment of helplessness.

I want to tell her, *You should laugh more often, you know. You're really very attractive when you laugh*, but I suspect it might not go down all that brilliantly.

'You can use it if you like. In the. In your performance.'

The level look returns. 'I don't really do ethnic humour.'

'Sorry?'

'I think you have to be Jewish to tell that gag.'

Now I think about it, perhaps I had made the three old ladies sound a little Chosen. I don't think of it as a Jewish joke, however. The comedy of losing one's mind is universal, I should have thought.

There doesn't seem to be anything to say now. So we sit there for a bit, each mulling over our private thoughts. I'm wondering what it would be like to go out with this spry, sexy, irritable woman. Would you have to tiptoe round her on eggshells, or would all the nonsense disappear once we'd . . . ?

A pair of desert boots lying on the bedroom carpet. The thought of the blue eyes at the moment of crisis.

The skin round her thumbnail, I notice, is red and worn away. She's sitting rather foetally hunched on her bar stool. I catch a wave of misery and loneliness off her. What sort of life can it be, waiting to face a room full of strangers with a pocketful of jokes in spidery handwriting? It occurs to me that she hasn't said a single genuinely amusing thing all evening.

'So, er. What made you flip through the *Guardian* and answer a few ads, then?'

A pretty innocuous way of framing the question, I should have thought, but she looks at me like it's the stupidest remark she's ever heard.

'Why do you think, Paul?'

There is nothing pleasant about the way she deployed my name just then.

'Was it to meet a nice man, Alice?'

There seems to be some sort of fury boiling up behind her brow. If her jaw sticks out any straighter, she'll be staring at the light fittings.

'Have I done something to annoy you?' I inquire. 'You seem a little . . .'

The word is *tense*. But in my experience, if you suggest to a person that they are in this condition, they are liable to respond by bellowing *I Am Not Fucking Tense* at an extremely high volume, quite possibly bursting a small blood vessel in their face.

She's shaking her head. 'I'm sorry,' she says. Now she's flapping her wrist. 'Ignore me. I always get ratty before a show. We should have met some other night.'

I am a producer. (Yeah, I know.) I understand about 'talent' anxiety. (Actually, I don't. Most of the stars I have worked with seemed nerveless to the point where I wondered whether they possessed even a gram of shame.) Nevertheless, I recognize that performers of all kinds are generally held to be a breed apart: exempt from the regular civilities; their otherwise appalling behaviour justified on the grounds that going up on stage, or reading the regional news on TV – as one of them once put it to me – 'is like pulling your trousers down and showing your bum'. (I have never been able to watch *Newsroom South East* in the same light since.) Part-shaman, part-fool, the performer is the one who exposes himself to the crowd. As a producer, you may roll your eyes behind his back. You may go *tsk*. You may privately resolve that if you never see this arsehole again as long as you live, it will be too soon. But ultimately you make allowances for him. If he wants a bowl of fucking Dolly Mixtures in his fucking dressing room, you provide a bowl. He is, after all, the fucking star.

Gently, ever-so-gently, like unwrapping the most delicate glassware from tissue paper, I do my producer thing.

Almost whispering, I ask, 'Have you worked here before?'

She nods. 'Yeah.'

'What sort of crowd is it?'

She shrugs. 'Drunks, mostly.'

Now the *coup de grâce*. Maximum sympathy. Maximum concern. 'Is there anything I can get you?'

Her eyes brighten. She does something novel with the set of her lips.

'You haven't got any chocolate, have you? I think I need a bit of chocolate.'

I am nervous for her. I am, really.

In the darkened upstairs room, about thirty people loll about in various stages of inebriation. There's a raucous table of office colleagues – I'm already worried about them – plus assorted dyads and triads. The singletons – silent shifty types with facial hair and serious glasses – I take to be television producers on the lookout for new talent.

Alice is on third. The two previous 'acts' have been poor, but forgivably poor. They were both in their twenties, at a guess, learning their trade on the nursery slopes of comedy. The first so over-projected it was as though he thought he was playing Wembley Arena. The second did a sort of slow-burn *is-it-the-world-that's-weird-or-is-it-me?* schtick. It was hard to say which was the less plausible.

Alice will not be able to invoke the youth defence. She is old enough to know better.

It's time. Our master of ceremonies – a reasonably grizzled old stager, clearly a father figure to many of the young pups – urges us to 'give it up' for my blind date.

My heart is banging behind my ribs as Alice springs on to the platform and grabs the mike.

'OK,' she booms. 'OK, here's a question for you. How do you know when your sister's having a period?'

When the hubbub – hard to say which is louder, the laughter or the hostility – when it has died away, she says, 'Actually, I only told that to get your attention. The rest of the act's quite respectable, really.'

If only.

To say she stinks would be an understatement, would not do justice to the excruciating aroma of ordure that comes rolling over our heads. It isn't just the material – an uncomfortable marriage of off-colour gags and 'observational comedy' – it's also her stage persona: arrogance fighting a transparent need to be liked.

Worst joke: I fucked a man with a wooden leg once. It was awful. Blood everywhere, splinters all up his arse.

Best joke: A friend of mine went to the doctor's complaining that every time she walked down the road, her upper thighs rubbed together making a whistling noise. She had to walk round the surgery to demonstrate. It was a sort of . . . *and here she did one of those feeble female whistles*. The doctor was mystified but agreed to record it and send the tape to a specialist in California. A week later the specialist replied. He said he had absolutely no idea what it was. As far as he was concerned, he said, 'it just sounded like some cunt whistling'.

At the interval, I beat a hasty retreat back to the bar. I find Alice sitting in a corner smoking a cigarette.

'Don't say a fucking word,' she snarls.

I've been trained. I know all the showbiz euphemisms for 'You stank big time.' My favourites are:

1. Well, you've done it again!
2. Only *you* could have done that!

3. That was so . . . *interesting*.
4. *What* can I say?

In the immediate aftermath of a performance, however, when the adrenaline is still banging round the capillaries, only a downright lie is acceptable.

'That was terrific,' I mumble.

'Fuck off. It was awful.' Not *I*, note. *It* was awful.

'Not at all. Must be very hard, I imagine. When there's hardly anyone in.' And you haven't got anything funny to tell them.

'Drink.'

'Sorry?'

'I need a drink. Could you get me a drink? *Please*,' she adds finally.

A number of thoughts pass through my head at this point:

1. Why are you quite so annoyed with everything? Surely a little more charm wouldn't go amiss.
2. In my fridge is half a roast chicken. I've videoed a documentary about dark matter, the exotic invisible substance that some believe keeps the galaxies from flying apart. Instead of spending my evening in a cruddy bar in NW1 being snapped at by a so-called comic, I could be at home, eating chicken and learning the secrets of the cosmos.
3. Will I look back on this encounter and wonder: if I'd pursued it harder, or differently, would something have shifted eventually, like a tectonic plate? Would we in fact have flown at

one another and mated with a surprising and altogether delightful intensity?

'Why don't you get your own damn drink?' I reply. 'You know something? You're about as funny as. As. As something not terribly funny. Mumps, possibly.'

There's a pause while she considers my last statement. Then she says, 'How did you get here tonight, Paul?'

'Northern Line,' I reply. 'Why?'

'Do you want me to refund your Tube fare?'

It was the funniest thing she ever said to me.

5

I AM CATASTROPHICALLY EARLY again. Browns at seven-forty on a weekday evening is thronging with the office crowd getting pissed enough to summon the courage to stagger off to Charing Cross and thence – Network Rail willing – to Esher, Aylesbury, or wherever it is those boys in the Hugo Boss suits come from.

Meanwhile, I am waiting for Gemma.

Confession: I know it is terribly superficial of me, but I simply cannot imagine marrying someone called Gemma. Sorry, I just can't. I feel the same about Rita, Stacey and Sabrina. (When I was a child, the people downstairs had a nervy little poodle called Sabrina, so maybe you can understand where I'm coming from on this one.)

I hadn't, however, raised this point with the Gemma in question when we'd spoken on the telephone the week before. Gemma – she worked 'in the medical profession' according to the message she left for me on the *Guardian*'s voicemail system – turned out to be a nurse.

'Were you hoping I'd be a doctor?' she chirped.

'Not at all,' I lied. 'I like nurses. Nurses are great.

They do a wonderful job. I'm rambling now, obviously.'

She laughed. Then she made a highly intriguing statement.

'I'm much younger than you, Paul.'

'Are you?'

'Do you mind younger women?'

'No. Not at all,' I replied generously. 'When you say younger . . . ?'

'I'm twenty-five.'

'Golly.' It just slipped out.

She is seventeen (or actually nineteen, depending how you calculate it) years younger than me. I find I am not opposed to this disparity *per se*.

'I get on better with older men. I find men my own age are still boys.'

'What sort of nursing do you do, then?' I inquired, very much hoping the answer wouldn't turn out to be geriatric.

'General.' She named a large hospital in a distant suburb of London.

'People are always bringing nurses boxes of chocolates, aren't they?'

I knew from visiting my father after his stroke that nursing stations were usually piled high with boxes of Belgian pralines, Black Magic and Ferrero Rocher. I also knew that, perhaps as a result, there were two types of nursing physique. There were the ones who were built like dockers, who were good at manhandling patients and flipping mattresses and the like; they were the ones who ate all the chocolates.

From the reference to being 'a bit of a keep-fit

fanatic', I had a strong suspicion that Gemma was one of the other sort.

I had a further thought: Nurses have seen it all, haven't they? They've borne witness to every human weakness and degradation. When you've been through the nameless horrors that nurses go through on a daily basis, you're not going to be overly shocked by someone who doesn't have quite as much hair as he once used to, are you?

After I informed her on this point, she went a bit quiet. 'I like bald men, actually,' she said in a low tone.

'Do you really?'

'I think it makes them look . . . *distinguished*.'

'May I congratulate you on your very mature grasp of things,' I quipped.

She laughed a laugh I could feel in my trouser pockets.

'Not everybody has such a positive attitude,' I added for good measure.

'I'm not everybody.'

'I can hear that straight away.'

We were flirting with each other within minutes. There seemed no reason not to book in a date there and then.

'Browns is such a zoo, though,' she said when I nominated it. 'Don't you know anywhere more exclusive?'

A nurse with *standards*. This was getting better and better.

'Let's meet in Browns. I'll think of somewhere else we can move on to.'

'Fuck *me*,' I said out loud to the empty sitting room when I replaced the receiver. 'Twenty-*five*.'

And later, as I was only half-watching *Newsnight*: 'A *nurse*!'

'Nurse, eh?' said Toby.

'Nurse.'

'Fucking hell, mate.'

'I know.'

He squared his jaw in a comically serious sort of fashion. Goggled his eyes a little. 'I knew a nurse. Met her in a hospital when I detached a retina. Christ, she was a horny little minx.'

In regard to irony: as with *totty* and *nookie*, with *minx*.

'Can women *be* horny?'

'Horny as all hell.'

'I mean, isn't it called something else when women are horny?'

'Jesus, she was a dirty bitch. I think they're drawn to it, nurses. The filth aspect.'

'It's not that being around death all day, they're more willing to . . . embrace life, as it were?'

Toby sniffed significantly. 'I've never known anyone so interested in bodily fluids.'

'How did you detach your retina?' I asked, moving on, sort of thing.

'She had a dirtier mind than any bloke I've ever met. She was clinically insatiable. And bloody kinky, actually. To the point where it became off-putting.

Sometimes, you just want to read the *Telegraph*, don't you? I did it playing cricket. Two of us ran to catch a ball.'

'You chatted her up in the hospital?'

'She said it was her. With a detached retina, it could have been anyone.'

'What happened?'

'In the end? She just stopped ringing. I was relieved, to tell you the truth. I aged five years in three months.'

Angela returned from the kitchen with another bottle of Chilean Merlot.

'Casanova's got a hot date with a nurse,' he told her.

'Toby's just been explaining how mucky they are. Nurses. As a species.'

Angela gazed upon the two of us with fond amusement on her face. 'You boys,' she said in an affectionately patronizing manner. Then her fingers flew to her lips. She'd remembered something. 'Actually! Actually, I once had an affair with a *male* nurse!' she screeched.

'Did he have an exaggerated interest in bodily fluids?' I inquired.

'He was from Thailand. No, Burma. He liked early music. Harpsichords and madrigals and stuff. I've never had to listen to so many bloody madrigals in my life.'

'Every relationship teaches you something,' said Toby.

'What did the horny nurse teach you?' I asked.

He did a squishy thing with his mouth to denote thinking. 'There's a technique . . .' And he trailed off, looking at Angela a bit sheepishly.

167

'What?' she exclaimed.

'What?' I echoed.

'Sorry. Shouldn't have brought it up.'

'*What?*' we chorused.

'There was a technique she knew for . . . no, I really can't. Sorry. There's an end to it. Change the subject.'

'Oh, for fuck's sake,' Angela cried. 'What?'

'It's OK,' I told her. 'He'll tell me, and I'll tell you later.'

Toby's face had gone a little queasy. In his imagination, he was back there. Being forced to adopt techniques . . .

'She did once show me how to perform an emergency tracheotomy with a biro.'

'That's not it,' said Angela.

'I was always very nervous of eating in front of her. In case of choking. She'd have been right in there with the old Parker retractable.' He performed a Psycho-like stabbing motion.

But Toby was right. Every relationship does leave you with something.

Going out with Morticia, oddly, had reawoken my interest in chess. For some reason she was keen on it – perhaps she'd read in *Vogue* that it was fashionable again – and I was obliged to reacquaint myself with the rules of the game that I'd last played at school. Where once I'd found it an appalling brain-strain, I now discovered a sort of pleasure and quietude in the contemplation of the little pieces. And happily, since she was reasonably crap, I wasn't forced to compete horribly. Playing chess together was the one companionable thing we could do when we had run out of things to say (apart from the other thing, of course).

What, however, had my latest date taught me?

Although the encounter with Alice was clearly a failure, it didn't feel like a disaster. Unlike the mad old hippie and the one who looked like an Aztec fright mask and the beautiful but unavailable one, Alice was at least in the right ball park. She felt *plausible*.

It felt like I was getting closer.

LESSON NINE:
Sometimes you learn nothing. Sometimes you just have to sit there and listen to some bad jokes and wish you were somewhere else. It's probably part of the process.

OK. It's eight pm on the nose. As we say in the television biz, cue the nurse.

She'll be late, won't she? If she's any sort of lady, she'll keep me twiddling my thumbs for another ten minutes at least.

Alongside me at the bar there's a band of colleagues having a few jolly drinks after work. They're some sort of team: three young men in suits and ties with bottles of beer and cigarettes, four young women in business skirts with white wine and cigarettes, and an older, fatter figure with salt and pepper hair whom they're grouped around. The way their heads bob towards him, the way they all laugh when he says something disparaging about 'Bill', the way they proffer him lights and Marlboros, and the angles of their bodies all suggest the way the power relationship lies. One of the women is very pretty indeed. I find it hard to take my eyes off her unclouded, doll-like face. For a moment her gaze flicks out of the circle on to mine before it is snatched back by the obviously amusing account of what Bill said to Jack when Jack made a total bollocks of the task Bill had entrusted him with. (Bill was not best pleased, apparently.) At the denouement – Jack evidently said to Bill, 'Well if you think you can do any better, why don't you fucking have a go?' – there is an explosion of hilarity that is almost painful to stand next to. Doll-face is helpless with laughter, her shoulders shaking, eyes glittering, wine leaping dangerously up the sides of her glass. One of the boys – a bit of an oafish brute with coarse standy-uppy hair – brushes against her shoulder in the merriment, and she turns a huge sunny smile on him, her face tipping sideways to signal goodwill and potential sexual availability.

I miss all this, I realize. The gossip. The banter. The flirting. The 'us against them' feeling of working with other people. I don't think I'd miss the fattish fucker with the s. and p. hair, however. His slower movements and senior-status growl. The solid way he plants himself on the floor. The horrible silvery watch band poking proud of the sharp white shirt cuff. Nor, I expect, would I particularly regret not seeing Mr Bogbrush every morning, with his sunken eyes and shit-eating grin, if you know the one I mean. Christ, I do hope Doll-face isn't thinking of taking up with this moron. The two of them have splintered off to form a separate conversation and she seems to be giving him the full set of green lights: the cocked-over head, the playful eyes; one slender hip is even pointing straight at the ape. He's doing his version of charm: fag and beer bottle in one hand, fingers of other hand splayed out wide like he's saying, *Look how big my hand is. I could fit plenty of you in it, I expect.*

I can't quite bear to watch any more, so I turn the other way. Two women of a certain age are perched on bar stools, a bottle of white between them. The one nearest throws me a sidelong glance and wipes something imaginary from the corner of her mouth with her ring finger, a gesture that so powerfully reminds me of Morticia, I almost flinch.

I was right about Morticia and Malcolm, it turns out.

About ten days after the birthday party, she and I had dinner.

'And how's himself?' I inquired politely.

She sniffed.

I knew that sniff.

It was the sniff that spoke louder than words.

'Oh. I see. Like that, is it?'

She sighed. Her eyes locked on to the middle distance. There was a good long pause, during which I had time to scan the specials on the menu (pan-fried lobster with chilli, lime and garlic sounded good). Finally she said, 'Malcolm will make a superb husband for someone one day.'

Here we go, I thought. 'Not for you, though.'

'He's loyal. Practical.'

'Good with shelves and what have you . . . ?'

She ignored my witticism. 'Romantic . . .'

'I heard about dinner at Le Caprice. Tickets for the ballet.' *The underwear*.

'He was *wonderful* with Daddy.'

Was this a slight? The irascible old git and I so clearly loathed one another on sight that it was almost reassuring. He hated everything about me – that I was Jewish, that I worked for the BBC, that I was penetrating his daughter on a regular basis – it brought me a great deal of pleasure to know how much I must have annoyed him.

His best-ever line: 'Elephant dung is supposed to be good for baldness. You rub it into the scalp. Or am I thinking of lion dung?'

My best-ever line: 'Beverly's an exceptional girl, Mr——, and I'm a very lucky man.'

'And he's. He was . . .' Morticia tailed off. I had a horrible feeling she was about to say *good in bed*.

'I feel a big *but* hanging over the rest of this sentence,' I quipped.

Her eyes grew wide. They moved beyond the middle distance to encompass the distant distance. They became a little moist in the process.

'I do sometimes wonder if I shall find anyone.' Anyone she could stand, is what she meant.

'Don't be silly,' I cooed. (Actually, twice-cooked tiger prawns with crabmeat and coriander could be interesting. Or were they the ones that fucked up the mangrove swamps?)

'Did *you* find him irritating?' she asked, seizing her chopsticks and snapping them together in a telling fashion.

'Oh, definitely.'

'He was always under my feet, somehow. Like a small child.'

'He was very fond of you, I expect.' Only God knew why.

'He wanted us to get married.'

'Really?' She shouldn't have revealed that detail.

'He wanted us to share the rest of our lives, when I couldn't face the thought of another weekend.'

I shook my head in wonderment at the black comedy that is the human condition.

'Was he very upset?'

She nodded. Stared down at the Chinese inscription on the empty plate. 'He's been phoning and asking to meet. I must have left him with the idea that there's a chink of hope.'

'Poor sap.' *Sup?* Where had that come from?

'He sent some beautiful lilies.'

'Those big white ones? With the amazingly rude insides?'

She nodded again, then looked up into my face. We allowed a pause for respect to pass.

Well, that was Malcolm then. Who's next, I wondered?

Now, rather in the manner of the footballer delicately floating the ball across the mouth of the goal, I said, 'Do you fancy the lobster, at all?'

'With the noodles? Or the special?'

'Dunno. Whichever you like.'

'Ooh. I don't know. Either. You decide.'

Eight-fifteen. Just the right sort of moment for my young nurse to arrive all breathless and full of excuses about people throwing themselves under trains at Liverpool Street.

Doll-face and Mr Bogbrush have rejoined the laughing circle, but I'm still worried about them. He, in particular, is continually casting glances in her direction. A long anecdote is under way; the porky bloke with the salt and pepper hair is growling his way through the history of what happened when Bill and Jack and another fellow called Duncan went to a conference in Malaga that seemed to involve rather a lot of golf and alcohol abuse.

I'm guessing that this lot are in sales. They have some of the piratical swagger that sales forces like to adopt in the evening. Malaga is exactly the sort of place that seniorish characters in sales go to play golf and get dribbling drunk in.

'So Duncan said, "I may be pished, laddie, but at least ah ken where to find ma fuckin scratcher."'

There is another eruption of merriment (what a wit this Duncan fellow must be). Mr Bogbrush shoots his hundredth shit-eating grin at Doll-face and she – may God forgive her – she chucks her head back in abandon, throws open her jaws and allows him to see all the way down her pink, perfect throat. She is intensely pretty rather than beautiful; the essential

174

mythological element is somehow missing. But I'm thinking, *Please* don't go to bed with him. He is so not worthy. I mean, just look at the great lunk. He can't believe his luck: admitted into human society, allowed to drink beer, have a job, wear a suit cut for an adult male . . . and now *her*.

The growl resumes. 'So on Monday, at the end of the dinner after the incentives presentation, Bill and Jack decide to go on to this *club*.'

Rather in the way that small children change their breathing when they're listening to a favourite story, the sales force settle in for the latest chapter in the continuing saga of Bill and Jack. Even Mr Bogbrush seems to want to know what happens in the end.

My view is: actually, I don't give a shit. I have already learned far more about these people than I ever wished to. Propinquity will do that for you. So my mind begins to wander on to my latest conversation with Angela. She'd phoned me the evening before to gossip about Toby.

'What about Toby, then?' she shrieked, unable to contain her excitement.

'What about him?'

'He's going to propose to Wasp Woman!'

I confess I was a little taken aback at this statement. Firstly, because Toby had specifically requested that I didn't tell Angela about his proposal plans (I concluded he must have invaded his own privacy on this one). And secondly, because the marriage story had since moved on in a rather dramatic fashion: Wasp Woman had turned him down.

'You're joking,' I replied when he broke the news to me over a drink.

'She didn't turn me down *flat*. She said she wanted to *think* about it. But it's still a bit of a slap in the face with a wet fish.'

Toby appeared rather crestfallen, a most untypical look which didn't suit him at all. He stirred limply at his Bloody Mary with the plastic stirring implement.

'It obviously came as a surprise to her. The proposal thing.'

'She was quite matter-of-fact, actually. No hint of waterworks.'

'Perhaps she's not the emotional sort . . .'

'She's a cold bitch.'

'Did you do the whole Savoy romantic thing?'

'Savoy was booked. We went to that really expensive Eye-tie near me. Bloody embarrassing, getting down on one knee . . .'

'You actually . . . ?'

'Oh Christ, yes. The full bizzo. First I say, Jennifer, actually I have something for you. Girl intrigued . . . I whip out the old padded velvet box, set it down in the breadcrumbs. She looks at me a bit oddly. I say, Well, aren't you going to open it? Horrible long pause while she looks like she's swallowed an egg. Then finally she pops the lid. Fifteen hundred quid's worth of engagement ring, socking great diamond roosting on the top, glinting and fucking winking like the Treasure of the Sierra Madre. Anyway, she's still looking unwell, so I take her hand and go down on one knee – the gap between the tables is *ludicrously* narrow considering

176

what they charge; I brought a packet of those bread sticks down with me, but I don't think she noticed – anyhow, I say, Jennifer, would you do me the greatest fucking honour . . .'

Toby swallowed hard.

'. . . actually, I didn't say *fucking* honour. What I said was . . .' He sighed heavily. 'What I said was, Would you do me the greatest possible honour by agreeing to become my wife?'

Toby was staring at me goggle-eyed. I had to suppress a powerful urge to hoot with laughter.

'The perfect romantic proposal,' I managed.

'So the cold bitch takes her hand away and starts fussing with her hair and begins um-ing and er-ing and I'm left squatting in the gangway like a prick. Meanwhile, Johnny waiter's hovering with two bowls of *fritto* bloody *misto* for the next table, and honestly . . .'

Thank God. Thank God, it was at this point in the narrative that Toby started giggling. 'It was fucking *outrageous*,' he squealed.

'Bloody. Hell,' I sympathized.

'Worse thing was, when I stood up, there was this sickening crunch of bread sticks.' And now he began shaking with amusement. 'Quite comic really, when you think about it.' Fat tears of laughter were rolling down his cheeks. 'And as I squeezed back into my seat, right . . .?' A mad cackle. Then in a thin voice, barely able to keep the hilarity at bay, 'I knocked over next-door's fucking carnation. The fucking carnation they put in those absurd . . .'

He was unable to complete the sentence. I, too, could hardly speak. Hysteria had us in its grip. I haven't laughed like that for years.

About an hour later, when the last of the shuddering convulsions had rolled away like a retreating thunderstorm, Toby shook his head and looked at me a bit seriously.

'Trouble is, I can't decide what to do next. Whether to mount a campaign. Woo her with flowers. A dozen red roses every day until she submits, sort of thing. Or tell her to go and fuck herself.'

To me, the way he framed the dilemma was highly suggestive of the probable outcome, i.e. the go-and-fuck-herself scenario. But here was another black bit straight out of the eternal human comedy. On the one hand, to ply her with blooms and the offer of a shared future together; on the other, the testy recommendation outlined above. Both possibilities seemed to carry equal weight in Toby's mind.

'Or how about this, right? On Monday I send her a single red rose. On Tuesday, I send two roses. Wednesday, four roses. Thursday, eight. Friday, sixteen. Saturday, thirty-two. By the middle of next week, her flat will look like Kew fucking Gardens.'

We sat and considered the mathematical consequences of that one for a moment.

'Bit of a nerve, though, eh?'

'Inexplicable.'

'I mean, what's to think about? Either you know, or . . .' He trailed off. 'I mean, if you have to think . . .' He crimped his lips, widened his eyes and shook his head slowly. It was one of those looks that said *Yup, life can be a real bastard sometimes.*

'I mean, many would think I was a fucking good catch!'

'Exactly.'

He raked his fingers through the flesh of his face. Then he brightened. 'Still. What about you? Nurse, eh?'

'Nurse.'

'Tomorrow, is it?'

I nodded. 'Listen. You know that er, *technique* you were talking about. Or rather not talking about . . . ?'

'Mmm.'

'Just out of interest . . .'

I am now beginning to get seriously pissed off.

It's five to nine. We have long passed the fashionable margin that girls are allowed to be late within and are now well into the territory where the excuses have to be very good indeed. Several possibilities occur to me:

1. There has been a major disaster. Her hospital's well-rehearsed emergency procedure has been activated, and our blind date has been forgotten in a blur of ambulances, oxygen masks and green surgical gowns.

2. She's one of those women who are pathologically, clinically, late. Who think that if what's been agreed is eight o'clock, then eight o'clock is when they should start getting ready. Who think it's enough to touch your hand, put on

one of those wincing *ooh-er* smiles and squeak, 'Sorr-eee.' Who think that if they turn up at all, that should be sufficient cause for celebration. Who might have been happier living in the eighth century when the arrangement would have been, 'See you on Tuesday.' Who make you suspect there may be some weird power-relationship thing going on; who (perhaps at an unconscious level) put themselves in the category of those who keep others waiting. Who, through some disturbance in their brain's time-control mechanisms, simply cannot compute how long is needed to wash one's hair, walk to the Tube station, buy a ticket and travel to Leicester Square.

3. She's here. And we haven't spotted one another. (Not v. likely. I seem to be the only tall man standing at the bar featuring not as much hair as he once used to.)

Gemma hadn't been the only respondent I called that evening. There had been two other new replies to my advert on the *Guardian*'s voicemail system.

Number one I congratulated myself on rejecting straight away. It was Annie again. She felt she hadn't 'done justice' to herself in the first message that she'd left for me, and wondered aloud whether that was why I had failed to answer. The lying old trout ran through the sickening list of her so-called interests and activities, and even had the nerve to bring up the subject of tennis. I shuddered at the memory of my panic-stricken flight from Peckham. Those rearward-sloping teeth.

The second I got quite excited about. Diana, mid thirties, was the publicity director of a little-known charity. In a pleasant, warm voice she revealed, 'I have to go to a lot of dinners, which is terribly dangerous of course, so I compensate by going to the gym. Usually twice, three times a week.'

Thanks to my new policy of *listening incredibly hard*, this single sentence told me an enormous amount about her.

1. It gave me a fix on her fitness levels. The gym, three times a week? She was fitter than the butcher's dog, most probably.
2. I also had a fix on her vanity levels. People who attend a lot of dinners are generally quite well turned out. She wasn't going to be some tragic slob, that was for sure. If it happened that she had a face like a mackerel, it would at least be a well-presented mackerel. A mackerel that had made the best of itself. (I was certain she was no mackerel, however.)
3. I'd got a fix, too, on her weirdness levels. This was clearly a ticklish one (cf. Alice, the angry comic), but all looked well at first inspection. Publicity directors of little-known charities weren't going to be carpet-chewing nutters, were they?

I decided to call her. We had a really excellent

conversation, travelling easily round books, films, theatres, universities, relationships, life and everything. She was clearly bright, and funny to boot. Only quite late in the day – as we were talking about maybe meeting up some time – did she mention the b-word.

Babysitting.

'Did I not tell you about my daughter in my message?' she said when I sounded a bit surprised.

'I don't *think* so.'

'It's a problem for you. I can hear it in your voice.'

'Not at all,' I lied. 'I love children. I went to school with children.'

She sighed. 'Actually, she's very funny at the moment.'

There was a pause while I struggled to remember what you are supposed to ask people about their children. Oh, yeah . . .

'How old is . . .?' Don't say *it*. '. . . is she?'

'Leone's six and a half.'

She had pre-empted my next question. So there was another pause while I rapidly tried to corral my thoughts on the single-mother issue.

Truth: I would rather there not be any children. If Diana and I were to enter some kind of a relationship, there would surely only be room for one immature, selfish and needy character at the centre of her life.

'She doesn't come on dates with me,' said Diana, reading my mind. 'She stays with her dad.'

'I see.' Then to sound a bit more upbeat about the whole thing, I added, 'That's handy.'

'Mario sees a lot of her anyway. He has her every other weekend. It's all quite amicable, actually.'

First Diana. Then Leone. And now Mario. Within minutes, I felt I had stepped into the middle of a family psycho-drama. I pictured myself drinking tea at Diana's kitchen table on Saturday morning, a friendly silent nod to Mario, framed in the doorway as he arrives to collect Leone. (For some reason, Mario is wearing a black T-shirt and long shorts with combat pockets. Why would that be, do you think?) The picture – I was surprised to realize – did not overly dismay me.

I said to her, 'Do you know Browns? On St Martin's Lane. It's easy to spot. There are two bloody great fiery torches fixed to the outside wall.'

.

I've been stood up.

She's not coming. She can't be now. No one is an *hour and a half* late, are they?

Even if she did arrive in the next few moments, it would be highly embarrassing. Any man with a modicum of self-respect would have stormed off ages ago. (Unless, say, he happened to have bumped into an old friend, for example. Who has perhaps only just left. Which explains what he is still doing here.)

The sales team have begun to disperse, the weaker members peeling off for their trains, leaving Doll-face, her suitor, their porky boss and one of the other women, a sturdy glum-looking creature whose face has blurred from an excess of white wine. They're playing that game where you have to say who you'd rather sleep with, A or B.

A lot of the names mentioned have been unfamiliar to me: 'Roy in accounts' rings no bells; nor do Spotty Nigel and Fat Brian, a duality which caused much merriment when Doll-face was asked to nominate a preference. The sturdy glum one has been particularly wicked in setting up oppositions, several times demanding that Mr Bogbrush choose between a good-looking male and a disastrous female. His visible discomfort over Glammy Robert in Traffic versus Smelly Gaynor was a joy to all who witnessed it.

I have a sudden vision. Three-quarters of a container of Singapore noodles and the congealed remains of a portion of salted spicy squid are currently lurking within my fridge. Having rested there for twenty-four hours, the little red and green chillies will have had time to further infuse through the noodles, and my mouth begins to water at the thought. In addition, there's an unwatched videotape about dark matter. I still haven't got to the bottom of the mysterious force that keeps the universe from flying apart.

But now the fat bloke in charge, for no apparent reason, says, 'Champagne, then.' It's the way he said *then* that I find interesting. 'I'm buying,' he adds, to clear up any confusion.

And then, fuck me, who should turn up but Jack and Bill.

Jack and Bill are tall, heavy, grey-haired men in well-tailored grey suits. Twin bellies swell powerfully against shirt fronts and trouser belts. Their complexions walk the tightrope between the tan of the golf course and the flush of the saloon bar. The taller, fatter and browner of the two I take to be (the more senior) Bill.

Jack and Bill have clearly enjoyed what is known in the trade as A Good Dinner. They order large brandies which they park on the long wooden bar and stand just out of reach of, like a pair of swimmers bobbing beyond the edge of the pool. They growl at one another and their junior colleagues in a highly coded fashion which I have to strain my ears to make sense of.

The other players have radically realigned themselves in the presence of the company's gods. Doll-face has wound her dial back to three drinks ago; Mr Bogbrush now seems incredibly callow; even Mr Salt and Pepper has lost some of his patrician ballast. He's standing straighter, somehow more nimble of foot. Jack and Bill, I realize, are what these characters aspire to become.

Only the sturdy glum-looking one with the blurred face seems unmoved by the high-level visitation. Her expression of bleary-eyed contempt is plainly indelible. It may have been in place when she arrived for work this morning.

'Where've you two been, then?' she mumbles. She obviously doesn't give a shit.

'We been in Sheekey's,' says Jack. 'With Pat and Roger from Birmingham.'

There follows some impenetrable dialogue about Pat and Roger, and their assessment of what the 'boys in Birmingham' think about the latest set of 'numbers' (they're not overly impressed, one gathers).

'What we need,' says Bill, floating up to the bar, draining his brandy balloon and signalling for another, 'what we need is for Pat to go on the board and Roger to be the new Pat.'

Then Bill says to Jack, 'Tell them Roger's story. About the bloke with the sheep.'

Jack takes a deep breath, blowing away the brandy fumes to make room in his head for the essential joke-recycling skills.

'There's this shepherd, right? Herding his sheep in the middle of bloody nowhere. Suddenly, OK, from out of this dust cloud, comes a brand-new BMW. The driver's this real flashy Herbert in a sharp suit, Gucci shoes, Ray Ban sunglasses and what have you. He leans out the window and says to the shepherd, "Here. If I can tell you exactly how many sheep you've got, will you give me one?" The shepherd looks at this bloke, and he looks at his sheep and he says, "Sure. Why not?" '

Jack pauses, checks how he's doing. His audience is totally with him. Even Mr Bogbrush's shit-eating grin has begun to spread out and make itself comfortable amid his Cro-Magnon features.

'So this bloke whips out his laptop, he connects it to his cell phone, he surfs to a NASA page on the Internet, then he connects to a GPS satellite navigation system to get a fix on his location. Which he then feeds to another NASA satellite that scans the area in, what's it called? Ultra-high-resolution.'

I fear Jack may be nearing the limit of his memory for technical details.

'The bloke then opens up this digital photo in, what

was it? Adobe fucking Photoshop. Then he exports it to an image-processing facility in fucking . . . Hamburg, and within ten seconds, he's got an email on his Palm Pilot that the image has been processed. Then he accesses the data through a SQL something. Uploads all the funny business via his Blackberry whatnot and, after a few minutes, prints out a full-colour, fifteen-page report on his hi-tech, miniature LaserJet printer. He says to the shepherd, "You have exactly 1,586 sheep." '

Mr Bogbrush can't help himself. He makes a muffled noise, like he thinks that was the end of the joke.

'The shepherd says, "Fuck me. You're absolutely right. You better take one of my sheep." Bloke picks one of the animals and stuffs it into the boot of his car. Then the shepherd says, "Listen. If I can tell you exactly what business *you're* in, will you give me back my sheep?" Bloke thinks about it and says, "Yeah, why not?" Shepherd says, "You're a consultant." Bloke says, "How did you guess?" "Simple," says the shepherd. "You turned up here, even though nobody asked you to. You want to get paid for an answer I already know. To a question I never asked. And you know fuck all about my business. Now give me back my fucking dog." '

Jack drains his brandy balloon in the tumult of laughter that follows. He told it rather well, it has to be said. Bill claps him on the back in congratulation.

'Home, home, jiggety-jig,' he adds.

Bill and Jack take a few steps away from the bar. And now everyone has begun looking at their watches and making those unmistakable signs that the party is over. Within minutes, Bill and Jack have lumbered off – I feel sure a car and driver are not far away – Mr Bogbrush and Doll-face have dissolved into the night (not with *each other*, please God). Only Mr Salt and Pepper and his sturdy blurred companion remain in place.

It's ten pm. She's definitely not coming now, is she?

'Bill's such a wanker,' growls Mr S and P.

His glum-looking colleague shoots him a glance of undisguised indifference and thuds off in the direction of the ladies'.

The two of us remain at the bar, nursing our respective potions. Officially, we do not know one another, even though I feel I have spent the whole evening in the company of this prematurely dour character. When I glance round again, I find him gazing at me.

'Never turned up, eh?' His expression is neither friendly nor unfriendly.

'Something like that,' I concede.

'Plenty more fish in the sea.'

I nod. 'Yeah. You're right there, I expect.'

We fall silent for a few moments. Something troubles me about the way the evening ended so quickly.

'Jolly crowd,' I comment.

'Piss artists,' comes the reply.

'What do you all do?' I ask as lightly as I can.

'Sales,' he confirms.

A few moments later, his glum-faced co-worker heaves herself back on to her bar stool.

'This gentleman was asking me what we all did,' he tells her.

Two sour eyeballs briefly rest on mine. 'As little as possible in the time allowed.' She doesn't betray a flicker of amusement and in the next instant has turned back to her drink.

When I wake on the sofa at three in the morning, lights on, video rewound, the remains of cold Chinese on the coffee table, I realize I have been dreaming about the mysterious force that keeps the universe together. The truth, when it had been revealed to me, had seemed so beautifully simple; it explained perfectly why the cosmos is exactly the way it is and no other.

Of course, I have forgotten it.

6

AND THEN, OUT OF a blue sky, love.

OK, romance.

But to begin at the beginning . . .

Gemma was incredibly apologetic when I called to inquire, in a manner of speaking, where the fuck she'd got to the other night.

'Oh, *fuck*,' she exclaimed – sincerely, in my view. 'I am *so* sorry.'

'I did begin to wonder . . .'

'I am so *fucking* sorry.'

'No. Well. Look, it's—'

'It's *all* my fault. I am *such* an idiot.'

'Really, there's—'

'Will you *ever* speak to me again?'

'We're speaking now, aren't we?'

'Paul. I am *mortified* that this has happened. I've got my diary in front of me. Can we have another try? *Please* say we can.'

Since she was begging, it seemed churlish to decline, though it was satisfying to be able to turn down the first three evenings she suggested.

'Shit. I bet you're out seeing gorgeous women.'

I let silence speak volumes on my behalf at this point. It was true that on the nights in question there were three names pencilled into my own diary: Diana, Lynne and Joy, although their respective gorgeousness levels had yet to be established.

We finally managed to agree a date about ten days in the future.

'You'll have met someone by then,' said Gemma, pretending to go all sulky on me.

'I doubt it,' I replied. After all, it wasn't as though ageing, balding, unemployed television producers were in such terrific demand. 'Anyhow,' I said, 'you haven't told me what went wrong the other night.'

'What went wrong is that I am a fuckwit,' she explained. And she added, with a bit of an edge to her voice, 'I'll make it up to you, I promise.'

'She says she'll make it up to me,' I told Angela when she inquired how my hot date with the nurse had gone. Toby and I were round at hers; we were midway through the second bottle of the Moroccan Syrah that her wine-tasting group had been raving about.

'Bloody right, she should,' said Toby. 'Disgraceful behaviour.'

'She'll probably offer to have sex with you,' said Angela.

'It would only be polite,' I agreed. 'After keeping me waiting like that.'

Then she asked, 'What do you think I should do about Bernard?'

Toby and I looked at one another.

'What happened to the trapeze artist?' he said.

'Fire-eater,' I corrected him, drawing a finger across my throat in a final sort of fashion.

Angela pulled a face. 'Little fucker. He's going out with bloody Rochelle.'

'The Incredible Clanking Woman!?' I couldn't help myself.

'Git.'

'He chose *her* over you?'

'Little fat shit.'

'Inexplicable,' said Toby.

'Maybe he needed some parts for his unicycle,' I suggested.

'But what should I do about Bernard? He keeps wanting to see me.'

'Sorry. Who's Bernard again?' I honestly couldn't remember. There was always some romantic lead either coming or going through Angela's life – sometimes both at the same time – and it was hard to keep up.

'You know. The estate agent.'

'Oh, *him*.'

Him. Not, from the sound of the bloke, one of those super-smooth, callow chancers who will say anything to make a sale, but a rather older figure. And a somewhat hopeless one too, according to Angela. They'd met when he came round to value her flat.

Toby said, 'Is he the clown who fell down the stairs?'

Angela sniggered. 'The last four steps where the carpet's loose. He could have sued, probably.'

Angela had pressed a packet of frozen peas against

his ankle and he'd been phoning her on and off ever since.

'Why don't you go out with him?' I asked. 'He's probably a decent enough sort.'

'I think he might be a Christian.'

'An estate agent who believes in God? Don't be ridiculous. What makes you say that?'

'He looks like one.'

Toby and I looked at one another again.

'He had grey socks,' she continued. 'I think he might have had that fish symbol on his car.'

'Jesus Christ,' said Toby.

'And he wants to take me ice-skating.'

'*Ice-skating?*'

'Good move,' declared Toby. 'Girl a bit unsteady on her pins. Chap extends the firm arm of support. Whiz whiz whiz round the old rink. Boom.'

'Whiz whiz whiz, boom?'

'Undoubtedly. Boom.'

'Ice-skating's not terribly conducive,' she insisted. 'The lighting's so harsh.'

'You're right,' I decide. 'The guy's a loser. Forget it. Who takes a girl ice-skating?'

'I've agreed to go, actually.'

Toby and I exchange a supplementary glance.

'So when you say, you don't know what to do about Bernard . . . ?'

'I don't really know whether I like him *that way*.'

'Ah.' Toby.

'Hmm.' Me.

'I suppose I could give him a chance.'

'His firm hands round your waist.' Me.

'Whiz whiz whiz, boom.' Toby.

'Perhaps he'll turn out to be the most brilliant skater,' Angela suddenly enthused. 'Perhaps he skated for his county or something and wasn't good enough to turn professional so he ended up being an estate agent. He might sweep me off my *feet*!'

Clearly the unfortunate realtor was going to need some sort of ace up his sleeve. Grey socks and the fish symbol weren't likely to cut it in themselves.

I considered entering my evening with Lynne for the World's Shortest Date competition. Seventeen minutes had to be a record, surely.

Lynne said she worked in the travel industry – travel agent, I guessed – but when we spoke on the phone, it turned out she was a 'flight attendant'.

'Air hostess, they used to call them,' I recalled playfully.

My mind went back to a student summer job I'd had on a railway station bookstall. One of the paperbacks – it might have been one of those soft-porn editions with the discreet dark covers – featured the libidinous adventures of a so-called 'trolley dolly'. It was entitled, hauntingly, *Coffee, Tea or Me?*

Despite the fact that our phone conversation was halting and unpromising – I have a feeling she may even have referred to outings to the 'thee-*etta*' – I went ahead and pressed for a meeting. My reasoning was as follows:

1. Air hostesses, in my experience, are almost always attractive. I've whiled away many hours on a long flight privately deliberating which air hostess was the most desirable. Sorry, flight attendant.
2. There is something about the proximity of violent death – occasioned by, say, a sudden catastrophic loss of cabin pressure – that can cause one to develop vivid sexual fantasies about young women in white blouses and close-fitting brightly hued skirts. I expect female passengers feel the same about those cheerful cabin stewards.
3. I had never had a date with a flight attendant.
4. Not really a reason, this. More a question; but what is it about women and cheaply made uniforms?

And also . . .

Also, I was rather getting into this blind-dating thing. There was a growing thrill attached to the act of waiting for a stranger. What would she be like? Goddess or haddock? There seemed no way of telling beforehand, and it seemed rude to request a passport snap in advance. All was up in the air until the instant our eyes met. Like rushing into the future at the cutting edge of a perpetual present, one felt, dare one say it, more alive. Devotees of the roulette wheel probably experience the same sensation in the moments before the circling ball tumbles into its slot and the man in the shiny suit says, 'Rien ne va plus.'

Lynne, however, did not fall into the goddess category. Nor, to be fair, was she all haddock, although there was something about her pale flesh and lifeless eyes that did speak of the ocean depths.

Her airline plied an uninteresting route between an unlovely airport in the south of England and an unfashionable destination in northern Europe. She was not one of those people who are in love with their job.

'What colour is the uniform?' I inquired, to seem perky.

The reply was a pigment that a painter of the Dutch school might have ordered in bulk when he knew he had a lot of fields in winter to colour in.

It was very clear that Lynne and I had nothing in common. My amusing definition of factual entertainment was received as though it were bad news from the oncologist.

It was obvious that I wasn't her type either.

After another roaring silence had fallen across our conversation, I suggested, 'This isn't really a great success, is it?'

'Not really,' she agreed.

'Do you think we should leave it?'

'Perhaps we should.'

'Return to the hanger with engine trouble, sort of thing.'

'Sorry?'

'Doesn't matter.'

I walked her to the Tube, although in truth I felt like skipping with relief. I had to fight the urge to say, *I hope you don't think this has been a complete waste of time*. It was far from it, in my view. We hadn't spent a moment longer than necessary, there had been no question of a second drink, let alone dinner together, and there were two powerful lessons to be drawn from the seventeen minutes during which the paths of our lives had merged.

LESSON TEN:
If the date is a disaster,
don't prolong the agony.
Life's too short. You'll be doing
everyone a favour.

LESSON ELEVEN:
Long-cherished fantasies around professional
uniforms are not a good basis
to make dates on.
She probably won't be wearing it.

Joy, whom I met twenty-four hours later, seemed so familiar that I felt I knew her from somewhere.

'Are you *sure* you don't know anyone in TV or journalism?' I asked. 'You seem . . .' She seemed like she could be one of my friends. Or rather one of my friends' friends, put it like that.

But Joy knew no one in my world. She worked in arts administration. And she was so transparently nice that it was actually off-putting. After an hour in her company, I wanted to yell, 'Haven't you got a bad word to say about *anything?*'

She was attractive, intelligent and, as I say, pleasant to a fault. There wasn't an atom of me that desired her. After two drinks, we had reached that point in the proceedings where we could raise the topic of dinner or alternatively say goodnight.

The words that fell from my lips, unmediated by any sort of conscious thought process, were these:

'It was really nice to meet you, Joy. I'm supposed to be seeing my sister in Charlotte Street at nine – I'm going to be a little late – can I walk you to the Underground?'

Rather to my amazement, a fictitious sister had emerged, together with a bogus assignation – including location – and the flattering detail that the present company had been sufficiently enthralling to set back my plans for the remainder of the evening.

She accepted my chivalrous offer. We shook hands rather formally outside Leicester Square Tube.

'Well, goodnight, Paul. Good luck with . . . factual entertainment.'

'Thanks. And you, with . . . with your things.'

We both knew we would never see each another again. I felt a small pang of regret. Joy was lovely. You know, a genuinely good person in a wicked world, sort of thing.

Then she said, 'Say sorry to your sister for me.'

'Sorry?'

'For making you late.'

I smiled. 'Not at all.'

'What's her name?'

'My sister?' Was there a microscopic pause before I answered? 'Charlotte.'

'And you're meeting her . . .?'

'. . . in Charlotte Street, yeah. How funny, it hadn't struck me as, er . . . funny.'

'Are you going to walk?'

'Taxi.'

An odd pause while she continued to look at me. 'Well. Goodnight, then.'

'Yeah. Goodnight.'

I don't know why it hadn't occurred to me before:

LESSON TWELVE:
Have a fallback position.
A tactful lie,
should the need arise.

As with all the best lies, it should make the liar sound better than if he hadn't needed to tell it in the first place. Like phoning to explain you'll be late for work because you've driven a neighbour to hospital (he fell and blacked out for a few seconds).

Keeping my sister waiting struck me as a masterful touch, in both its authenticity and the positive light it threw upon the receiver of the information. Oh yeah, and . . .

LESSON THIRTEEN:
Attend to the details. If you're going
to the trouble of inventing a relative,
get their name sorted out in advance.

* * *

I don't know how the plan arose to put Toby together with Morticia. I think I may have just woken up with it. Following the incident in the Italian restaurant, shares in Wasp Woman were sinking through the carpeting.

'There's no way back,' said Toby decisively. 'Once she's said she's got to think about it, boom, game over.'

'Boom.'

'Momentum lost. Train derailed. It's the exact opposite in business.'

'Sorry?'

'In business, someone comes to you with an investment opportunity, right? You know right away if you don't like the smell of it. You give it what I call an Instant No. But if you think there might be something there, you proceed more slowly. You take weeks, months, to do the research, interrogate the business plan and whatnot. Arriving at what I call a Slow Yes.'

'Yes.'

'Exact opposite with women. Yes is either instant, or it's a No.'

'And mounting a campaign? Flowers and what have you?'

Toby did something ugly with the shape of his mouth.

'You seemed rather good together,' I persisted.

'If you've got to think about it, ka-boom.'

'Really?'

'Oh, definitely. Anyhow, how's it going with the blind dating?'

'Yeah, fine. I think I'm getting the hang of it now.'

'Had any nookie?'

I shoot him what I think of as an old-fashioned look.

'Seen that nurse again?'

'Next week.'

'Anyone you think I might like?'

'How do you feel about women who are *painfully* nice?'

'What are we talking here . . . ?'

'Saint-class.'

'One does like a *touch* of wickedness.'

I nodded in agreement. 'How about Morticia? She's free.'

'Your ex?' Toby did something interesting with the angle of his head. 'She's not overly nice, is she?'

'Nice isn't the first word you'd choose to describe her. Or even the last.'

'Bloody striking woman.'

I nodded in agreement, and not without a certain amount of pride.

'You think she'd be amenable to a tickle?'

'I don't see why not. Women are always flattered to be asked . . .'

'What's the downside?'

'What do you mean?'

'What are her negatives?'

'You've met her loads of times.'

'Always seemed rather a good thing to me. Can't understand why you two didn't make it to the altar.'

'The *altar*!? With Morticia!?'

'Bloody good-looking girl.'

201

'I'll invite you both to dinner. You can have a proper tête-à-tête.'

'That chap she was with. Off the scene now, is he?'

'History. Toast. Heavily carbonized toast.'

'Like that, is she? Chews them up, spits them out?'

'Not really.'

'And you wouldn't mind? What with her being . . . ?'

'My ex? I'd be delighted for you both.'

'What a good sport.'

'Listen. I should tell you. She's not the *easiest* person . . .'

'Uphill? Moody? Trouble on a stick?'

'Sort of thing.'

Toby assumed a mask of supreme indifference. He shook his head. 'No problemo.'

'You feel you'd be able to deal with . . . with that side of things?'

'Momentum's the key. If you're the one creating the momentum, they're too off-balance to cause trouble.'

I neglected to mention that, in a suitably dark mood, Morticia could create as much momentum as a Saturn Five rocket. 'Good luck, mate,' I added.

'No problemo.'

Diana the publicity director for the little-known charity is exactly on time: a novelty, in my experience. I recognize her instantly, first from her own description, but also in a deeper sense: she conforms perfectly to the idea of her that I hold in my head. Another novelty.

202

She is no mackerel. No sort of sea fish whatsoever.

'I *really* need a drink,' she says, settling herself on the next bar stool, fussing with her hair and the strap of her handbag, and endearing herself hugely to me in the process.

'Difficult day?'

I had spent the morning tapping idly at my novel. The early afternoon on the sofa re-reading *Brideshead Revisited*. The late afternoon stroke early evening shaving and bathing and generally getting ready for tonight.

'A little trying,' she smiles. 'Have you ever had one of those days when you want to creep up behind your boss and . . . I don't know.'

'What?'

'What's piano wire?'

'It's wire they string pianos with.'

'And strangle her with piano wire.'

'Garrotte. I think the technical term is garrotte.'

'What's the difference?'

'Garrotting's more French. It sounds nastier than being strangled.'

'Would there be blood?'

'Probably. The wire might go through the flesh.'

'That sounds fine. I'd like to garrotte her with piano wire.'

'This woman has displeased you in some way.'

Diana downs a mood-altering quantity of the Cabernet Sauvignon provided.

She says, 'Do you think it's healthy to have violent fantasies about authority figures?'

'Oh, vital, I expect. For your mental well-being.'

Diana looks quite pleased with my flippant remark. She's gazing at me in a promising way. Blue eyes shine in a strong squarish head. Her short businesslike hair and modern-girl trouser suit lend her an attractive gamine quality. I can imagine her in fishnet tights playing the lead in *Dick Whittington* at Christmas.

'Have you been out with lots of women, then?'

'Not at all. Half a dozen. Maybe eight. Nine, perhaps.'

'That sounds like quite a few.'

'Well, most were. You know.'

'Mistakes.'

'I was going to say duds.'

She laughs. 'Do you know immediately?'

I nod. 'I think so.' I think of Toby. *Boom boom. Kaboom* and all that.

'I think one does,' she agrees.

'They say it takes women longer. Women being notoriously less superficial and more inclined to look deeper and so forth.'

A slow, satisfied smile starts to spread itself out across Diana's face. It seems to take about a quarter of a minute to reach all the relevant parts, curling into the various features and bedding down among the pre-existing contours.

'I think women know pretty instantly as well,' she purrs. 'I always do.'

I have to restrain a very powerful urge to swallow hard.

'So have you answered lots of adverts, then?' I

inquire. To my own ear, my voice sounds like it might have ascended a register or two since it last said anything.

'Not lately.'

'But you've done it before?'

'I had a few dates with a chap. He worked in the City. It didn't really lead to anything.'

A pause, to consider this.

'When you say, *It didn't really lead to anything*, do you mean you slept with him, and it didn't lead to anything? Or was the thing that it didn't lead to . . . would that have been sleeping with him? Just to be clear. Only you looked a bit sad when you said it just then.'

Much as I'd like to, I don't voice this question. Instead, I reply, 'I see.'

'He did economic forecasting.'

'Really. That must be useful.'

'He knew all about the housing market in South East Asia.'

'Fascinating, I expect. When one delves into it.'

'Cambodia's the coming place, apparently.'

'Not Margate, then. I keep reading about Margate.'

'I knew pretty much instantly with him that I wasn't interested.'

'Ah.'

'But I thought: give him a chance, Diana.'

'Very sporting.'

'He might be all right, really.'

'And the economic forecasting, that could have come in . . .'

'Whereas, tonight . . .' She trails off, and becomes

fascinated by a tiny speck of cork floating in the remains of her drink.

A criminally long time seems to pass before I have the wit to pipe up, 'Do you feel like another? In fact, shall I order a bottle?'

For all his bluster, Toby was right.

Boom.

Or, to put it another way:

Ka-boom.

We've moved ourselves from the bar to one of the little round tables on that raised area by the window. Menus have been offered and accepted; neither of us seems likely to recall an appointment with a fictitious sibling.

We Like Each Other.

Full-on reciprocal flirting behaviour is under way, including overlong eye contact, postural congruence, tugging at earlobes, fiddling with hair (where appropriate) and light touching of the other's wrist; in general, all the non-verbal funny business that usually signifies a call to arms in the circuitry of desire. In addition, a creature – it may be an electric eel – has begun coiling through my guts. As this is a purely local effect, the fact of its presence is not available to the other party to form any kind of view upon.

It turns out that it is a good thing that I am not an economic forecaster. It turns out that being a TV producer – even an unemployed one – is a much more interesting thing to be. And being a would-be novelist is just about the best thing of all to be, topped only perhaps by being an actual novelist.

'I would love to have the time to *read* a novel, never mind write one,' says Diana.

'I didn't really choose it, the trying-to-write-a-novel thing,' I explain. 'It's more like it chose me.'

'So brave.' She looks genuinely impressed.

'Doesn't really feel all that brave, to be honest.' Feels like I can't think of anything I'd prefer to do.

'What if it's a disaster?'

'That could happen.'

'No, I didn't mean it like that.'

'Definitely, it could be a disaster. That's actually one of the likelier outcomes.'

She laughs. Then her head falls to one side. 'Gosh. I do *like* you, Paul.'

'Me too. I like you too.' It just popped out.

We allow a few moments to pass, just staring into one another's faces.

Then she says, 'There's no point not saying it, is there?'

'None at all.'

'There isn't enough time to not say what's on your mind.'

'I totally agree,' I reply, although I do not share the present contents of my mind owing to the adult, indeed explicit, nature of the material.

We talk enjoyably of our careers, she with an attractive mix of sincerity and cynicism about the little-known charity, its infuriating boss, the rigorous programme of dinners she has to attend, and the compensatory sessions on the running machine. For some reason I find myself picturing the sweat stain that would form in the hollow of her back.

'What music do you listen to?' I inquire. 'When you're running.'

She looks embarrassed. 'I'll tell you when I know you better.'

'Just tell me it's not the Venga Boys.'

She smiles and shakes her head. 'Not them.'

Instead of the stumbling fool I found that I had turned into in the presence of . . . what was her name? The Beautiful But Fundamentally Unavailable One . . . Julia, that was her. Instead of thinking, as I had with Julia, if we could just fall into bed together first and talk afterwards, I should be a much more sparkling conversationalist, with Diana I feel a powerful sense of events unfolding at their own pace. Nonetheless, it does occur to me to wonder: if we found ourselves going back to someone's flat tonight – or house, in her case – whose would it be?

'Did you say you live in Barnet?' I ask by way of keeping the ball rolling.

'High Barnet,' she replies with a bit of a twinkle.

'The end of the Northern Line.'

'Very much so.'

'Bloody long way from anywhere, if you don't mind me saying.'

She smiles. 'You're right. And I don't. I did think of moving, but Leone's happy at her school. And Mario works not far away. And we've got this big old comfortable place. It needs loads doing to it, but

Leone's friends all come and sleep over. We've just got a cat, did I tell you?'

The awesome prospect of family life raises its food-smeared, wax-crayoned head.

'A cat.'

'Gnasher.'

'Just the one?'

'She hung round a lot, and then just sort of moved in. They do that, I think.'

'Yes,' I say weakly.

'We put up notices. Has anyone lost a cat, and so forth, but no one claimed her.'

'Lucky old Gnasher.'

'Would you like to see a picture of her?'

'Of Gnasher?'

'Of Leone.'

'Sure.'

Diana fishes into her handbag while I wonder: How un-cool is this? Surely you don't show the kid's photo to the guy you've just met. Surely, at this stage in the proceedings, the kid should be That Thing Of Which We Do Not Speak. Same goes for Mario in the combat shorts.

'This is her. And that's her dad.'

A rather beautiful brown-eyed child stares solemnly out of the photo. Alongside her is a smiling brown-eyed man with offensively curly black hair.

'He'd be . . . Italian?'

'Greek.'

'She's a bit serious,' I quip.

'She actually is a bit serious.'

'Good-looking girl.'

'She inherited the best bits from each of us.'

I feel a little out of my depth in this talk of other people's mates and their progeny. I am suddenly very aware of a world where my attractive, sexy date is known as Mummy. At the same time, a voguish phrase, strictly speaking a voguish acronym, that I have just come across pops into my head. When I first learned what MILF stands for – Mother I'd Like to Fuck – I failed to see how it could possibly ever apply to my own life.

Diana retrieves her picture.

'It's all right. You need never have to meet them,' she says with a slow smile on her face. It's a statement that raises as many questions as it answers.

But I find myself saying, 'No. I'd like to. Well, her maybe. Perhaps not him just yet.'

It's late. It's already creeping past eleven. Food, further wine – and on my part, a large brandy – have been taken. If everything else was equal, this is the point where I might suggest that we cab it back to my flat and 'have a bit of a nightcap'. However, it has been made clear that Diana must return to High Barnet this evening, ready to receive Leone first thing in the morning – Mario having to leave early for work – then on to school, then back into town for another day at the little-known charity; not forgetting, at some point, to provide fresh food for Gnasher.

'All sounds a bit exhausting,' I commented. My plan

for the following day was: Get up. Read newspaper. Tap away at novel for a bit. Check *Guardian* Soul Mates system for further replies. Fling self on sofa and burrow into *Brideshead Revisited*. Possibly fire off the CV to a few people.

'It is exhausting,' was the frank reply.

'So, er . . . ?' What I was about to say was, When can I see you again?

'Are you free, not this weekend, but the weekend after?' she asked. 'Leone will be staying over with her father. Maybe we can do something together.'

There had been nothing at all suggestive in the way she said *do something together*. But I now had a very clear vision of the two of us in my sitting room, my right hand on her hip, the fingers of my left hand in her short, businesslike hair as we subsided on to the carpet.

'I'd like that,' I said quietly.

We walk to the Tube station. Even though I am about to plunge down the same stairwell and also travel home on the Northern Line (albeit the Edgware Branch), for some reason I feel we should part on the pavement and not in a crowded Underground carriage at Camden Town.

'It's been really good to have met you,' she says like she means it.

'Yeah. You too.'

'We'll speak on the phone, then.'

'Definitely.'

'And we'll go out, not this weekend, but . . .'

'. . . the weekend after. Yeah.'

'Maybe see a movie.'

'Or go for dinner. Or both. Or neither: Maybe I'll come up with a totally radical idea. Like, Go-Karting in Docklands followed by a roller-disco in Hoxton followed by this incredibly groovy cutting-edge club that hardly anyone knows about yet.'

'Sounds exhausting.' She smiles promisingly.

We stand staring at one another, the way that parting couples do when they don't quite want the evening to be over.

'You're sure you can't drop back for a nightc—'

'Im. Possible,' she says sweetly.

Her lips taste of Cabernet Sauvignon and the herby fish dish she ordered. There's female flesh in there too, and a particular perfume that I've smelt before but cannot name. I'm rather horribly aware of all the people streaming past us into the station concourse. After about a minute, the next time my mouth is favourably configured to make a brief statement, I mumble, 'You're absolutely certain you can't . . . mmmfff?'

I'm not sure how long the second part of our embrace lasts. And eventually, I even lose awareness of the passing public. Finally, her teeth sink into my lower lip in a way that seems to signal *That's All, Folks*, and I find myself staring into her face.

'That was quite . . . quite something for a first date,' I comment.

She smiles, a little woozily. 'Was rather.'

'Shall we do it again?'

'Definitely.'

I close towards her, but she spreads a hand across my chin. 'Last train.'

'Damn.'

'Not this weekend . . .'

'. . . yeah, the weekend after. Fuck it, how am I going to wait that long?'

She performs the international hand signal for *We'll speak on the phone*. And then she is sucked down the swirling vortex that is the entrance to Leicester Square station.

My matchmaking dinner for Toby and Morticia is a curious affair. The two principals accept their invitations readily enough, but I can't seem to find any other takers. In the end, Angela agrees to come, but only if she can bring Bernard.

'What, the Christian?'

'Don't be horrid.'

'The ice-skating Christian.'

'I'm not coming at all if you're going to be like that.'

'Only kidding. Did he take you skating?'

'He was quite good, actually . . .'

'Firm manly hands round your waist, sort of thing?'

She giggled. 'Until he fell over.'

'He didn't?'

'It wasn't his fault. There was a child going round the wrong way.'

'What happened?'

'We went to casualty. They think he's cracked his wrist. Listen, you won't be horrid about it, will you?'

'Not at all. I'll do a menu he can suck through a straw.'

She cackled. 'He's very keen, you know. He tried to kiss me.'

'With an arm in plaster?'

'He says I'm the most attractive woman he's come across since he transferred to the Tufnell Park office.'

Bernard is younger than I thought he would be. He's one of those overgrown, ill-fitting schoolboy types whose biros leak in their pockets. I can imagine his colleagues in the sharp suits taking the piss out of him something rotten. He shrugs apologetically about his bandaged right wrist when I offer to shake it.

'Ice-skating,' I begin. 'So unusual these days . . .' To find an adult male mucking around with it, is what I mean.

'I love the sense of freedom,' he says winningly. 'You know, screaming across the ice. You feel so . . . weightless.'

Angela is beaming in his direction like she might be falling for the chump.

'Do you do that thing where you go backwards?' I ask. Where you stick your bottom out and try not to bark it on the advertising hoardings.

Bernard produces a rueful smile. 'That's how I did this.' He waves his bindings in triumph.

Toby and Morticia arrive at the same moment, which I take to be auspicious. She's in what I'd call Seductive-Lite: skirt, pearls, pink cashmere cardigan. He's in Weekend-Stockbroker: clean blue jeans with creases, striped shirt, dark blazer. I have to say they look made for one another. (Angela and I have made no effort whatsoever. Bernard is already a walking disaster area.)

214

'And where's Jennifer this evening?' inquires Morticia, displaying her tactical intelligence and ferociously good memory at one and the same time.

Toby pulls a face. 'Finito,' he adds brusquely.

Her head – she can't help it – drops fractionally to one side. 'I'm sorry.' If one didn't know her better, one might have imagined she meant it.

'Oh, don't be. I'm not,' says Toby. 'Anyway, where's . . . er. Himself tonight?'

Morticia does something with her face that speaks of forbearance in the face of tragedy. She flaps a languid hand, as though shooing away an insect in a Thirties tropical drama.

'You too, eh? Well, let's get stuck into the sauce and drown our sorrows.'

The first course – my mother's recipe – is cold borsht with sour cream, hard-boiled eggs and spring onions, accompanied by hot new potatoes. All the guests, with the exception of Skater-Boy, have had it a million times before.

'Much as one enjoys this traditional starter from Eastern Europe, one does suspect the chef may be running out of new ideas.' There is quiet amusement at Morticia's waspish remark. She, I notice, is the only one here eating the soup in the 'correct' manner, i.e. spooning it up away from herself.

'Yeah. Come on, mate,' piles in Toby. 'Where's the originality? The vital element of surprise to make us gasp in delight.' He shoots Morticia a big conspiratorial glance, and blow me down if she doesn't shoot him one right back.

Boom. Maybe even *Ka-boom.* I honestly wouldn't like to say.

'Yeah,' says Angela, warming to the fun. 'This tastes like *sick.*'

Everyone laughs, but Bernard looks a little shocked. 'Not that bad,' he mumbles through a mouthful of ingredients. A trickle of purple fluid spills from one corner of his mouth. 'Quite nice really, once you get used to it.'

The main course is a recipe I tore out of a Sunday paper. It features a huge lump of lamb, implausible quantities of shallots and garlic, plus the best part of a bottle of wine. You combine the ingredients in one of those whopping great Le Creuset dishes and leave the whole shooting match to bubble on a low light for bloody hours on end (I paraphrase).

'Fortunately,' I declare, 'having no actual job to go to as such, I had all day to shop for and then lovingly prepare this meat treat for my special friends.' Murmurs of anticipation rise with the steam as I raise the lid. 'And you too, Bernard,' I add.

The lamb is a hit. It does indeed fall from the bone, as advertised. Even the hapless estate agent has no trouble forking it away with one hand. Toby makes a great show of keeping everyone's glass topped up – especially Morticia's, I can't help noticing.

'What happened with the nurse? No, with the charity woman?' he says. 'Bloody hard to keep up with Don Juan here.'

He fires another little bit of body language in Morticia's direction and is rewarded with a half-smile, half-wince. (*Yes, amusing, but don't push it* too *hard*, would be the rough translation.)

'Yeah. She was nice. We'll see each other again, actually.'

'Paul put an ad in the lonely hearts,' Angela informs Bernard.

'The manager of our office did that,' he replies. 'He ended up going out with a policewoman.'

'Really?' splutters Toby. And before he can stop himself, he adds, 'Did she take down his particulars?' A speck of food flies from his lips as he hoots with laughter and lands, very visibly, on the side of Morticia's wine glass.

There are two ways this can go, I'm thinking, and it will be instructive to discover which way she leaps. She can freeze in horror at the uncouth vulgarity, or she can endorse the warmth and humour of the moment. What she does, I'm relieved to see, very stylishly, and smiling all the while, is to make a tent of her napkin over her index finger and vanish away the offending morsel.

Toby touches her wrist. 'Sorry,' he mumbles, still a little creased with amusement.

She returns his touch, bats her eyelashes. 'Excellent lamb,' she declares to the room.

Angela and I exchange glances. And I'm thinking: Toby and Morticia . . . why didn't I think of it *before*?

The next morning there are two telephone calls.

'I wanted to congratulate you on a most agreeable evening.' A pause. And then straight in, no messing, 'I liked your friend Toby.'

217

'You've met him before.'

'Yes. He's not usually so entertaining, is he?'

'Toby? He's always full of fun.'

I'm being a little wicked. I know perfectly well the purpose of this call.

'It's entirely over between him and Jennifer, is it?'

'History, I believe. All ancient history.' I leave out the stuff about how he asked her to marry him.

A bit of a silence falls on the line.

'Why?' I inquire eventually. 'Are you interested?'

A deep breath. 'He seems solid.'

'He is a bit overweight . . .'

'No, that doesn't bother me. In fact . . .' She decides not to pursue this line of thought. 'What I mean is, he feels . . . substantial.'

'A proper person.'

'Exactly. Drinks too much, of course . . .'

'Well, who doesn't . . . ?' She wasn't exactly a shining example of moderation herself.

'I thought there was a mild frisson,' she admits.

'Oh, definitely. Moderate to good, I'd say.'

'You think so?'

'With fog patches.'

'What?'

'Forget it.'

'So what happens next?'

'What do you mean, what happens next?'

She sighs, like she's dealing with a difficult child. 'I assume you'll let it be known that an approach wouldn't be unwelcome.'

You have to take your hat off to Morticia. When

she wants something, she doesn't mince her words.

'I'll let it be known.'

'Now tell me about Angela's new beau,' she adds, moving on to other business.

'The estate agent?'

'In urgent need of modernization, I should have said.'

'Plenty of potential, we think.'

'Hmm. Not sure. Might be best to demolish and rebuild.'

Toby calls about five minutes later. He sounds as jolly as I have ever heard him.

'I'm besotted, mate.'

'Don't be silly.'

'No, seriously. You saw what happened. We got on like a house on fire. Ka-Boom. Bingo.'

'Bingo?'

Highly uncharacteristically, he begins to sing the lyrics of the song '(I'm Just A) Love Machine'. They claim, if you recall, that the singer is a hugging, kissing fiend.

When he stops chuckling, he adds, 'No. This is it. I'm stricken.'

'You poor thing. I'm so sorry.'

'Sorry? Whatever do you mean? It's a wonderful thing that you've done.'

'Listen, you've met Mort—, you've met Beverly loads of times. Why did you never think of her in that way before?'

'She always had some bloke in tow. I was always with some piece of totty. Context, in other words.'

'Beverly's not really totty. I suppose you know that.'

'Oh, they're all totty. But I take your point; she's a special lady and all.'

I'm not sure I warm to this new tone of Toby's. He seems far too certain about everything for his own good. I need to remind him: Morticia is not your everyday sweetness-and-light girlfriend. We're talking hardcore uphill. For connoisseurs only, most probably.

'So did she say anything? "I like your friend, Toby," sort of thing?'

'Funnily enough, that's exactly what she said.'

'I'll call her right now.'

'It's twenty past nine in the morning.'

'And your point is?' He starts chuckling again.

'Listen. She can be . . . quite prickly, you know.'

'Oh, I shouldn't worry about that. There's not much that a rare steak, a bottle of decent red and a good fuck can't put right.'

'I think it might actually be a *bit* more complicated than you—'

'Does she like horses?'

'Not that I know . . .'

'Chap gave me a pair of tickets for those Viennese horses who do tricks and whatnot.'

'I'm not sure that's *absolutely* her thing, to be—'

'They're marvellous, according to this chap.'

'I think she's more one for the ballet and the op—'

'Girls adore horses. It's the unconscious idea of all that rippling muscularity between their legs.'

220

I am defeated. 'Good luck, mate,' I sign off weakly.

'Luck, my old friend, will not come into it.'

After my passionate snog with Diana, it feels vaguely disloyal to be embarking on a date with someone else. But Diana and I aren't exactly going out . . . and this is unfinished business. I am here at the second attempt to meet Gemma, the self-styled 'fuckwit' nurse. Sickeningly, as I plonk myself on the familiar bar stool at Browns, I find myself next to the porky sales bloke with the salt and pepper hair and his sour-faced female companion. I catch the names Bill and Jack, and the words *Groundhog Day* have just enough time to pass through my head before a young woman has insinuated herself at my side.

'*Paul.*' She looks absurdly relieved to see me.

'Gemma?'

'I didn't think you were going to turn up. I wouldn't have blamed you if you hadn't.'

It's not a classically beautiful face; nor even a pretty one, particularly. Her eyes are on the small side, and a fraction too close together, the lips ungenerous, the brow a tad over-pronounced and shiny; the proportions just generally *off*, somehow. And yet.

I wave away her apologies. 'What can I get you?'

She's wearing a sleeveless shimmering print number that's doing an excellent job of demonstrating her advertised commitment to the keep-fit movement. Red high heels either clash hideously with the rest of the

221

ensemble or set it off expertly, you probably need to be a woman to tell.

'I'm nervous as a kitten,' she states, looking anything but. 'Do you think they serve White Russians?'

'Oh, they're not fussy. They'll serve anyone in here.'

She shoves me in the shoulder. 'You,' she says. All of a sudden I feel like some embarrassing older relative who's cracked a stale gag at a wedding.

'Just remind me, what's a White Russian?'

'Vodka, Kahlúa and milk. Or cream. Do you know *The Big Lebowski*?'

'Of course!'

The Big Lebowski (1998, Coen Brothers) is one of my favourite movies. The central character, The Dude, played by Jeff Bridges, drinks a river of White Russians which, together with the very large amount of grass he consumes during the course of the picture, serves to explain his relaxed attitude to the various improbable events that befall him in the plot.

'I *love* that film,' I add.

'Me too!'

I order two White Russians – they clearly hold no mystery for the man behind the bar – and admire the perky way she mounts the adjacent bar stool. She crosses her legs, leaving the toe of a red high heel pointing straight up at me, a famously promising piece of non-verbal communication, I seem to recall.

'So have you had a busy day in Hospital-Land?' I ask breezily.

'I've been off today. I've been to the gym.'

'Oh, you too?' It just slipped out.

'Do you go as well?' She seems to find it a surprising idea.

I shake my head. 'Loads of people I know do. I rather hate the thought. Those . . . *machines*.'

'They're good for you. Come on–' She sets an elbow on the bar and assumes the position for arm wrestling. There is obviously some sort of expression on my face because she says, 'Come on. I won't hurt you.'

My hand laces up with hers – her fingers are surprisingly cool – and in an instant my knuckles are grazing the woodwork. She's actually come off her stool to achieve her surprise victory.

'Hey. That was cheating. I wasn't ready.'

'OK. Again. You count it in.'

There's a bit of a look in her eye which I don't know whether to find encouraging or deeply worrying. It is rather nice, however, to intermingle our fingers and jostle elbows. The second time, I can just about maintain my arm at the vertical, though I'm not sure how long I could have lasted, and I'm certain I would never have toppled her.

'I'm actually a bit squeamish about this,' I admit. 'Haven't people broken bones?' The terrible report as one's radius snapped.

'I do martial arts as well,' she informs me with a smile.

'So basically, don't mess with you. That would be the message.'

'Yeah. Something like that. Cheers.'

We clink our White Russians together. It tastes like a high-voltage milk shake.

223

'These were an excellent idea,' I congratulate her.

'Let's order two more *immediately*,' she suggests with enthusiasm.

The barman has heard this exchange and his hand hovers over the cocktail-making impedimenta.

'Go for it,' I confirm.

A few minutes later, when I look again, I realize that hers is the face of a murderer. Or a murder victim. One of those odd young women you see in newspapers who have killed a rival or have themselves been killed. Who are attractive perhaps by dint of their youth and strangeness, but for no other reason.

An hour and a half later, we have both drunk more White Russians than the British government guidelines on alcohol consumption currently advise. In addition, Gemma has also flagrantly ignored the very well-documented evidence of the adverse effects of smoking upon health, by working her way through a box of Lambert and Butlers.

'I know, I shouldn't,' she replies when I state the obvious.

'Then why do you?'

'Oh, fuck off.' She punches me, not without force, in the shoulder.

'Are you hungry at all?' I ask.

'I can drink or eat. I can't do both.'

'How terrible. Can you get treatment for that?'

She sucks down another dose of her cocktail and blasts a jet of cigarette smoke just past my face. We're

224

not so much flirting with one another as joshing with a sexual overtone.

'Let's all go back to my house,' I suggest brightly. 'I've got milk and vodka in the fridge. If we pick up a bottle of the other stuff at Oddbins, I can make us some more of these.'

'I can't come home with you. We've only just met.'

'Don't be ridiculous.'

'My flatmate will be worried.'

'Ring her.'

'I need to be home tonight.'

'I'll call you a taxi.'

'It's a long way.'

'How long?'

'Cockfosters.'

'You're not serious?'

'It's at the end of the Piccadilly Line.'

'I know where it is. Come back to mine first.'

She gives me a look like she is seriously contemplating the idea. Then:

'Have you got any decent music?'

'Loads. Yards of the stuff. What do you like?'

'Have you got any——?' She mentions an artist I have never heard of.

'I think I might, actually.'

'Which album?'

'The new one.'

'I fucking *love* that album.'

'Really?'

'And the other thing I love at the moment is——'
She says a long word I don't really catch. It could be the

name of an artist or it could be the title of an album, it isn't clear.

For some reason I find myself asking: 'Have you ever heard any Phillip Goodhand-Tait?'

She shakes her head in confusion, as well she might. Phillip Goodhand-Tait is a singer who wasn't even particularly well known in the 1970s when I had one of his LPs, as they were called then. There was one song on it I liked. I think I dragged his name into the light to demonstrate the eclecticism of my tastes.

'Oh, you should,' I assure her. 'And Pluto Shervington.'

'Who?'

'You don't know Pluto Shervington?'

'You're taking the fucking pee.'

'We've got to go home right now and listen to Pluto.'

Gemma assumes a look of extreme scepticism. 'You'll *definitely* be able to call me a taxi?'

My heart does a little lurch. 'Definitely.'

'This is a lot of sad-old-bastard crap.'

I've made us a couple of White Russians and she's kneeling on my carpet going through the tottering heaps of CDs.

'*Some* sad-old-bastard crap, I admit . . .'

'Leonard Cohen? Bob Dylan? *Tosca*?'

'You're looking at all the wrong stuff.'

I kneel alongside her and begin hunting for something acceptable to the younger generation.

Unfortunately, in order to read the tiny writing on the spines in the low light, I have to perch my glasses on the top of my head and peer at them from a distance of about six inches, which makes me feel like some dusty old historian poring over the parish records.

'Where's——?' She mentions the long word again that I didn't quite catch.

'It's not alphabetized. He's in here somewhere . . .'

'She.'

'Sorry?'

'She's a she.'

'Here,' I exclaim, waving a small plastic box in triumph. 'You have simply *got* to hear this.'

Neil Young's *Harvest* isn't a perfect work of art, I'm prepared to concede. For a start, there is the small matter of Track Three ('A Man Needs A Maid'). But when you consider it was recorded in 1972 . . . . well, I wonder whether the artist with the long name will still find people listening to her material in thirty years' time.

Gemma scrutinizes the CD case as though it harbours a dangerous bacillus. She seems particularly interested in the photograph of the musicians on the rear cover (the haircuts, it must be said, are of genuine historical interest).

'This is sad-bastard music,' she concludes and shoves me so hard in the shoulder that I actually lose balance and roll over on to the carpet. Fortunately, being in such a relaxed state, I rather enjoy the sensation. When I regain the vertical, I see she is examining a CD of television library music, a collection of themes, scores and twiddly bits that programme makers use in their shows if they don't have the budget to get something specially composed. I must have taken it home to find a suitable piece in the days when I was a TV producer.

'What's this like, then?' she inquires.

There is something about the way she has folded herself in front of my CD player that makes me very much want to spill her on the carpeting in a reciprocal sort of manner.

'Stick it on,' I reply.

The opening track, described on the inner sleeve as 'a powerful, rhythmic, building theme with female voice, ethnic percussion and shakuhachi', does not meet with her disapproval.

'Cool,' she declares, though it sounds to me like the sort of tune you might hear on *Newsnight*, say, under a montage of shots of Singapore's business district.

'Would you like me to demonstrate my martial arts skills?' she says.

'Sure,' I reply. 'As long as you promise not to break anything.'

'Pretend to come at me with a weapon.' She steps out of her red high heels. We are standing about six feet apart. I drain my White Russian and set down my glass.

'What sort of weapon?'

'Doesn't matter.'

'OK,' I say, making a fist. 'This is a World War Two hand grenade.' I 'bite' the pin out, lob it at her and make one of those quiet bomb-explosion noises. *Booffff*. She rests her hands on her hips in a way that serves to further stretch the shiny, shimmery material of her dress against the contours of her body.

'Don't be stupid.'

'OK. Sorry. Right, this is a . . . a proper weapon.'

'A knife.'

'Yeah. A knife.'

'Come on, then.'

I take a step towards her. In a flash, I am somehow bent double across her left flank, one hand on the carpet, the other up behind my back. 'I could break your wrist now,' she adds cheerfully. Judging from the precarious angle at which she clasps it, I have no doubt that she could.

I am rather enjoying the way her body presses into mine, however. 'Do it again,' I request.

The second time, it's just as hard to work out the trick. Even on the fourth or fifth repetition, I can't see what to do to avoid ending up staring at my shoes. The next time she releases my wrist, I roll on to the carpet and tug her down with me. Her knees land heavily on my hip, and she sort of tumbles across me in a pleasingly drunken fashion. There's a moment where we stare at one another at this unusual angle, then my lips gain hers and everything goes quiet for a bit.

She tastes of vodka, milk, and Lambert and Butlers. The documentary theme music playing in the background makes me feel I am in . . . well, a documentary, probably.

'You promised to order me a taxi,' she says when we pause in the way that kissing couples do.

'I will do,' I assure her.

She grasps my ear painfully and pulls me towards her. No one says anything in words for at least twenty minutes.

'Stay,' I mumble at the end of the last track, 'Globalization 2' ('Strong, driving industrial rhythms').

'I'm not going to sleep with you,' she murmurs blearily.

'Why not?' I mean, why ever *not*?

'Just not.'

'This isn't really our first date, you know. If you count the one where you didn't turn up, you could argue this is actually the second . . .'

She takes my wrist and bends it forward upon itself.

'Call me a cab, or I'll break your fucking wrist,' she adds playfully.

'OK, OK. But just one thing . . .'

With my spare arm, I reach forward and hit the PLAY button. The compact disc, *Power and Imagination* ('Reflecting the changing world of business, industry and corporate power') starts again from Track One.

'North London, 1999,' I intone like a documentary voice-over. 'In a second-floor flat, Gemma and Paul abandon themselves to the mysterious forces that have conspired to bring them to . . . mmmfff.'

7

THE NEXT MORNING, AS I am lying in bed, still half drunk, half hungover, half delirious from the epic smooching session on the carpet, the phone rings. *Woman's Hour* is playing on the clock radio, so it must be after ten.

'Paul. How's things?'

It's someone I used to work with in the wacky world of television. Let us call him ... ooh, I don't know. Jason.

Jason runs a tiny independent production company that makes programmes on tiny budgets for TV stations with tiny audiences.

'Jason! Things are good. How are your things?'

'Not bad.' The little pause, and then on to the point of the call. 'Listen. I need to find someone to produce a one-off for me. It's a pilot, actually. I was wondering whether you might have a convenient gap in your diary.'

Had I sent Jason my CV? I cannot remember. I am intrigued and simultaneously nauseated by the prospect of imminent re-employment.

'I *might* have. What sort of thing are we talking about?'

'Essex builders do up an old property. A real wreck. A shell, practically. But here's the twist, OK? It's in France. They're a terrible bunch of oiks from Romford, of course they don't speak a word of the language, and they have to tangle with all these difficult French people. Local officials and suppliers and resentful peasants and what have you. It's a fascinating clash of cultures; docu-soap meets travel meets home improvement.' He names a highly obscure television channel. 'They're going bonkers for it.'

'Nice idea,' I comment. If you like that sort of thing.

'Thanks.'

'So what are the builders like?'

'Well, we haven't actually found the builders yet.'

'Ah.'

'Or the wreck. But that isn't a problem. France is full of them. The place where Nikki and I go for weekends, the estate agent in the town square always has masses of falling-down farmhouses in the window. You can pick one up for about sixpence. Do you fancy it?'

The full horror of the task unfolds before me. I would need to scout out a bunch of colourful telly-friendly builders from East London (who won't want much in the way of payment); locate a suitably dilapidated building in France (whose owners won't want much, if any, money); somehow bring the two together – with all the associated logistical problems like accommodation and transport – and make an amusing and informative telly programme out of what happens next. With next to no help. And in next to no time. Ten to twelve weeks would be my guess.

'How long have they given you?'

'In an ideal world, they'd like to see something in five or six weeks, but we could probably push them on that.'

I feel sick. The first invitation to resume my career as a TV producer that I have received, and it is a 24-carat, 5-star nightmare. From hell. On a stick.

Squared.

'What's the budget, Jason?' I ask as lightly as possible.

There is an ominous pause.

'We're being asked to develop the idea. They've said they're willing to put in . . . well, the phrase she used was "a few pennies". Which I guess means thousands.'

'So there isn't really a budget.'

'We would pay *you*, of course. But we would need to control the other costs.'

'Could I think about it?'

'Of course.'

A silence falls on the line. Out of respect, perhaps, for the monumental folly of the project.

'It would be quite a . . . a complex shoot. What with the builders, and the house and that.'

'Yeah,' he agrees. 'It wouldn't be simple.'

'Television rarely is,' I add wearily.

'You're right there, mate.'

'I'll get back to you, then.'

'Sure.'

'When do you need to know?'

'Oh, you know. Yesterday. The usual.'

The job offer bothers me all morning. Now that the

threat of work has thrown its dark shadow across my existence, I begin to realize how much I have come to appreciate my life of . . . I was going to say idleness, but perhaps a better way of putting it would be economic inactivity. Writing (OK, *tapping* at the keyboard) in the morning, reading in the afternoon (maybe a snooze, too, somewhere in between), followed by a blind date in the evening seems an entirely agreeable way in which to pass one's time. Jason's TV show sounds at best irksome, and at worst hellish. That it might prove to be irksome, hellish *and* a disaster to boot is an entirely plausible outcome; indeed, there is a high chance of the whole thing being a thoroughly unpleasant experience ending in ignominy and failure, for which I would receive not less than 100 per cent of the blame.

On the other hand, someone has offered me a job.

The dilemma laps round my head, together with images of Gemma from last night. Her powerfully lithe body pressed into mine. Those ungenerous lips, at first urgent, then languorous. A third vignette adds itself to the mix: Diana and I outside Leicester Square Tube.

Isn't it all exactly like life?

Nothing for ages, then everything at once.

Toby, the selfish bastard. All he wants to talk about is him and Morticia, when all I want to talk about is me and Gemma. And me and Diana. And going back to work (well, possibly).

'I think she *did* like the horses,' he says expansively, settling back into his chair and plainly preparing to regale me with a full account of the proceedings. 'They *were* terrific seats, even she conceded that. We were close enough to get a whiff of that earthy smell you get around horses . . .'

'It's flatulence. Horse flatulence.'

'. . . and they do some bloody impressive stuff. Even she was impressed.'

'Why do you keep saying *even she* like that?'

'Well, I don't think horses are really her thing, to be honest.'

Heavy sigh. 'Really?'

'She's more of an opera and ballet girl. But she took it in good part. There was a *little* bit of a snooty expression round the chops, but she was generally game, which I liked.'

'I finally met that nurse the other night.'

'So afterwards, right, I booked a very posh Italian in Knightsbridge. Manager made a big fuss of us, she positively *glowed* with all the flim-flummery. And she looked fucking fan-*tas*-tic, did I say? Done up to the . . . well, it was beyond nines. We're talking tens or elevens. A lovely floaty clingy number, dead sexy, totally classy. And we had this *very* satisfactory flirty conversation – *loads* about you, most entertaining – and we seemed to be getting on like the proverbial house. Did you know her father used to be a driving instructor?'

'The old bastard? I did, yes. Why?'

'She doesn't seem the sort.'

'When I first met her, I thought her dad must be a Lord. At least a Lord.'

'Hmm. Anyhow, it turns out we've got stacks in common. The same view on the world.'

'Aside from the horse business.'

'You see, this is where you go wrong, my friend, if you don't mind me saying so. You should open yourself up more to new experiences . . .'

'Performing horses . . . ?'

'Why not?' Toby becomes animated. 'Why *not*? When we do something we've never done before, we learn. We grow.'

'As people.'

'You may mock. But I've suggested to Beverly that we do something completely new every week.'

'Jesus. What did she say?'

'She's up for it, mate. Like I said, she's game. Game as a pigeon.'

'So, what are you . . . ?'

'Cycling on the South Downs.'

'You have got to be joking.'

Toby claps his hands together in glee. 'Next weekend. We're driving to . . . wherever it is you drive to, hiring bikes, cycle-cycle-cycle. Fresh air, softly folding hills, gorgeous country hotel, good dinner after a hard day in the saddle. Boom.'

'Boom.'

'Oh, boom. No question, boom.'

'You haven't told me what happened after the Italian in Knightsbridge.'

'Ferried her back to hers. Park up outside. It's been

a wonderful evening, really good to have met you properly, blah blah blah. She agrees, but no invite to pop in for a quick Nescafé. Anyhow, there follows a bit of a snogette in the jam jar; polite, full of promise, but nothing too grievous. Then a strange thing. She shakes hands formally. Odd, that. Don't know what to make of it. But anyway, we're all nailed on for the South Downs.'

'Boom, then.'

'As I say, boom. Where are the South Downs, by the way? Any idea?'

'South, I imagine. And down, most probably.'

'You don't mind me talking like this? Her being your ex and everything?'

'I'm delighted for both of you young puppies.'

'She was very nice about you.'

'Perhaps I don't need to hear this bit . . .'

'She said she was enormously fond of you . . . despite everything.'

'What's that supposed to mean?'

'Didn't explain. Thought best not to go into it.'

'What else did she tell you?'

'Thought you didn't want—'

'Tell me one nice thing she said.'

'Hmm.' He has to think about this one for a bit. 'She said you were always trying to make her laugh.'

'That's true.'

'That she'd have preferred it if you hadn't because laughing gave her lines.'

'Fuck. I'd forgotten that little detail.'

'She does have a sense of humour, though, don't you think?'

'It's a very . . . particular sense.'

'She definitely made me laugh. I laughed like a drain when she told me your great chat-up line.'

I suddenly begin to feel a bit sick. 'That I *definitely* don't want to—'

'It's right up there, mate. One of the all-time greats.' His shoulders are shaking with merriment. 'I won't be using it myself. Out of courtesy, if nothing else.'

Famously – it had entered the mythology of our relationship – the winning endearment I had mouthed at Morticia was, 'So, listen. Are you coming to bed with me, or what?'

True, the line did not reflect well on me, although in my defence it should be stated that I was drunk. But why bring it up with Toby? Why paint yourself as the sort of person to whom such lines are delivered?

'It worked, though, didn't it?' I point out. 'Perhaps the moral of the story is, when you've got all your little ducks lined up in a row, it doesn't matter what you say.'

Toby does the ugly thing with his lips and the faraway stare and I find myself thinking of my friend Elizabeth, who met the love of her life at a party in the eighties. He was eating a whole raw carrot at the time. When he noticed her watching him he said, 'Do you know where I'd like to put this?' Without replying, she walked up to him and kissed him. They slept together that evening and began living together later that week.

And in answer to the obvious question: sorry, I have no idea.

But what if it had been a radish?

Or he'd said, 'Do you realize carrots are an important source of Vitamin B within a balanced diet?'

Would passion have engulfed them with such awesome rapidity if he'd merely been nibbling on a baton?

Elizabeth and Carrot-Boy are no longer lovers. But on such words are relationships launched.

What if Morticia had replied to my overture, 'What. I'll take what, please.'

Or if she'd thrown me out into the street.

I expect there's a parallel universe out there in which she did.

A day or two later, with the greatest reluctance and the heaviest heart, I summon the strength of will to call Jason again. I guess if people offer you work in your chosen profession, it ill becomes one to turn it down. I tell myself it could be quite amusing to tour the bars of Essex in search of characters whom the public could take to their hearts like Maureen from *Driving School*; or that camp bloke who worked at the airport. Nor would it be the worst job in the world to pootle round France in search of a tumble-down shack in need of restoration. Nevertheless, I have a powerful sinking feeling when Jason comes on the line and – deep breath – I tell him I'll do it.

'Oh, listen. Sorry. This is a bit of a cock-up, actually. You didn't sound terribly keen, so we've found someone else.'

'Ah.'

'I sort of assumed when you didn't call . . .'

'No, please. Don't worry.' A large crowd has begun cheering in my head.

'I'm really sorry, Paul.'

'Not at all.' My heart is surging with joy.

'There will be other stuff coming up . . .'

'Fine. Honestly. Not a problem.' I am so happy I could cry.

'I'd like to talk to you at some stage about a celebrity-based treasure-hunt idea we're punting round. Two teams of glamorous girls running round the forest looking for clues. I'm calling it *Babes in the Wood*.'

We both have a bit of a laugh about that one.

Then I say, 'Hasn't there already been a show called *Babes in the Wood*? A sitcom about girls who live in St John's Wood?'

'Has there? Doesn't matter, I expect.'

That evening, I celebrate my lucky escape by buying a bottle of champagne and taking it round to Angela's. Toby and I have browbeaten her into roasting a chicken for us, although she has reserved the right to phone for a takeaway if she 'simply can't be bloody bothered', as she put it.

'Narrow squeak,' says Toby, raising his flute in tribute to my successful brush with the spectre of gainful employment.

'Fuck. You know, I could really feel the hounds at my heels there.' I could, actually. The warm breath of the pack.

'Never does any harm to turn down the odd job,'

240

asserts Toby. 'Gives people the idea that you can afford to.'

It's true, probably. I have always felt that my so-called career was shaped as much by the jobs I didn't get as those I did. Somewhere in that parallel universe, there's a version of me who was offered the sub-editing job on the *Blackpool Gazette* that I unsuccessfully applied for; who then perhaps stuck with newspapers rather than branching into broadcasting; and now . . . well, who knows? Perhaps I'm – perhaps he's – the editor of the *Blackpool Gazette*. And in another universe, there's another version of me who got the job of press officer at the University of the West Indies in Jamaica. It was the Blue Mountain campus, as I recall; the advert seemed particularly enticing on a rainy Monday in November in North Wales, where I was working as a junior reporter on the *Wrexham Leader*. In a third universe . . .

But you can go on like this for ever.

Occasionally, it occurs to me that my whole life turned on the twitch of a university accommodation officer's pen. If he or she hadn't assigned me a place in a particular corridor (F) in a particular hall of residence (Grosvenor Place), I would never have met the people I did there, one of whom (Alistair) had a friend (Richard) who knew there was a vacancy in the North Wales newspaper scene, which led me to phone the editor of the *Wrexham Leader* . . .

Actually, you can go mad like this.

If my father hadn't met my mother in that bus queue in Rome. Or rather, if he hadn't met my mother's *sister*. And if she hadn't invited him back to their house . . .

'So how are things between you and the stunt-estate agent?' I ask Angela.

'Fine, thanks. Don't be horrid.'

'He hasn't damaged any more limbs since we last met?'

'Actually Bernard's taking me to the country at the weekend. We thought we might go to the South Downs.'

'You can't go there,' splutters Toby. 'I'm going there. With Beverly. Go somewhere else.'

'They are quite big, as I understand it,' I chip in helpfully.

'Bernard comes from the South Downs.' She smiles like she's played the ace of trumps. 'He's going to take me to all of his favourite places.'

'I'm sorry. You'll have to think of somewhere else. What about Wales?'

'So what about you?' she asks. 'Where are you going this weekend? The South Downs are nice, I hear.'

'Actually,' I reply, 'since you ask, High Barnet.'

I've been here before. I used to spend rather a lot of time coming and going to the Barnet General Hospital when my father had his stroke. At that time, the hospital was laid out like a Second World War intern-ment camp. One day, when I came to visit him as he lay stricken in one of the low barrack-like wards, I brought along a chess set. Chess was my father's lifelong passion; he'd learned the game in Poland as a boy, and in his eighties, although he still found the occasional opponent, more commonly he would play by himself, brooding for hours over a particular position, humming softly and rocking in his armchair like a Sufi mystic. A game of chess, I reasoned, would help us test the gravity of the cerebral insult that had scrambled his speech and robbed him of the ability to swallow properly.

He was propped up in bed wearing a dressing gown when I arrived. I sat in the chair alongside, wheeled the bedside table between us, unfolded the board and opened the box of familiar pieces.

'Game of chess?' I suggested.

The look of surprise that appeared on his face was a wonder to behold. To his disappointment, I had always disliked playing chess against my father; he was many leagues too good for me, and I was ill tempered about accepting his advice on the superior moves I inevitably failed to make. It had been at least thirty years since I had last framed such a proposal.

I unilaterally decided to play black and began laying out my side of the board. After a few moments, my father's stubby yellowed fingers joined mine in the biscuit tin that contained the old wooden pieces. Slowly, and not without the odd clumsy moment, as though there might be a gap in his vision, he painstakingly set out white's back row. Finally he looked at me as though we were ready to start. The muscles in part of his face had been slackened by the stroke, but his eyes still held something of the challenging expression he always wore at the beginning of the timeless ritual.

All eight of his white pawns were still in the box. My exact, non-medical thought at this point was, *Oh, fuck. He's lost it, big time.*

'The pawns,' I said, motioning to the open biscuit tin.

I was oddly happy to see the brain injury had done nothing to degrade my father's ability to look at me as though I were an idiot.

'Aren't you going to put out the p—?'

He closed the biscuit tin. His face said, *Now shall we begin?*

Did he *realize* half of his pieces were absent, I wondered? Was the lesion actually constricting his ability to make sense of the world? And why was he now motioning for me to start? In chess, white always opens.

And then, with a mixture of astonishment, relief, and a feeling of helplessness that went all the way back to my childhood, I understood.

He hadn't neglected to set out his row of pawns because of damage caused by the cerebral haemorrhage. He'd done it to demonstrate that such was the level of contempt in which he held my game, he believed he could still beat me with eight of his pieces missing.

It didn't, as it happened, quite pan out like that. After a powerful opening attack from depleted white, we got bogged down in mid-game skirmishing and eventually, after several distinctly odd – illegal – moves on his part, agreed to pack it in.

So like I say, I've been to High Barnet before.

Diana opens her front door, ignites a big smile – there's a friendly peck on the lips – and walks me straight through the house to the patio, where we agree it's still warm enough to sit out and have a drink. Within seconds she's produced a chilled bottle of Chablis and two glasses.

'You don't mind *too* much, do you, being dragged all this way?'

'Not at all,' I reply in a good-natured fashion. 'Anyway, it's nice to get out of London every so often. Cheers.'

In her weekend wardrobe, Diana is, if anything, even more attractive. Some sort of scooped close-fitting top tapers into black jeans that are filled, I can't help noticing, with an admirable mix of restraint in certain quarters combined with exuberance in others. Chopped blond hair emphasizes the strong lines of her face. I am suddenly very glad that we decided not to travel into the West End this evening to shout at one another in some alcoholic bear-pit.

Actually, our choice of venue had not been a delicate negotiation. Even though Leone was spending the weekend with her father, Diana felt she wanted to be around, 'in case. In case of what, I don't know. Just in case.' It was she who'd suggested that she cook dinner and I was happy to accept. I felt a quiet certainty that we would end up in bed together. I mean, you don't slog all the way up to bloody High Barnet just for salmon *en croute* and profiteroles, do you?

Large plastic objects litter the lawn: a slide, a

space-hopper and some kind of climbing apparatus. This, I realize, is my first second date; the one with the nurse didn't count, despite the argument I tried to mount on the living-room carpet.

'Terribly grown up, isn't it?' The words are out of my mouth before I can stop them.

'What is?'

'Owning garden furniture,' I mumble.

'Owning kids' furniture, you mean,' she says with a bit of an ironic smile. 'Owning kids.'

It was true. All the way through the house, the clues were there. From the miniature pink plastic wellingtons by the door to the tricycle in the hall to the naive school daubings on the fridge.

'I can't pretend she doesn't exist. Or that she's not the most important thing in my life,' she says entirely reasonably.

'Why should you?' I reply with equal common sense, though some sulky part of me is rolling its eyes and going *tsk*. 'My friend Toby, who you haven't met, has got this deal with this woman where every week they try something totally new. They're cycling in the South Downs as we speak.'

To my ear it sounds like a non sequitur, but Diana seems unperturbed by the statement.

'What would you do?' she inquires, the smile moving from the irony part of the spectrum into the flirty.

'Ooh. Dunno. I've always fancied going to one of those deserted warehouse places where you get to sneak up on people and fire paint balls at them. Or a creative-writing holiday, perhaps.'

'I thought you were going to say something else,' she purrs.

'I wouldn't mind doing a helicopter ride over London . . .'

'I thought you were going to say . . .'

'. . . or, where's that really posh place in Mayfair? I wouldn't mind going there and eating, like, a mountain of caviar.'

'What I thought you were going to say was . . .'

'I'd quite like to swim with dolphins. Or maybe just hang out with them by the edge of the pool, or something.'

'. . . was, have an affair with a single mother.'

Her words reverberate into the silence. It's become rather dark, I realize, and the wine is almost finished. The slide and the space-hopper have turned into shadows.

'Well . . .' I discover that I have to clear my throat to continue. 'Yeah. That would certainly be a novelty.'

Diana stands up, and for a moment I think I have offended her somehow.

'I'll open another bottle, shall I?' she says softly.

'That's one of my favourite sounds,' I quip. 'Waves sucking on pebbles; the intro to "Whiter Shade Of Pale"; and a human voice saying, "I'll open another bottle, shall I?"'

High Barnet lies very still as I wait. A dog barks in a distant garden. From somewhere further drifts the pleasing clonking of a Tube train coming home to roost. Nearby, two cats begin an argument (or it could be the other thing, it's hard to tell).

Diana sets a fresh bottle and a corkscrew before me.

'Dinner will be ages,' she says, in a way that I find curiously reassuring.

Oddly, it's rather like the lamb dish that I cooked for Toby and Morticia. It involves lamb, of course, plus little onions and potatoes, the ingredients listed above all baked to fuckery. She does tell me the title, even the fact that it's a Nigel Slater, but frankly I am so pissed and hungry at this point, I don't really absorb the information.

'Bloody good,' I mumble approvingly.

We are seated at the dining table, not opposite one another, but side by side around a corner. With the arrival of the grub, Gnasher has rolled up from somewhere and is rubbing himself against my ankles in an insinuating manner.

'I'll put him out if you like,' offers Diana.

'Not at all. I rather like it,' I reply playfully.

The sitting-room lights have been dimmed. The bottle of Australian Shiraz that I brought along has been pressed into service. A romantic candle flickers. Some of Diana's pantomime-boy edge has been blurred by the wine and the labour of cookery and the fact that it's the end of a long hard week, I expect. I feel the powerful sense that we only need to get this lamb down our necks – and whatever follows; not bloody crème brûlée, I'm hoping – before we can retire to the big old sofa and start tugging speculatively at one another's garments.

'How's that boss-woman of yours?' I inquire by way of making conversation. 'Have you felt the need to garrotte her again?'

Diana's fingers fly to her lips. 'I did an awful thing,' she confesses.

'What? No, let me guess. You gobbed in her tea.'

Diana looks at me a little wide-eyed. Maybe the gobbing-in-the-tea thing is a boy revenge fantasy.

'Actually,' she says. 'Actually, I can't tell you. Change the topic.'

I set down my knife and fork with a bit of a stage report.

'You can't do that,' I tell her. 'You *have* to say. You're required to say by law.'

She shakes her head. 'I honestly can't.'

Under the table, my right hand finds her left knee. With my thumb and index finger, I take a tight grip on the top part just above the bone and begin squeezing rhythmically. 'Tell me,' I hiss.

It's as if an electric current has been passed through her body. She emits a long girlish squeal and threshes frantically in her seat as she attempts to prize my fingers from the powerfully ticklish region. I must say, it all makes for a highly arresting sight.

'All right! All right!' she implores. 'I'll tell you.'

I allow my grasp to weaken and she wriggles free. I take up my cutlery and begin eating again as if nothing has happened. Diana sighs heavily.

'I put a curse on her.'

'What do you mean, a curse?'

'I put an ancient curse on her.'

'What? Are you a witch or something?'

'It's a long story, but I know the words for this ancient Greek curse. You're supposed to scratch them on a piece of lead and bury it on your neighbour's property. Well, one afternoon, Catherine – that's my boss – she really fucked me off. So I went back to my office . . .' She trails away. 'You're going to think this is so incredibly childish . . .'

'Not at all, this is *great* . . .'

'. . . and I wrote out this curse on the foil wrapper from a Kit-Kat. I folded it up and hid it in her office.'

'Where?'

'Where, what?'

'Where did you hide it?'

'I dropped it down the back of one of her wooden units when she wasn't looking.'

'Diana, that is so great. I'm really impressed.'

'No, it's awful. She's been off sick for the last two days.'

'Excellent. It worked.'

'It could be serious. She says it's flu, but you don't know, do you?'

'Good point. Lots of very serious illnesses start with what they call "flu-like symptoms".'

'Paul, it's not funny.'

'I think you must have a gift. I shall be taking great care not to upset you in any way. Smashing supper, incidentally.'

Now Diana sets down her knife and fork.

'I have to get it back somehow. The bit of silver foil.'

'Steal into her office and root behind the wooden units un-noticed, sort of thing?'

'It's only the first time I've ever tried it. Well, the second.'

'Who was the first?'

'Mario. When we broke up.'

'Did anything . . . ?'

'He broke his leg skiing. But only months later.'

'Listen. You wouldn't mind giving me a copy, would you? I can think of a few people . . .'

'It's actually a bit scary. What if she, you know . . . ?'

'What if she dies?' Diana nods. 'Result.'

'No, seriously . . . ?'

'Seriously . . . she won't. And even if she does, and even if the death is thought to be suspicious, and even if the police search her office and find the Kit-Kat foil, and even if they spot the writing and have it translated and somehow link it to you, what are they going to do? Charge you with murder by means of invoking an ancient curse?'

Diana's earnest face cracks into a slow smile. 'I suppose it would look rather silly.'

'But I'm still not taking any chances. That was a magnificent dinner. I couldn't eat another morsel.'

'Oh. But there's dessert. Crème brûlée. I've even got one of those blowlamps to scorch the top.'

How did I know it would be crème brûlée? Because it always is, I guess. Crème brûlée must be the official dessert *de nos jours*. Without excessive difficulty, I manage to smash my way through the hardened outer casing and gobble up the cold custard within.

'Delicious,' I declare. 'Can we go and sit on the comfy chairs now?'

We move across the floor to the sofa, where we pause for a few moments, breathing heavily and staring at the table we have just vacated. Gnasher seems to have discovered something under my dining chair. He is sniffing at it circumspectly in the way that cats do, and once he has satisfied himself about aspects of his find, begins licking it up.

'Sorry, I think I must have dropped . . .'

'Don't worry. Gnasher's dealing with it.'

'Isn't Gnasher actually a dog's name?' I inquire. The animal in question has made short work of the fallen morsel and has begun cleaning himself in a thorough if intimate manner.

'What do you mean?'

'Isn't he Dennis the Menace's dog?'

'I don't know. It was Leone who decided to call him Gnasher.'

Oh, shit. Me and my big mouth. There it is again. The L-word. In all the talk of ancient curses and general flirting I'd almost managed to forget about *her*. In an instant it's as if the six-year-old has materialized between us on the sofa, bumping her feet together and sucking her thumb. A minute ago, I was doing sophisticated late-night chatter with cool, sexy Diana and now . . . well now, all of a sudden, she's Mummy. The insidious acronym – MILF – flashes through my head; the strangely provocative idea it contains; its uncomfortable similarity to the word *milk*.

There must be something written in my face because she says softly, 'Aren't you going to kiss me, Paul?'

'Me? Of course I am,' I reply. 'Whatever made you think that I wasn't going t— mmmfff.'

She tastes of lamb, and crème brûlée, and that perfume I've smelt before but cannot name. This time there are no crowds flowing past us into the hellish bowels of Leicester Square Underground station. I am very aware that we are perfectly alone in a living room in High Barnet; a naked flame dances on the table and a cat's on the loose somewhere, but otherwise, it's just us. Diana and I lock on to one another with an unexpected ferocity and subside into the depths of the sofa. No one says anything for a very long time; not even when my hand drifts behind a cushion and makes contact with something that feels very like a Barbie doll.

'You've missed your last train,' she murmurs at some point in the period that follows.

'I came by car. You knew that.'

'I was being funny.'

Then, later: 'So can I stay, then?'

'If you'd like to.'

'I would, yeah.'

'Good.'

Later still: 'I found this.'

She giggles and tosses it through the open living-room door, where it lands in the hall. It was a Barbie doll, by the way.

And even later still, perhaps because I'd so recently been reminded of it by Toby: 'So, listen. Are you coming to bed with me, or what?'

'I think it's more the other way round, isn't it?'

'Mmm. Whatever.'

Diana shoots me a bit of a square look across the kitchen table.

'So how many times have you done this?' she asks. She's not being unfriendly, exactly. But not entirely friendly either.

'What? Had breakfast? Ooh, thousands of times. Tens of thousands, I expect.'

'Gone to bed with some woman you met in a newspaper.'

'I don't like to think of you like that,' I riposte gallantly. 'We didn't meet *in* a newspaper. And you're not *some* woman.'

'Yeah. But.' She punches a great big hole into the corner of a piece of toast. 'Admit I'm not the first. Tell me there were others.'

'A gentleman never tells,' I assure her. Except in a properly published memoir, obviously.

Next mornings are always a bit grisly, in my experience; trapped in someone else's premises with a pounding hangover, too enfeebled by sex and alcohol to inquire where the powerful painkillers are kept. When we woke, and after a short reprise of last night's main theme, Diana wriggled into a towelling bathrobe and headed downstairs, from where there soon issued the unmistakable sounds and smells of coffee being brewed and toast being browned. As a concession to keeping it casual, I appeared without socks. I hoped she noticed.

'There's a paper, if you'd like to see one,' she said brightly, like the proprietor of a seaside guest house. It was the Saturday *Guardian*, of course. The one with all the lonely hearts in.

I think we're both a bit embarrassed, to be honest.

'Anyway. How many times have you done this?' I ask her.

'Never,' she replies. 'This is the first.' She seems to sit and stare at me for rather a long time. 'I don't know what I think.'

'Think about what?'

'About . . . about all this. About meeting like this. We're practically strangers.'

'Not now, we're not. Not after . . .' My eyes drift upwards in the direction of the bedroom floor.

'Hmm. Perhaps not,' she concedes. 'Would you like a boiled egg?'

Diana is looking rather lovely and unkempt this morning, all parcelled up in her towelling bathrobe, the chopped blond hair even choppier after a night adrift on the seas of romance. If she were a tent, I'd say that one or two of her guy ropes had snapped. Not that mine feel anything like secure. The fact is that I'm not at all sure What This Is, if you know what I mean.

Is this:

1. A meaningless night together. Very pleasant and all that, but essentially a one-off?

2. A meaningless night together that we repeat a couple of times just to make sure about the meaninglessness?
3. The Start of Something a little unfocussed and confusing and ultimately frustrating?
4. The Start of Something rather intense and powerful and ultimately frustrating?
5. The Start of Something which, after an initial period of confusion and lack of focus, gradually solidifies into a richly rewarding relationship where everything goes swimmingly for about two years and then collapses under the weight of its own contradictions, unravelling horribly quickly in bitterness and recrimination and possible deliberate damage to men's knitwear?
6. As above, but without the period of confusion and lack of focus?
7. The One? As in, *The One*. Where one finally finds a co-pilot for the remainder of life's journey. To include posh hats, confetti and irritating relatives. And maybe – gulp – the b-word.
8. None of the above?

Diana smiles. 'What do you mean, you don't know?' she says. 'You must know.'

'Sorry?'

'I only asked if you'd like a boiled egg.'

'Ah. Not a desperately difficult one, is it?'

'If you'd like some more time to think it over . . .'

'No, it's fine. I won't, thanks, but you go right ahead.'

Diana walks round the kitchen table towards me and does something rather surprising: she lowers herself on to my knees. I resist the temptation to contort my face into a rictus of pain and inquire whether she's thought about losing weight (a joke that probably only works when you know someone reasonably well).

'So what are your plans for today?' she asks.

'Don't know that I've got any,' I reply truthfully. 'What about yourself?'

'Tesco. Washing. The garden. The garden's a disaster area, perhaps you noticed. Hairdresser. Yoga. Computer-repair place. Blockbuster. And a friend's coming over later. We're going to sort out her love life.'

'Fucking hell. Busy *busy*.'

'And then *after* lunch . . .'

'You're kidding, right?'

She gazes upon me fondly. 'Can we do this again, Paul?'

'Sure. Do what?'

'This.' She nuzzles my ear.

'Oh, yes. Definitely.'

'Good.'

'I mean, why wouldn't we?'

'Exactly.'

'Be a shame to stop now.'

'That's what I think.'

'When are you free, then?'

'Are you sure you don't fancy a boiled egg?'

'I. Er. Mmmmfff.'

I thought about it all the way home in the car, the thing she'd asked me: Can we do this again?

And I repeat: Yes, of course we can. But what, I wonder, is this *this* that we're doing?

The hounds are getting closer. The following Monday afternoon, I find myself in west London, sitting in what's known as a 'bubble' – a glass-walled office within a larger open-plan workspace – listening to someone I shall call . . . Jacqui. Jacqui is explaining 'the thinking' behind the new TV show she has been put in charge of. I know Jacqui vaguely; she phoned me in a panic first thing this morning and asked if I could come in straight away.

'I see this very much as event television,' she says. 'Part magazine, part chat show, part platform for surprises. Something totally unexpected will happen every evening. Something to make the viewer go . . . *shit*!'

Jacqui's eyes have grown rather wide at the thought, although it should be stated here that the programme in question will only be available to viewers with access to cable, satellite or digital television, and only then if they make a special effort to tune in.

'Shit. As in . . . I wasn't expecting that to happen.'

'Exactly!'

'Shit as in, that was good. Rather than . . . shitty shit.'

'Yeah. Shit, as in . . . *wow*.'

Jacqui seems to have undergone some kind of irony bypass. Maybe it helps, if you intend to prosper in factual entertainment after a certain age.

A thought drifts through the empty windswept plaza of my mind. 'How about . . . ? I'm making this up as I go along, so let me run with it. How about, on *some* evenings, right, there's *no* surprise? Which is, in itself, surprising. I mean, if there's a surprise *every* night, the concept of the surprise could lose some of its, er, surprise value.'

Jacqui looks at me like she can't decide whether I'm a genius or an idiot; or whether maybe, like most decisions in TV, this one can't also be put off to a later date.

'There'll be a different producer for each night,' she says eventually. 'We'd be looking at you to do Tuesday.'

'I see.'

'With its uniquely Tuesday-ish feel and tone.'

'Mmm.' Undoubtedly.

'What does Tuesday night say to you?'

'What does Tuesday night say to me? Very. Good. Question.'

I stare out of the window for inspiration. Among the chimney pots, a male pigeon has puffed himself up into a right old state over a lady pigeon. He's banging his beak up and down on the roof and waddling about and generally summoning up the nerve to ask her out.

Jacqui decides to help me. 'Say we booked Nicole Kidman. Would she be right for Tuesday, do you think?'

We both know the chances of Nicole Kidman appearing on this show are indistinguishable from zero. Nevertheless, she asked me politely and I feel she deserves a reply.

'I see her as a terrific guest for Monday. Bang! Get

259

the week off to a flying start, sort of thing. Or a Friday, perhaps. With that Friday thing going on. Actually, to be honest, she'd be a fucking fantastic guest wherever you played her . . .'

Jacqui concurs with my acute commentary. 'Yeah. She would, wouldn't she?'

She sighs heavily, and I use the opportunity to change the subject. 'So *who* are the presenters again, Jacqui?'

She mentions a handful of names, none of whom, I swear, I could put a face to. One, I admit, does sound vaguely familiar, but only because I may be confusing him with someone I used to buy drugs from at university.

'They're all rather untried, aren't they?' I suggest delicately.

'That's the beauty of it,' she counters.

'They don't know what isn't considered possible . . .'

'They'll push the envelope. Exactly!'

'It sounds *very* exciting,' I tell her, struggling to keep the great fat smirk off my face.

'Of course, I've got a few more people to see.'

'Of course.' A great flood tide of happiness chooses this moment to surge through me.

'We'll be in touch.'

'Look forward to it.' I think a celestial choir may have joined the celebrations.

'Say hello to—— for me.' She mentions someone I barely know.

'I certainly will.' That scene in *The Producers* where

Zero Mostel and Gene Wilder are dancing outside the New York Metropolitan Opera and suddenly, joyously, the fountains burst into life.

Of course, I've got a few more people to see. She'd actually said it. As I travel down in the lift and hit the street, I can't fight the stupid smile off my face.

When they tell you about the other people they're seeing, it only means one thing, doesn't it?

That you haven't got the job.

'So when do you start?' asks Toby.

'Monday.'

'Shit,' sympathizes Angela.

'I know.'

'Still, look on the bright side,' says Toby. And then he can't think of one.

'I was so sure they weren't going to offer it to me.'

'Think about the money,' counsels Angela.

'The money's crap, and I haven't spent all my existing money yet.'

'There would have come a time,' says Toby.

I shake my head sadly. I am already in mourning for my lovely lifestyle. We are sitting in Angela's garden, some way into the second bottle of the Argentine Cabernet-Merlot.

'Anyhow,' I attempt to console myself, 'they haven't sent me the letter. They might change their mind. Or go bust. Or the Martians might invade earth and cancel all the television. They might put out their own programmes.'

Angela says, 'Like, Martian chat shows and whatever.'

Toby does that facing-the-brutal-facts thing with his mouth. 'There's an old Navaho saying. *If we don't turn round now, we might just get where we're going.*'

'I'm sorry, I fail to see how that helps.'

'There's another one: *No one, in the entire history of the world, has ever washed a rented car.*'

'That's Navaho as well, is it?'

'Anyway,' says Angela, 'don't you want to know what happened with me and Bernard on the South Downs?'

From the look on her face, and from the way she's hugging her sides, I'd say the answer is all too clear.

'Let me guess. He slaked his foul lust upon your pale, trembling body.'

She giggles. 'Don't be horrid.'

Toby looks at her a little sourly. I have a feeling that his own bicycling trip to the country did not prove quite so satisfactory.

'He's *very* romantic,' she swoons.

'When he's not falling over.'

'He bought me flowers. We went for lovely long walks.'

'Can't come to much harm walking,' snorts Toby.

'Actually . . .' And now she has to stifle a powerful squeal of laughter. She flaps her hand in the air to regain the ability to speak. 'Actually, he fell into a *hedge.*'

We can't help ourselves. We roar.

'What's the matter with the fellow?' guffaws Toby.

'He can't see a patch of ground without throwing himself down on it.'

'Oh, *don't* be horrid. It could have happened to anyone. It was his weak ankle; the one he did on the stairs here. He turned it over on a cobble and just sort of top— Just sort of top— Just sort of toppled into this h—' She can't complete the sentence for the great cackle that erupts from within her.

'He managed the other thing all right, did he?' I inquire when the hilarity has died down a bit.

Angela pulls a cat-that's-got-the-cream expression. 'Mmm,' she confirms. 'Definitely.'

'Funny you didn't bump into each other,' I suggest to Toby.

He waggles his eyebrows about for a bit. 'Fussy sort of creature, Beverly, would you say?'

'She knows what she likes, yes. Why?'

'She put on the boot face when we arrived at the charming little hotel I booked.'

'Ah.' I think I see the problem. The give-away word in the sentence above is *little*. And quite possibly *charming* as well.

'I say hotel. Actually, it was more of a bed and breakfast place. But it was scrupulously clean; low beams and horse brasses everywhere; lots of those daft dog pictures all over the walls – dogs dressed up as lawyers, playing cards and whatnot. I think she rather took against it.'

'Beverly doesn't really do quaint.' The Ritz-Carlton would probably be more her style.

'She perked up for the knife and forker. I took her

to this very reassuring posh restie straight out of the *Good Food Guide*; full of businessmen and magistrates; dessert from a sweet trolley. She loved all that.'

'And boom-wise? Was there any . . . any boom at all?'

Toby makes a face. Like he's just swigged half a glass of vinegar. 'I think I might have mistimed my run to the crease on that one.'

'You didn't jump on her, did you?' inquires Angela.

'Of course not. Just . . .' Heavy sigh. 'Well, I hired these bicycles, right. And she's bloody fit, as you know; I suppose I was imagining a nice leisurely tootle round a few leafy byways, but she set off at the most un-believable lick. Practically mowed down an old boy out walking with his dog. Anyway, it took me about twenty minutes to catch up with her – we were already in the next county by then – I found the puff to say, "Hey. Slow down a bit there, racer-girl," and she replies, "Oh, *do* try to keep up!" She didn't actually add *you fat bastard*, but she might as well have. So all day long I'm struggling along behind her, watching this magnificent arse in action; no wonder I'm feeling a little frisky by nosebag time. Anyhow, like I say, that side of things is a hit, there's a fair amount of fluttering of eyelashes and twizzling with strands of hair, and when we get back to the hotel, I suggest a nightcap from the honesty bar. So we're all alone, hunkered down by the inglenook with a pair of vast schooners of firewater, when in comes this other couple. He's some arrogant twat who works in the City and she's this brainless floozy, and the lounge is so small, we've got no option but to talk to them.

Well, I *suppose* I could have mounted some sort of conversation with Bugalugs about the cricket, or something, but the women *loathe* each other; the hate's crackling off them like electricity. Anyhow, they show no signs whatever of buggering off, so I sort of signal to Beverly, time for Bedfordshire, and she duly trots along behind me.'

'You booked separate rooms?' I ask. More to see if my mouth is still working than anything else.

'Indeed. Well. At the top of the staircase, I say to her – moment of truth – I say to her, I've found this very interesting book about birdwatching in my room; would she care to take a look at it? And she's wearing this rather promising smile, and says, yes, all right. And I'm thinking, bingo.'

'Bingo.'

'I'm thinking ka-boom. So we're both perched on the edge of the bed, which is a bit tricky because it's under the eaves. And she's flipping through this old Reader's Digest bird book, and I say, Beverly, I have so enjoyed spending the day with you. And she says vice versa. And then I say that I think she's a great girl, and she says . . . actually, she doesn't say anything nice about me at that point, but she accepts the compliment. And then . . . well, and then I snog her.'

'You dog,' says Angela.

'And she's snogging me back – you don't mind hearing this, do you, being as how . . . ?'

'Not at all,' I reply. 'I'm riveted.'

'And she's snogging me back. And it's all quite intense and everything. And then – and then, I *swear* I only put my hand on her knee. I mean, I swear it was only her knee.'

Toby looks a little shaken at the memory.

'What?' gasps Angela.

'Never seen anything like it, actually. She shot into the air like a rocketing pheasant.'

'Why?'

'Fucked if I know. I don't think it would have been nearly so bad if she hadn't cracked her head on the beam.'

Angela fails to stifle a laugh.

'She didn't black out, but she took a hell of a knock. I was incredibly solicitous, of course. She was effing and blinding about what a pokey little dump I'd brought her to; unbelievable language, actually. She calmed down eventually, but it totally ruined the mood.'

'It would.'

'I know the knee is a sensitive area. Would you say – without going into areas of unpleasantness – would you say she was excessively sensitive? In that way, at all?'

I shake my head. 'It's a mystery.'

'It's more than that, my friend. It's a riddle. An enigma.'

'So when are you seeing her again?' I ask.

'Friday. We're going to the pictures.'

'But you've done that before,' I jest.

Toby bowls me one of his square looks. 'We haven't seen this *particular film* before. Anyhow, what did you get up to this weekend?'

'Well since you ask, I went to High Barnet to—'

266

'Actually, before you say anything, can we order? I'm still fucking famished from all that pedalling.'

The *Guardian* must have run my advert again, because there are seven new messages on the Soul Mates telephony. I don't know what to think about this development because I have already opened an account, as it were, with Diana.

Naturally, I listen to them.

After all, what harm can it do to listen? It's not like we're going out or anything.

Well, is it?

The first is from a divorced Greek woman who is 'into computers and art'. She says she's in her mid thirties, but she has one of those gravelly Greek voices that suggests someone much older. Like, you know, sixty or something.

The next two, weirdly, are both 'mental-health professionals'. The first says she's down to earth, a member of a book club, sings in a choir and enjoys walking holidays. The second likes jazz, dance, theatre, cinema and cafés. (I feel it is interesting that she should specify cafés. I mean, what's not to like about cafés?) I wonder if they know one another. Maybe I should introduce them.

Respondent four, Amy, confesses to being 'slightly older' than me, recently divorced, and 'slimm*ish*'. She reveals she is looking for someone to 'put the sparkle back' into her life. I suspect it may fall to someone else to fulfil that role.

Jane teaches Media Studies at an institution in the

south of England. She enjoys tennis, reading, going to art galleries, and tells me she has a 'wide mouth', a detail, I confess, I find alarming.

Laura, who sounds like she's reading from a prepared text, says she's 'as comfortable slobbing around in old jeans and a pair of wellies' as she is in 'heels and a skirt'.

And finally there's Ruth, thirty-five, a lecturer in Classics at an American university who teaches and performs dance. There is a quiet intelligence about her voice that appeals to me. Despite the fact that she's five two – I would stand a whole twelve inches taller – I pen a fat exclamation mark alongside her details in my notes. A dancer! She's not going to be built like the back of a 134, is she? And a brainy one, at that.

In addition, I put exclamation marks against Laura (was it because she bothered to write a script, or more the phrase *heels and a skirt?*) and also against wide-mouthed Jane.

I spend the rest of the morning tapping away at my novel. The central character has solidified into a foolish young television producer who has developed something of a crush on one of his female colleagues, and apart from a slightly worrying absence of plot, I admit to finding it moderately amusing. They do say, don't they, that if one's own work doesn't entertain one, then how can it be expected to amuse anyone else? In other words, that authorial satisfaction is a necessary though not sufficient condition for reader satisfaction. But can this be true? It seems to me there are a variety of responses to the work, both public and private, that can perhaps best be summarized by the following table:

Author's view	Reading public's view	Result
Work of genius	Work of genius	Heroic triumph
Work of genius	Load of cobblers	Shattering disappointment
Cobblers	Genius	Delightful surprise
Cobblers	Cobblers	I knew it was shite

In the grid above, clearly, the genius–genius outcome is the most desirable, although cobblers–genius makes for a better story structure. As regards cobblers–cobblers versus genius–cobblers, I'm not at all sure which would be ultimately more depressing: to know it was all crap from the beginning, or only to discover it at a later stage. There are obviously an infinite number of further possibilities (not that bad–not that good; it stinks–it's quite amusing in parts, and so forth). Why am I telling you all this? In truth, fruitless agonizing about the future seems to be something deeply ingrained within my psyche. It's easier, probably; a softer option to engage in endless speculation about what will happen than to get off one's butt and actually make it happen. Perhaps it's a Jewish thing.

Or there again.

Anyway, who knows?

The untypical thing about my blind-date project is its proactivity. As others – well, Angela actually – have commented, It's Not Like Me.

But I take this to be a good development. That even after forty-two years (or forty-four, depending how you calculate it), change is possible. That when we do something we've never done before, we learn.

We grow (as people).

Nevertheless, the prospect of three new dates in the wake of the Diana episode is unsettling. I think myself back into the scene in her bedroom in High Barnet. All that filthy sex – as someone I knew once described it – all that was jolly good fun, and there seemed to be a genuine fondness between us. But there was also a sense of distance; a sense of her other life, the sense that the centre of her world was occupied by a six-year-old and that our relationship would always be peripheral unless and until it turned into something fairly major.

On our first date, Diana had given me her business card from the obscure charity. Now I decide to send her an email.

From: Paul Reizin
To: Diana@——
Subject: Hello.

Good morning. How is You Know Who? Are thousands of locusts swarming from her open mouth as we speak?

PXX

Ten minutes later, I check to see if she's replied yet. I know you shouldn't. That you should just go about your business and only check your email once, maybe twice a day. But I'm not like that. Anyway, she has:

From: Diana@——
To: Paul Reizin
Subject: RE: Hello.

**Back at her desk, thank goodness. How are YOU??? The
heating has broken down here and we are all wearing
coats. Am writing endless press releases about our
forthcoming 'Day'. Can you think of other ways of saying
'courage in the face of adversity'? Drinks tonight at the
House of Lords (with our patron)!**

Best
DianaX

I am faintly outraged by *best*.

Best is a signifier of professional courtesy. You write
best to your lawyer, or your estate agent. You surely
don't write *best* to the bloke you've spent half the night
wrestling around in the sack with. To a bloke you've . . .

As I say, I am faintly outraged.

From: Paul Reizin
To: Diana@——
Subject: RE: Hello.

**Very disappointed about failure of curse. I should like the
details nonetheless, as I can think of a few people I
might try it out on. Am tapping away at the magnum
opus, but unsure whether it's a light and amusing
confection or a steaming great pile of horse droppings. I
enjoyed our night in High Barnet. When are you free to
come out to play again? Have a nice time at the Lords. I
always liked that story about Bertrand Russell who got**

into a taxi and told the driver, 'I'm as drunk as a Lord.
But then I am a Lord, so what does it matter?'

PX

In view of *best*, I decide to dock her an X and ignore
her request for courage-in-adversity synonyms.

From Diana@——
To: Paul Reizin
Subject: RE: Hello.

Leone this weekend. So it'll have to be next, I'm afraid.
Hope that's OK? I enjoyed it too!

DX

PX plays DX. *Best* has been dropped, but now it's
gone, I find I rather miss it. Her two-line missive seems
positively curt beside my own light and amusing confection. It occurs to me: perhaps she's busy, or
something. She is at work, after all.

I click out of email and return to my novel in
progress. By going into the Tools menu and selecting
Word Count, I discover that I have written 9,914
words. Or, to put it another way, 44,752 characters
(without spaces) or 54,409 characters (including
spaces), a statistic that contains the remarkable impli-
cation that I have created almost 10,000 spaces. If I
manage to write another 86 words I shall have
written 10,000 words. Aside from the central

character's erotic obsession with his lithe, willowy colleague, I have absolutely no clue what's going to happen next. I hope all goes well for him.

The phone rings on the desk beside me.

'Is that Paul?' asks a female voice.

'It is.'

'Have you done anything about your sad-bastard record collection yet?'

It's Gemma. Gemma the fuckwit nurse.

'*Hello*,' I drool, like late-period Leslie Phillips. 'How the devil are *you*?'

8

'. . . AND HE SAYS, As a matter of fact I've been breeding bees. Really? says the bloke. Yeah, really. In fact I've managed to breed a bee this long.' Between my index fingers, I indicate an insect about six inches in length. Gemma looks at me like I might be a bit simple or something.

We are in my sitting room, on the carpet with our backs against the sofa. Somehow, I keep ending up on the carpeting with this woman.

'I don't like to tell you how much I paid for that sofa,' I told her.

'I like it better on the floor,' she replied.

'Fine. I suppose I paid for the floor too,' I added. 'The carpet. The underlay. Hardboarding. The bloke who came to fit it. It mounts up.'

'You.' She thumped me rather hard in the shoulder.

'You've bred a bee *this* big?' I do the thing with the fingers again. 'That's amazing, how many have you got? How many have I got? Let's see. Ooh . . . ten thousand, maybe. Just a sec, you've got *ten thousand* bees, this big?' Once more, the tips of my index fingers suggest a creature approximately fifteen centimetres from stem to stern. 'Where do you keep them? Where do I keep them? I keep them in a *hive*, of course. Where else would I keep them?'

It's so late, and we've downed so many White Russians, that it barely matters how well or otherwise the bee joke's going down. Once again, the library disc of theme music for TV shows is playing on the stereo.

'What *is* this?' she'd asked. 'Like, ambient-techno-lounge fusion or whatever?'

'Yeah. Something like that.'

'You keep ten thousand bees *this* big?' I do the fingers thing. The fingers thing is important in the bee joke. 'In a *hive*? How big's the hive? Ooh, says the bloke. Let's see. The hive's maybe . . . this big by maybe this big.' With my hands, in the manner of a fisherman estimating the size of the one that got away, I indicate a structure about three feet long by about two feet tall. 'Just a sec, says the first bloke, let me get this straight. You're telling me you keep ten thousand bees *this* big . . .' Fingers. 'In a hive this big . . .' Hands. '. . . by maybe this big?' Hands. 'Bloke says, yeah. That's right. I do. Bloke thinks about it for a moment. Then he says, don't they all get *squashed*?'

We're nearly there. Gemma has a somewhat sour face on, readying herself for what she instinctively feels will be a crappy punchline.

I deliver it.

But now, God bless her, she actually laughs. Well, she titters. 'I thought it was going to be something else,' she admits.

'I love that joke,' I tell her. 'It's not even a joke, strictly speaking.'

'You're weird,' she murmurs.

And then she tells me a bit of a story. About a man called Andrew. An older man with a sick wife whom she'd nursed when she'd worked briefly in a private clinic. It was one of those 'instant' things, apparently, that took them both equally by surprise.

'To be honest, I was a little disgusted at the beginning.'

'With him?'

'With myself.'

It had felt wrong – with 'her' all festooned with tubes and wires and hooked up to drips – to be 'shagging like bunny rabbits', as she put it, in the marital bed. Andrew loved his wife very much, but 'we just couldn't keep our hands off each other'. It had been an 'insane time'.

'What happened?' I ask, with a bit of a frog in my voice.

'She went into remission. I still see him every now and again. As friends. For coffee and whatever. And we talk on the phone. He's a very important person in my life now.'

'How old was he? Is he?' I don't know why I ask.

'Fifty-five. Sixty. Don't look so shocked. I told you I like older men. It's a daddy thing, probably.'

Gemma's story rather disturbs me. I suddenly have the feeling that alongside me on the John Lewis carpeting is a powerfully sexy – albeit crackers – member of the medical profession.

'Andrew would like that joke,' she tells me. 'He's a great one for funny stories.'

'Really? Well, let's call the old bastard up. Get him round here. We can have a fine old time, swapping gags and snappy one-liners. Have you heard the one about the old man who fucked his sick wife's nurse?'

No. Much as I'd like to, I don't say it. I merely think it.

'What do you do if you see a herd of elephants coming over a hill? That's one of Andrew's.'

'I don't know. What do you do?'

'Run like hell. No! *Swim* like hell. Fuck, I ruined it.'

'Man goes to the doctor's. Says, Doc, I think I'm a moth. The doctor says, I'm sorry, I can't really help you. You need to see a psychiatrist. The man says, I know. But I was just passing. And your light was on . . .'

There's rather a long pause as the joke fights its way past the White Russians to the part of the brain that deals with elderly comedy material.

'Oh. I get it. He thinks he's a moth. Andrew might like that one . . .'

'Do you think – sorry to be rude – but do you think we could stop talking about bloody Andrew? Only it's just that . . . mmmmfffff.'

There's a nasty clash of dental enamel as she falls at me, although not serious enough to halt the embrace and check for damage. We roll around the floor enjoyably for a bit; I feel sure her closely cut lady-trousers in an artificial fibre will be picking up a lot of carpet fluff, but decide not to mention it. When we get a bit too near the fireplace and a fragile blue vase that I'm fond of, I have to contrive to reverse our trajectory. At one point she breaks off long enough to declare, 'You. You're a fucking mad one, did you know that?' which puzzles me, but it seems like the wrong moment to ask for further commentary.

'So, er.' I have a horrible feeling we may have rolled over my glasses.

'Yeah?' I can't help noticing she's breathing as hard as I am.

'I was wondering . . .'

'What?'

'You don't have to get back to Cockfosters or anywhere, this evening?'

'I would have said if I did, wouldn't I?'

I suppose she would have. 'Or call your flatmate?'

'She's away.'

'You haven't got a plumber arriving at eight in the morning? To fix a dripping tap. Leaky washer. What have you.'

Not easy, I imagine, to look at someone as though they are a complete idiot when you're lying directly beneath them, but somehow Gemma manages it.

'No, Paul.'

'Ah. Well, in that case . . .'

'Ye-es,' she says slowly, as though to a backward child.

'Are you coming to bed with me, or what?'

'Fucking hell,' she says, rising to her feet. 'I thought you'd never ask.'

* * *

'And was I right?' inquires Toby.

We are sitting in a gastro-pub waiting for Angela and Bernard. These two are now officially an item, a thought that for some reason makes me feel a little gloomy.

'About the muckiness?'

'Without going into the gory details, obviously.'

'Obviously.'

'In the most general of terms.'

'She was quite . . . enthusiastic, yeah.'

'Told you.'

She was, actually. Although, without going into the GDs, I'd have to say there was a curious lack of intimacy. Her manner I would characterize as erotic-brusque; indeed, if it weren't for her deliciously anatomically correct female body, I should imagine it was rather like going to bed with a man. At times, I felt a bit of a cipher, although compared, say, to raging toothache, or cholera, feeling like a cipher isn't the worst feeling in the world, clearly. In fact, to be blunt about it, if it's cipher or nothing, give me cipher any day.

And she didn't mention Andrew once.

Well, she did. Just the once. She didn't state his name, but she began mumbling something about 'older guys' that made my stomach lurch and I had to put my hand across her mouth to stop her from completing the sentence.

'When are you seeing her again?' asks Toby. 'When you can next walk straight, yeah?'

There's a lascivious grin on his face that I don't much care for.

'Wasn't like that. Anyway. What about you and Morticia?'

'Who?'

'You and Beverly.'

'What did you call her?'

'My little pet name. On account of her dark side.'

'I'm taking her to the pictures on Friday.'

'Sounds a little . . . how can I put this? Low rent.'

'Ah. That's the beauty. When you have no expectations, you cannot be disappointed, my friend.'

'Is there a plan, as such?'

'Very much so. I pick her up from Chez Beverly. Drive to the local fleapit. View film. Repo sharpish to a nearby Indian, or Italian, as the fancy takes us. Natter-natter-natter about what we've just seen and matters arising. Then I drop her home. Perhaps she asks me in for coffee, perhaps she doesn't. It is immaterial. I am a rock. A safe, dependable character in choppy seas. Shifting sands. Whatever.'

'You won't put your hand on her knee?'

'Not without written permission in triplicate. What do you think?'

'Might work.'

'How's the job going?'

'All off. I thought I said.'

'Sorry. Or congrats. I can never tell with you.'

Actually, I'm not quite sure which it is with this one. I had almost convinced myself that producing the Tuesday night edition of the chat-stroke-magazine-stroke-platform-for-surprises show for the digital channel might be something of a laugh, so long as one didn't have to take it too seriously. So long as one could 'have fun with it', as they say in Tellyland about projects where no one has much of a clue what to do. The thought of the daily commute down the North Circular to the studio near Heathrow Airport wasn't a pleasant one, but the idea of a job to go to, having colleagues, leading a small team of keen young people, these things had an appeal. There was even talk of the programme, if successful, 'transferring to terrestrial', which was plainly bollocks, although it demonstrated that somebody cared about it more than I did, which was in itself reassuring.

However, when the personnel woman failed to ring me as promised to discuss detailed terms, and I phoned Jacqui to find out what was happening, I found her clearing her desk.

'Did they not let you know? What a fucking shambles, honestly.'

'What's happened?' I asked, trying to quell the hysterical laughter rising in my throat.

'The fucking channel, right? The one we were going to make the show for, right? It's gone fucking belly-up.'

'Oh dear.'

'I called my mate at——'. She named a well-known independent television production company. 'I'm starting there on Monday; doing a thirteen-parter about people and their gardens. I'll let you know if they've got anything going, if you like.'

'Thanks.'

'You're well out of this abortion, that's for sure.'

'Whoops. Look out. Here come Anthony and Cleopatra.'

Angela and Bernard are walking in holding hands like a pair of teenagers. She has the look of a contented, well-satisfied woman, which makes me feel a little unwell; he's a little blinky and bothered, as though maybe a biro has begun leaking and he hasn't quite worked out what that funny sticky feeling by his left nipple is all about.

'Sorry we're late,' says Angela. 'Bernard's been helping me put up a shelf.'

'Really?' I reply sourly. 'I've never heard it called that before.'

And blow me down if the chump doesn't blush like a ripe tomato.

So now I am seriously confused.

In recent days I have been to bed with two separate women, one of whom is attractive and sensible but not available again until the weekend after next; and the other of whom is as mad as a squirrel – a very sexy squirrel, admittedly, but a squirrel nonetheless. The thing with the squirrel feels weird and maybe even a bit dangerous. I can imagine her breaking my wrist or injecting my veins with mercury should I displease her in some way. We've made no firm plans to see one another again.

'I'll call *you*,' she'd said as she left the next morning, with heavy emphasis on the *you*.

I really can't decide: Is it a good idea or a bad idea

to have a mad, sexy nurse in one's life? Which would be better: that she turn up on my doorstep in the next few days, or that I never hear from her again? Perhaps the very fact that I've asked the question suggests the answer. On the other hand, she laughed at the bee joke. People who laugh at the bee joke can't be entirely dismissed. On the *other* other hand, Morticia sniffed when I told her the bee joke, and we went out successfully with one another for eighteen months. Yet on the other *other* hand – and this strikes me as significant – I hadn't felt the urge to tell the bee joke to Diana. Was that because we seemed to be getting on fine without it, or was there a deeper reason?

While these issues remain unresolved, I decide to phone Jane, Laura and Ruth, if only to eliminate them from my inquiries.

Jane (wide mouth, Media-Studies lecturer) sounds so like me, it's spooky. Not the voice so much – more the flip, cynical attitude.

'So what's it like living in——?' I ask, referring to the south-coast town where she now lives and works after moving from London two years ago.

'Oh, you know,' she replies, her words freighted with ennui.

'Like that, is it?'

'Exactly.'

'A breath of fresh air and yet. And yet . . .'

'And yet . . . not a breath of fresh air.'

'Dull at times, possibly. February, for example.'

'February is *cruel*.'

'Still, I expect the students are an inspiration.'

'Yes, thank God for the students.'

'Those eager young minds. All thirsting for knowledge, sort of thing.'

'It can be humbling.'

'Moving, even, I expect.'

'Some mornings, it's hard to fight back the tears.'

'So what did you do before you did this?' I ask. I am picturing one of those long sinewy women at the other end of the telephone; sprawled languorously on a chaise, perhaps, possibly with a cocktail cigarette smouldering at one end of her notably wide mouth.

'Before I taught Media Studies? I was at the BBC.'

'No!'

'You sound surprised.'

'Which bit?'

She names a semi-respectable department within the Corporation's Factual Group.

A little amazed, I tell her, 'I bet we stood next to each other in the queue at the canteen.'

'Are you a BBC person?' she asks.

I explain the latter part of my so-called career; the bit before I became a full-time novelist-to-be. I name a few of the less disgraceful programmes I have been associated with.

'I know you,' she says. I observe that a note of disappointment has crept into her voice.

'Really?'

'You know me.'

'*Really?*'

'We know each other.'

'That's . . . that's ridiculous. Are you serious?'

284

'Think about it.'

I do. And nothing happens. 'I'm sorry,' I respond. 'I don't know anyone called Jane. Actually, I do know one Jane. She's Jayne with a Y. And you're not her. Unless you're disguising your voice.'

There is silence on the connection from the seaside.

'Not being funny, how well do we know each other?'

'We've spoken several times. Once at length.'

'Face to face?'

'Face to face.'

'I must be going senile.'

She does not take the trouble to contradict me.

'Give me a clue,' I demand. 'Was it at the BBC?'

'Actually, not.'

'So, where . . .?'

'I should be offended that you say you don't know anyone called Jane. Apart from your friend with the Y.'

'Please. I've had a hard life.'

'Shall I remind you of the last occasion we met?'

'I'd be terribly grateful.'

She names the wedding of an amusing character I used to be quite friendly with until about nine months ago. Something must have happened after then, because he stopped returning my calls. Possibly his wife disapproved of me; or it was felt that my wedding gift wasn't quite up to snuff. (True, it had been a little underpowered. They'd probably have preferred vouchers.)

And then it comes to me.

'Oh, fuck.'

'Have you remembered now?'

'Jane. I'm so sorry. How are *you*?'

Not the smouldering sinewy cocktail-cigarette smoker, but a short, dumpy, enjoyably cynical young woman who was pally with my former friend. We'd got chatting at one of his parties; she was attractively flirty and she did have, it was true, a dramatically wide mouth, but I probably fancied her as much as she fancied me, which was not nearly enough.

'So, when we met at the wedding, right? Oh yeah, I think you did say you'd moved to——'

'I would have.'

'Well.' Deep breath. 'How is it down there?'

'Oh, you know.'

'Like that, is it?'

'Exactly.'

'A breath of fresh air, and yet . . .'

'And yet.'

I get off to a seriously bad start with Laura, from which we never really recover.

After the opening pleasantries I ask, 'So, are you slobbing around in old jeans and wellies today, or is it heels and a skirt?'

(I thought I was being funny.)

There's something of an Arctic pause. 'Neither, actually,' she replies. Then she adds, 'Why do you want to know?' Like I'm a pervert or whatever. Like I'd asked what colour her knickers were.

'I don't want to know,' I explain. 'I was being satirical.'

Another silence follows. If I listen hard, I can hear the wind moaning across the frozen tundra. 'I'm sorry,' she says. 'Are you trying to be funny?'

There's a position in chess – it's called the Pin; it probably sounds better in French or Russian – but when you're in it, whatever move you make, your opponent on his next move will inevitably capture one of your pieces. Your only choice is to select which piece to preserve.

I feel in just such a position.

'I was trying to be funny, yeah. Sorry. It didn't come off.'

It's late in the day to be still learning these lessons, but it feels like an important one.

LESSON FOURTEEN:
Don't take the piss – however well-meaningly –
in the first sixty seconds of the opening phone
call. Wait till you know her a bit better, probably.

There doesn't feel much of a way back now.

'So you're a lawyer, then?' I chip in lightly (she said she worked for a big City law firm in her message).

'And you work in TV,' she ripostes. 'What have you worked on that I might have heard of?' She doesn't actually attach the words *you worthless maggot* to her inquiry, but they seem to be dangling there.

'Ooh, all sorts.' For some reason I elect to name a show at the shallower end of the factual-entertainment spectrum. '*Auntie's TV Favourites* with Steve Wright. That was one of mine.' When the Siberian chill descends on the line again, I quip, 'Don't tell me you missed it?'

Look at it this way: it would never have worked.

My third call is to Ruth. This is altogether a much more promising exchange, and since it turns out she lives only a couple of miles away from me in north London, we arrange to meet at my local Café Rouge. I offer her a brief description, starting with my new glasses which, I tell her, 'make me look like a German architect'. They are narrow, in the popular new style, with gun-metal-grey arms and frames.

'I shall probably be sketching plans for the rebuilding of Berlin on the back of a napkin,' I jest.

'What colour hair have you got?'

Her question is a bit of a sickener. I seemed to have forgotten all about that side of things.

'I should probably explain.' Heavy sigh. 'I don't have as much hair as I once used to. What there is . . . is brown,' I concede.

She accepts this news in good part – well, she doesn't slam the phone down – and reveals that on the evening in question she will be wearing a dark coat with a scarf containing a fish design.

I hang up, genuinely impressed. Ruth is a classicist; currently working in the States, at no less a seat of learning than Princeton University. And an Egyptian dancer; she both attends and leads workshops. What's more, she didn't sound in the slightest way nuts. When I'd asked subtly, 'So, what's with the dance thing, then?'

she hadn't told me to go and fuck myself. Rather, she had quietly explained that dance was something that she had always been drawn towards and that Raqs Sharqi, to give it its Arabic name, was particularly interesting to her because of its traditional emphasis on movement of the hips.

Hmm.

Make that hmm-squared.

Actually, in the immortal words of Eric Morecambe, make that *wey-hey-hey!!!*

I am early. Really painfully early. Not this time from a pathological fear of being late, because I know I can walk to Café Rouge from my flat in exactly eight minutes. I am early this time because I am nervous.

Why else have I turned up a good fifteen minutes before blast-off – to which may be added the ten minutes by which she will be late – if not to sink a quick glass of house red and generally appear the relaxed and happy character rather than the gibbering fool.

'What size would you like?' inquires the waiter in response to my request.

I try not to look at him as though he were an idiot.

'Large, please,' I explain patiently.

Dark hair, dark coat, fish scarf. It's not a lot to go on, but I suspect we shall not have a problem identifying one another. Café Rouge on a Monday evening is far from busy. Apart from myself, there's almost no one here who resembles a German architect. I am in my black uniform: black trousers, black leather jacket, black roll-neck. I should own an Alsatian dog called Rudi and there should be a silver Audi parked nearby with a lot of Kraftwerk CDs in the glove compartment. Back home, in our minimalist apartment in Cologne, Heidi will be putting little Helmut and Otto to bed . . . but hey. I'm getting ahead of myself here.

At eight pm on the dot, a short dark-haired woman in a dark coat steps through the doorway. My heart sinks. Sorry, but it does.

She's no haddock, although on the goddess–haddock axis she's definitely up the haddocky end. The instant her eyes alight upon mine, she ignites a big smile and comes marching over to my table. I attempt to hoist a pleasant expression on to my face. Through the back of my head runs the thought: if we can get this over with quickly, I can go home and finally watch that video about the mysterious dark force that holds the universe together.

'Hi,' she says cheerfully. 'Are you Marcus?'

I am temporarily lost for speech. Somewhere within me, an entire stadium erupts with the sort of pandemonium that the eighty-ninth-minute match-winning goal normally brings on.

I shake my head, trying hard to keep a great fat grin off my chops. 'No, sorry. I'm not,' I croak.

She takes the information well – she doesn't burst into a fit of hysterical sobbing, for example – and retires to a banquette to await the arrival of the Marcus in question.

Ten minutes later, I check my watch. When I look

up again, another small dark woman in a dark coat is standing in the doorway. This one is rather beautiful, and not dissimilar facially to the actress Kristin Scott Thomas. I believe I actually gulp.

'Are you Paul?' she asks.

The remainder of the evening is recorded in my diary thus:

Ruth – Wow!!

Despite the schooner of house red, I spend the first fifteen minutes of our encounter just . . . just babbling, I guess, so bowled over am I by the glamorous elegant creature who has materialized out of the night to sit and talk to me. (To *me*.) I am on auto-pilot; I could be saying anything out here; I'm just hoping it's not total drivel. At the same time, I realize, I'm barely listening to what *she* is saying – it seems to be something about Classics; I clock the word *Byzantine* as it goes past – I am far more captivated by the sight of this . . . sorry, but glamorous elegant creature are *les mots justes* on this occasion. Indeed, I find it remarkable that a GEC like the one before me should ever have been flipping through the *Guardian* in search of men. Rather, I should have thought the situation would be one in which she would be fending them off with a shitty stick. (I do not voice these innermost feelings, however, for fear of somehow phrasing them badly and ruining the moment.)

But then a stroke of luck. She asks me what sort of

TV shows I produce. For some reason, rather than go into my pre-recorded sound-bite on factual entertainment, I tell her about the last programme I actually made for the BBC: an hour-long tribute to the late writer and satirist John Wells that had been shown a few months previously.

'I saw it,' she exclaims.

'No!'

'I watched it with my parents at Christmas.'

'How very extraordinary.'

'My father specifically wanted to see it.'

'Did you . . . ? Would you say you . . . ? What exactly . . . ?' Heavy sigh. 'Did you like it? At all? In any way?'

Ruth thinks about this for a moment, eyes shining, head on one side. 'Yes,' she says finally. 'It was quite good, as far as I remember.'

I am not offended by the mealy-mouthed words of praise (doesn't she know the only acceptable review in Tellyworld is 'I *loved* your show'?). I begin to tell her stories about meeting all the famous people who wanted to say nice things about Wells: how we'd gone to interview Jerry Hall at home and bumped into Mick ('he's in absolutely fantastic condition, for a man of seventy-five'); how Tom Stoppard spoke in scarily complete sentences; how one of Wells's posh female friends had castigated our sound man when he, in reply to her inquiry 'How do I look?', had replied, 'Fine.' 'If my husband told me I looked *fine*,' she'd hissed in return, 'he'd be sleeping on the sofa for a week.' If I saw one console table heaped with auction catalogues and copies of *Country Life*, I tell her, I saw twenty. I was treated politely, but I knew my place. I tell her that I felt rather like a piano tuner, or the man who came along to deal with wasps' nests: the bloke from the BBC who comes round to take away your old memories when someone dies.

For some reason, I don't feel the urge to tell her about *Auntie's TV Favourites*. Or the hidden-camera pilot with Dale Winton.

I suppose I am trying to impress her.

We discover another connection: that we had both been to the same exhibition at the Royal Academy a few months ago on the same day; the final Saturday before it closed. It was a show of work by Charlotte Salomon, a young German Jew who painted in hiding during the Nazi period and died in Auschwitz in 1943. We attempt to speculate that we may even have been in the gallery at the same time, but it doesn't work; we weren't.

But we are clicking, all right. Despite our very different paths in life, I can feel all manner of small correspondences and shared ways of looking at the world.

'Do you, er? Do you feel like eating anything at all?' I suggest.

We move to one of the banquettes, not so very far from where the first short dark woman to arrive this evening is currently in conclave with Marcus (a Marcus to his toenails, I should have said). Menus are produced and scanned, orders for food and further wine placed. She asks me whether I want children one day. In *theory*,

I reply carefully. One of those nice theoretical children who don't crayon on the walls and tantrum in front of everyone in Tesco's. She says she feels exactly the same way. We get talking about our families. I tell her the story about how my parents met one another – first the fiction about the pile of oranges, then the rather duller, more authentic tale. She begins telling me about her own family.

Some time afterwards, Ruth wrote her own version of events up to and including this evening. She has kindly given me permission to quote from it here:

Monday 15th was one of the first warm spring days. I remember that detail because I'd been working at home with the window open and heard great Arabic drumming coming from the open window of one of the terraced houses opposite. I went out to investigate and found Mahmoud, who became my live drummer for dance workshops that summer. (He and his friend thought I was coming over to complain about the noise.) At least I'd have something to talk to my date about, I thought.

I chose my highest heels to minimize the embarrassing height difference, a long straight black and charcoal grey skirt, low-cut tight-fitting black top and a tight-fitting grey cardigan with a plunging v neck: dress code – serious but sexy, I hoped. And the brown coat and Liberty's scarf, of course, for ID purposes.

I caught the Tube over to Hampstead but found I was about ten minutes early, so I walked to Waterstone's to look for an exhibition catalogue for my mother. That's why I ended up being five or ten minutes late. No problems spotting him; he was sitting by himself at a small table by the bar, directly in view of the door. Black polo, the glasses, and a large glass of red wine. 'Are you Paul?' I asked.

I can remember bits and pieces of the initial conversation. He pointed out a woman who'd asked him if he was Marcus. I showed him the exhibition catalogue. It was one he'd seen, and we worked out that we'd seen it on the same day that January. Weirdly, I remembered looking round the visitors at the time thinking, this would be a good place to meet people, but how do you start the conversation?

I wasn't bowled over immediately. I'd been anticipating this meeting but it felt a bit flat at first; it clearly wasn't going to be a disaster, maybe just another pleasant evening with someone I wouldn't otherwise have met. I asked him about the book he was working on but he said he didn't like talking about it. I said I found the opposite, that it helped to talk about my book, so I talked about it as briefly as I could. We talked about our personal lives: he didn't seem fazed by the fact that I'd continued living with my ex after we broke up. He wanted someone in his life. 'Being single's rubbish,' he said.

We'd originally agreed to meet for a drink. Choosing Café Rouge (his idea) left the option of dinner open, and things were going well enough to move over to the comfortable seats on the other side of the café and order something to eat. I sat on the red velvet banquette, he sat opposite, and we talked more; he told me a brief *version of his parents' history that he had clearly told many times before. Then something I said made him give me a different look. His eyes narrowed slightly (in a nice way, an interested way) behind the steel frames. He said, 'History must be important to you.'*

I honestly can't explain what happened next. It seemed to come out of the blue: I swear I looked at him and found myself thinking: 'This is what it's like to know you've met The One.' It was a feeling like coming home. I could feel the years ahead of us. I thought, if this man asked me to marry him now, I'd say yes, except I know it would be crazy – it's crazy for me even to be thinking about it; I don't even know *him – and he's not going to.*

So when we got to the end of the meal and he asked me if I wanted to come back to his flat for a drink, I agreed. At the back of my mind there was still a little voice saying, 'But you don't know he's not a mad axe murderer,' but I knew it was going to be all right.

In the kitchen, he offered me a White Russian (with Sainsbury's organic milk) but I went for the lemon and ginger tea. We sat at either end of his big leather sofa and I remember the tension. I wanted him to touch me, to kiss me, but at the same time I didn't; it was a first date, after all. So I perched at the far end of the sofa, keeping a safe distance.

I do remember at one point he told me a rather strange joke about bees.

'So let me get this straight, says the first bloke. You're

telling me you keep ten thousand bees *this* big in a hive this big by maybe *this* big? The second bloke says, Yeah. That's right. I do. The first bloke thinks about it for a moment. Then he says, Don't they all get *squashed*?'

To be honest, I don't think I should be telling Ruth the bee joke. She's smiling patiently; she hasn't yawned or looked about for something to read even once, but somehow I don't think this one's for her.

On the other hand, the bee joke is a strange and mysterious phenomenon. And in a sense, it's not about her; it's for *me*. It's my desire to tell the bee joke that is significant, not the response of the other party.

'And the second bloke thinks about it for a moment.' Here I gaze into the air, as if attempting to picture the tiny hive packed with ten thousand over-sized bees. 'Yeah, he admits, they do.' And then – remaining in character as the bee-keeper – I shrug, one of those fatalistic Eastern European shrugs, and flapping a hand in helplessness, deliver the final, killer line.

'Ah, fuck 'em.'

Ruth does not bellow with uncontrollable amusement, or spill her lemon and ginger infusion in her hysteria. But nor does she assume the boot face. Her measured reaction lies somewhere between the two possible extremes. It's as if she can see why other people might find the joke funny without viewing it as irresistible herself.

Before I can tell her another, she skilfully changes the subject.

It hadn't been difficult to ask her to come back to my flat for a drink; we seemed to be getting on reasonably famously. She talked about her family for a while; her father's interest in World War One; growing up in the Midlands; going off to Oxford to do Classics. At one point, when she fell silent, and it was obviously my turn to say something – I hadn't really been concentrating; I had been gazing at her face and wondering how I should ask her back for a drink – I put on what I think of as my piercing intelligent expression and, hoping for the best, said something as uncontroversial as possible: 'History must be important to you,' or some such anodyne remark.

I first came across this technique – of sounding on top of things whilst really not having much of a clue – when I was employed as a reporter by LBC Radio during the early 1980s. There, I fell under the influence of a deeply loveable, if flawed, character who declared himself to be 'the laziest cunt in the office', a view from which there was no serious dissent. It was he who vouchsafed to me the three key questions that could be safely asked of *any* interviewee on *any* occasion, thereby obviating the necessity to know anything about the story. The first, to be delivered with maximum urgency and sincerity, was, 'Fred Bloggs . . .' (Pause for additional drama.) 'What's it all about?'

Thus inspired, Fred Bloggs would rabbit away for a minute or so, providing the reporter with a helpful summary of the issues. *It* was usually a dispute. (Actually, during the early years of Margaret Thatcher's first term in office, *it* was *always* a dispute.)

Once Fred Bloggs had got his opening peroration off his chest, with suitably narrowed eyes (to show a rich appreciation of the complexity of the situation) the second question could be pressed into play: 'What's the atmosphere like?'

Poisonous or cordial, this was usually good for another forty or fifty seconds.

Finally, when the atmosphere had been fully described, came the moment for question three. In an appropriate tone, reflecting the degree of entrenchment of the two sides and the hopelessness or otherwise of the position at hand, one inquired: 'So where do we go from here?'

By the judicious use of these three simple questions – What's it all about?/What's the atmosphere like?/So where do we go from here? – and any supplementaries one was able to think up along the way – union officials and government ministers, health-service administrators and local protesters could be efficiently delivered of two to three minutes of 'news radio'.

'History must be important to you' – although not a question, strictly speaking – was only the latest in a long line of what my friend the lazy cunt would have called 'pebbles in a pond'. His view was that all one needed to do was drop a pebble in a pond and observe where the ripples spread.

It was the ripples that were the point, not the pebble.

I'm not sure where he is working today, but I still rather miss him.

It's the age-old problem, of course. A desirable woman at the other end of the sofa, but how to move the conversation to the romantic plane without coming over like some creepy old letch?

'*You really do have the loveliest eyes.*'

'*Do I?*'

'*Er, yes. You do, actually.*'

'*Thank you.*'

'*Not at all.*' Pause. '*And a fabulous arse.*'

'*Sorry?*'

'*Nothing. I didn't say anything.*'

'*I think you better call me a taxi.*'

'*OK, you're a taxi.*'

How to engineer the moment so it feels like a natural development to bring one's lips together with hers rather than a surprise event completely against the run of play? (Something of the kind, I imagine, must have happened with Toby and Morticia. When she stood up and brained herself on the beam.) Of course it always helps if both parties have swallowed a river of aperitifs; but Ruth has been relatively abstemious. She only drank a couple of glasses at Café Rouge and her request for herbal tea was not especially encouraging.

'*Can I say something?*'

'*Sure.*' Pause. '*What?*'

'*I'm . . .*' Heavy sigh. '*I really like you.*'

'*Oh.*'

'*There. I've said it.*'

'*Yes.*'

'*Well?*'

'*Well, what?*'

'*Aren't you going to say you like me too?*'

'*Actually . . . actually, it's getting late.*'

300

We talk about dreams. I tell her a recent one in which, for some reason, Bob Hope was the president of the USA. How I'd thought about it for ages until its meaning suddenly came to me: it wasn't the president, but the *precedent*. Hope was the precedent. In other words, that which I hoped for would come to pass. She tells me then in the ancient world, dreams were thought of as messages from the gods; they predicted the future if one knew how to interpret them correctly, rather than following the Freudian model of offering commentary on the past.

'*All this talk of dreams . . .*' I leave the sentence hanging.

'*What?*'

'*It's making me want to lie down.*'

'*Aren't you feeling well?*'

'*Perfectly. I just thought it might be more comfortable. We might be more comfortable.*'

'*I'm fine, actually.*'

'*Really? You're sure you wouldn't rather . . . ?*'

'*Absolutely.*'

But this is a first date. You don't on a first date, do you? Well, you don't if you're a nice girl and Ruth is very clearly in that category. And I want her to feel secure; I want her to feel that she is safe to look all elegant and glamorous sipping tea on my leather sofa. And that I can be relied upon to contain my Inner Sleazy Lothario, if not for ever, then at least for a little while longer.

'*Wouldn't you care for something . . . a little stronger?*'

'*No, thanks. This is fine.*'

'Something a little more . . . exciting?'

'Hmm.'

'Go on, you know you want to.'

'Well, if you're sure it's no trouble . . .'

'Au contraire.'

'OK then.'

'Excellent. Now what can I get you?'

'Do you have any mandarin and lychee?'

When the minicab bears Ruth away – not even a chaste peck on the cheek, just smiles, a handshake and 'Nice to meet you; see you again, I hope' – I return to the sofa to nurse my White Russian and wonder if I have played it all wrong. If, in fact, I should have come on stronger, been a touch more predatory.

Women viewing persistence as attractive, in and of itself.

And fortune favouring the bold, as I have heard it argued.

'And . . .?' says Toby, a bit meaningfully.

'And what?'

'And did you?'

'No. We didn't, actually. Somehow the mood of the meeting was against. Or not entirely in favour, put it like that.'

He sniffs philosophically. Does something with his eyebrows that I've never seen him do before. In the past, Toby would have jumped on to my last statement. Would have talked about pushing on closed doors; how the act of pushing and shoving on the closed door was, in and of itself, perceived by the door as seductive. Now it seems like he's undergone some kind of personal conversion. There's a slacker look to his face, to the set of his jaw. He looks – yes, he does – he looks a little rocked. I have a horrible feeling that I know what has happened.

'How, er, how was your trip to the pictures with Morticia?' I inquire lightly.

Even though his gaze is fixed in my direction, its focus lies some distance beyond my own eyeballs. Maybe about ten inches. Call it a foot.

'Beverly,' he says reflectively, 'is a very remarkable woman.'

'I wouldn't argue with that,' I confirm.

'She knows her mind. To a remarkable degree, really.'

'You think so?'

'Oh, she huffed and puffed all the way through the film. Didn't mind one bit letting me know how ghastly she thought it was.'

'What did you see?'

'On the way to the Chinky she absolutely lacerated it. Hacked steaming great lumps out of it. Said she could see the twist coming a mile off. *Five* miles off.'

'This was . . . ?'

'She called it the worst kind of puerile Hollywood claptrap.' Toby is plainly still reeling from the onslaught. '*The Sixth Sense*. I didn't mind it. I thought it was quite good, actually.'

'She can get quite snooty about movies. I remember she got very shirty after *Muriel's Wedding*.' I think she might have used the p-word then, too.

'She didn't seem to blame me for choosing it, to be fair. And things definitely perked up over the old flayed duck and pancakes. She drank a good bit, too, which I took to be a good sign.'

'Ah.'

'Although she did pick the second-most-expensive bottle of wine on the menu.'

'Oh.'

'My policy is always to go for the second-cheapest.'

I can't really say *ah* or *oh* again, so I go with 'Hmm.'

'No funny business about paying the bill. She let me take care of all that. And when I dropped her off, there was no nonsense about would you like to come in for coffee?' He goggles at me a little open-mouthed. 'It was *Park in that spot there – no, that one there! – There, between the Merc and the nasty little purple car*. Then she practically frog-marched me up the front steps.'

'Blimey.'

'And then.' He sighs heavily. 'Well, by then, I rather got the idea.'

'The idea.'

'The idea that I was expected to make a pass.'

'She didn't leap into the air and concuss herself?'

'If you want to know her exact words . . .'

'I'm not sure I do, to be honest.'

'She said, "If you don't kiss me soon, I shall be forced to switch on *Newsnight*." '

'Blood. Dee. Hell.'

'I mean, no contest, obviously.'

'Obviously.'

'And then . . .'

'No more, please. I beg you.'

'Just let me tell you this bit, OK?' Toby snorts with amusement. Discovers he has to cover his mouth with his hand. 'Actually, I can't really tell you that bit. Wouldn't be right.'

'I'm relieved. Thank you.'

'Anyway, it's all your doing and we're both eternally grateful.'

'You are?'

'Eternally.'

'Blood. Dee. Hell.'

'I know, mate.'

'At the risk of repeating myself.'

'Please. Be my guest.'

I made another trip to High Barnet. As Diana and I dined at a local Italian, the thought that passed through my head most frequently was *What the fuck am I doing here?* It was no consolation to realize that many before me must have framed the identical question when they too found themselves stranded in an unexciting north London suburb on a Friday evening.

We both had clearly gone to some trouble to make ourselves look presentable for the occasion: Diana's carelessly chopped blond hair looked like someone had been at it recently with the garden shears. I had picked out my best black roll-neck (the one that didn't feature the shadow of a food-strike in the shape of the Falkland Islands).

And yet.

And yet I felt we were only going through the motions. I *appeared* interested as she *appeared* to chatter animatedly about the latest outrage on the part of her boss at the obscure charity; but I couldn't be certain that we weren't just actors in a scene. Even when she put her arm through mine as we strolled through deserted lamp-lit streets to her house, there was a sort of detachment on both our parts. Even when we found ourselves smooching on the sofa again, it was all rather pleasant of course, but I couldn't help wondering what was the *point*, exactly? Even when . . .

Actually, there's nothing remotely sensible that can be said about *that*.

What was definitely a little alienating happened the next morning. Over the post-coital tea and toast, the doorbell rang, immediately followed by the sound of the front door opening. The next moment the kitchen was swarming with Mario and Leone and several of Leone's little pals. While the children stood about kicking the furniture and picking their noses, Mario – who looked *very* surprised to see me – extended a gruff nod in my direction and explained to Diana that they'd stopped off for Mumfy. Mumfy – whom I took to be one of Leone's stuffed companions – was a key player, evidently, if their trip to the coast was to be any kind of success.

'Mario, this is Paul,' said Diana, seeming a little flustered herself. 'Paul, this is Mario,' she added for symmetry.

Mario nodded at me again. He was one of those squat, swarthy chaps with rather too much dark curly hair sprouting about his person. In the photo she'd once showed me, he'd looked friendly enough; this morning I couldn't be 100 per cent certain he wasn't going to poke me in the eye.

I found myself alone as everybody stomped up the stairs in search of Mumfy. I drank tea and listened while they thumped around overhead, my reverie only disturbed by Gnasher, who let himself in through the cat flap, offered me a sour look, and padded off in search of the action.

Finally, when Diana returned, after she'd waved them all off and the house was silent again, she sat down and sniffed back a tear.

'Sorry,' she said. Another loud sniff followed.

'Not at all.'

'I'm probably not very good at this,' she asserted. Now a snort and her fingers flew to her face.

'Hey.' I went round to her side of the breakfast table and put a hand on her shoulder. 'Hey,' I repeated a little uselessly.

Now she shook her head violently and snorted *exceptionally* loudly. Not as loud as a factory hooter, say, or even one of those novelty car horns that play Colonel Bogie, but it was a powerful blast. It may have been her way of staving off a full-blown episode of waterworks, because she came up *sort* of smiling and said 'sorry' once more.

'So who else have you met?' she said after a bit.

'Me? No one,' I replied. 'Nobody,' I added for emphasis.

'Don't be silly,' she insisted. 'Of course you have.'

There seemed no point in persisting with the fiction.

'Actually, there is a woman. She does Egyptian dance.'

Diana laughed. 'What? A belly dancer?'

'She actually does the classical form of Arabic dance that belly-dancing is a bastardized – vulgarized – form of. It's called ... I can't remember the name. Raqs-something. She's from Highgate,' I added for some reason. 'Well, not *from* Highgate, but she lives in Highgate. I don't know where she was born, to be honest.'

Maybe I mentioned it because Highgate was, and remains, on the same branch of the Northern Line as High Barnet.

'So,' said Diana, with a bit of a look in her eye. 'When are you seeing her again?'

Our second date is at my favourite Italian restaurant in Crouch End. As he greets Ruth and me at our table, Arnie, the maître d', displays all the tact and diplomacy for which the natives of his home town – Venice – are justly famed.

'Hello, Mr Paul,' he says. 'You married yet?'

Attempting to keep a pleasant expression on my face as I reply in the negative, I notice Ruth is quietly amused by the preceding bit of dialogue. I accept Arnie's recommendation of a particular white wine and hope to God he will not return with the giant pepper mill and grind it suggestively while delivering saucy comments about girls who 'like it hot'.

We chat. And as we do, I am once again struck by Ruth's sense of poise, of stillness – it occurs to me that maybe it's a *dancer*'s sense of stillness – behind which there is plainly a keen intelligence and a busy brain.

As a waitress brings the wine and begins to pour, I notice something terrible floating about at the bottom of the bottle: it's an insect, or spiny sea-creature; some kind of small crayfish, the length of my finger and a sickening beige colour. The sort of colour, or absence of colour, achieved by ancient life-forms that live in rock pools at the far end of caves, a long way from daylight.

'I, er, hardly like to mention this, but . . .'

A replacement bottle is rapidly produced, but it seems like an unpromising augur. At a nearby table, a very new baby lolls helplessly over its owner's shoulder, eyes boggling at the world he has been born into.

'It wants to fall asleep,' says Ruth, 'but it's too interested.'

'I've been to parties like that,' I quip.

She talks about her work, and in particular about her specialist interest, a topic called *Ekphrasis*. Resisting a terrible urge to blurt out, 'That's a big word for a pretty lady,' I struggle to concentrate as she explains how *Ekphrasis* is all about the way that words paint pictures in the mind, a skill that the rhetoricians of antiquity strived to possess. The most effective speakers were the ones who could conjure up the best images (wrathful gods, scary invasion fleets and the like).

'Quite technical, then,' I flounder.

'Well, yes and no.' (*Ekphrasis*, I will discover, contains rather a lot of yes and no.)

'I mean, if I described a certain scene, and then asked you all sorts of questions about it – including things that I'd never mentioned, like, I don't know, the colour of the wallpaper, or the design of some character's outfit, or the particular breed of dog in the scene – would it be *Ekphrasis* if you had an answer, a picture in your head that I hadn't put there? That you'd put there yourself, as it were?'

Ruth thinks about this one for a moment.

'Well, yes and no.'

Now I ask a really stupid question. 'The Egyptian dancing. And the *Ekphrasis* thing. Would there be a connection at all?'

She assumes an expression I cannot read anything into.

'Hey, dimbo. How would that work? Just think about it for a second.'

No, she doesn't say it. But perhaps she would have liked to.

As we drift into less ambiguous material – growing up in Rugby, living in north London, teaching in the USA – I am struck by how comfortable I feel talking to her, how attracted I am to her – how we seem to be 'clicking' on a personal level, on a *meteorological* level, if I can put it like that (our emotional weather systems feel compatible) – but how our interests could not be more different. For example, I have never been terribly interested in dance, per se. Dance, to me, is getting sufficiently pissed to throw myself around the dance floor at a friend's wedding without feeling like a total pillock. Dance, for me, is 'Pretty Woman' by Roy

Orbison; 'Love Shack' by the B52s; 'I'm A Believer' by the Monkees. And as for this *Ekphrasis* business . . .

Oddly, however, I find it reassuring. There's something about the very strangeness – *otherness* – of her world that I find familiar somehow. Authenticating, even.

The *authenticity of the weird*, one might call it.

When I stop the car outside her house, I don't really know what to expect.

'I've enjoyed it,' I say, just to say something.

'Would you like to come in?' she asks. Then she adds, 'I've got a bottle of old brandy somewhere.'

Somewhere. Love that *somewhere*. If I had a bottle of old brandy, I would know *exactly* where it was. Anyhow, if there was any serious doubt about whether I would agree – and there wasn't – this is the clincher.

Her flat is one of those small girl flats – picture a doll's house, converted some time in the Seventies – one of those where you knock something over if you turn round too quickly. While she goes to fix me a drink I study a wall full of books. Most appear to be academic texts; the only ones I recognize are *The God of Small Things* and the London *A–Z*. A laptop rests splayed open on a desk. Postcards of ancient pottery are jammed into a mirror frame.

I sit on a small sofa, she on a nearby chair. She tells me of her professional plans: she will, with some reluctance, be returning to Princeton in the autumn unless she gets the highly sought-after job she has applied for in London. Princeton is a great institution, she explains, but no place for a single woman. She pours me another brandy.

We get talking about dreams again. She tells me about a recent one in which she is in a moving train. Through the window she observes a smouldering wooden post.

'What's that about, then?' she asks playfully.

With a sagacity and insight that I didn't know I possessed, I suggest the post is a *university* post. The one she has applied for. The dream expresses her anxiety that it may go up in smoke. She seems slightly shocked by the interpretation, by the idea that her unconscious could be arsed to construct such an elaborate symbolic depiction of her inner state.

I cheer inwardly at being cleverer than her on this occasion and pour myself another brandy to celebrate.

I am troubled by the room's geography, however. I rise from the little sofa; in two paces I have reached the window. I draw back the curtain and look across the road into the windows of the house opposite. A man is watching TV; the shadows on his wall jump around to the picture cuts. From their rhythm, I'm guessing it's the Ten O'Clock News. When I return to the sofa, she is still sitting on her chair.

Now she rises, stands for a moment, as though lost in thought, then sits, very gingerly, at the edge of the sofa; as though any second they will call her flight. She is to my left and rather forward of me, affording an excellent view of her finely wrought profile. She is staring into her lap.

'Do you know that bloke over the road?' I ask.

Although I could be saying, 'How do you fancy England's chances in the Eurovision Song Contest?'

Or even, 'Yibble, yibble, yibble.'

I barely know what words are coming out of my mouth.

When we kiss, I feel her heart hammering against my chest like a canary's.

And shortly after nine the next morning, we are both startled when my mobile phone explodes into life.

Ruth tells me later that she automatically assumed it was an urgent call from the world of television. But it turns out to be my mother. Worried that she couldn't reach me at home all last night and again today.

'For God's sake,' I whine. 'I'm . . .'

I'm about to say I'm forty-four years old, but just manage to stop myself in time.

'I *am* a grown-up, you know.'

9

TOBY IS A CHANGED MAN. From the confident, not to say cocky, not to say Mr-Bloody-Cleverclogs-Know-It-All character of a few weeks ago, Toby has become the epitome of agnosticism. Rock-solid certainties have dissolved like the morning mist. All is contingent. Alternatives exclude. He vacillates; he is bewitched, bothered and – yes – he is bewildered.

So, of course it's love.

I'm happy (and worried) for him.

'I'm happy for you,' I say over dinner.

'I'm happy for me,' he replies. 'And worried.'

'Why so?'

Toby looks a little haunted. 'Her. She's . . . she's something, wouldn't you say?'

'Oh, she's something, all right. Undoubtedly something.'

'The question is. Really, the question is how to hang on.'

'Hang on to the runaway racehorse, sort of thing?'

He nods moodily, as though the struggle were already lost. Fires up a Marlboro and allows his eyes to defocus somewhere over my left shoulder.

'What about momentum? The keeping her permanently off-balance business.'

He shakes his head. 'It's way beyond that now.'

'Just a sec. When did you start smoking again?'

'Not smoking,' he says absently. 'Having a cigarette.'

'*She* won't approve.'

He fails to reply, continuing to stare philosophically into the Great Wherever and generally displaying all the signs of the heavily fuck-struck human adult male. Seconds tick by. Followed by further seconds. Additional seconds ready themselves for possible tickage. Entire minutes are placed on standby.

'You see, I need a plan,' he says eventually. 'A man is nothing without a plan,' he adds with a bit of a dying fall.

'Be her rock,' I say gently. 'Be the rock upon which her waves can dash themselves. Be the rock that endures. Be the string to her kite.'

Even as I'm saying it, I know it's the wrong way round. If anyone's the kite or the boiling waves, it's Toby. He offers me a suitably sceptical look.

'Just . . . cherish her,' I suggest 'Be nuts about her. Worship the ground she walks on, sort of thing. Girls love that shit, don't they?'

The sceptical look only grows in intensity. Then it moves away from scepticism into the sort of facial territory reserved for sick dogs who've crapped on the sofa for a third – and possibly final – time.

I try another tack. 'There's a PG Wodehouse story, right? One of the Bertie Wooster ones where Bertie's friend Gussie Fink Nottle has fallen for a girl and he's desperately trying to think of ways to impress her. So Bertie comes up with a plan for the girl's annoying little nephew to fall into the lake, and for Gussie to be miraculously on hand to rescue him.'

In his mind, I see, Toby has already placed the call to the vet.

'OK. How about this? Become indispensable.'

A flicker of interest, so I pursue it. 'Make it so she can't imagine her life without you. Get her friends to like you.'

'Freddie,' he says weakly.

'You've met Freddie, then.'

'She said he was priceless.'

'I could never see it, myself.'

'He's a ridiculous cunt.'

I am pleased to see the return of Toby's critical faculties.

'He is a bit, isn't he?'

'There's absolutely no getting round it. He's the most ridiculous cunt I've ever come across.'

'I guess we've all got friends who our other friends disapprove of. Sometimes that's the point of them. To be the grit in the oyster.'

'The git in the oyster, in his case.'

'Hey. That was quite funny.'

'It's bollocks. Who's *your* friend who everyone else thinks is a tosser?'

I give Toby a funny look and allow the silence to tell the story.

'Oh, fuck off!' he exclaims when he gets it, and kicks me under the table. 'No. But I like it. Become indispensable. There could be something to that,' he concedes.

'We've got to think of ways for Toby to become indispensable to Beverly,' I tell Angela, when she finally arrives from her Pilates class.

Angela assumes her seriously-thinking-about-it expression. 'There has to be a crisis,' she concludes. 'And Toby reveals himself as a tower of strength. That's how you really find out what men are made of.'

Her words ring true. I quail slightly as I think back to my time with Angela and wonder how I measured up in the crisis-management department. Fortunately it was all a very long time ago – the world was young, as I say – and I find I have only retained the good things about us.

'She's right,' I agree. 'A crisis will develop – one always does – and you must be a brick.'

Toby is nodding. His mouth is doing that unpleasant *Yup, that's the way the world is, better get used to it* thing that it used to do.

'Crisis? *What* crisis?' he says, as though a decision has been made.

'*Exactly*,' affirms Angela.

'So where's the great property expert tonight?' he inquires.

Angela pulls a face. I draw a finger across my throat. She giggles.

Toby is genuinely surprised (he really hasn't been keeping up). 'All over?'

Angela nods pretend-sadly.

'I'm sorry,' he says.

'He was a bit of a berk,' she reminds him.

'Bernard? Of course he was. But you were always telling us not to be horrid about him.'

I cough lightly. 'I think you'll find there's a new fish under the grill.'

'Don't be horrid.'

'Another one!? This woman has more lovers than . . . than. Than whoever it is that has a lot of lovers. Joan Collins or someone.'

Angela is hugging herself. Saying, 'Mmm.'

'Who is he, the lucky devil?'

'He's called Augustin,' she replies, sprinkling loads of herbs and garlic into the pronunciation. 'He's a composer.'

'Really?' says Toby, plainly impressed. 'Symphonies? Operas?'

'Adverts, mostly. He's incredibly good-looking. He's *very* nice – I mean *really* nice, OK. And he makes absolute *shit*-loads of money.'

'I hate him,' says Toby.

'Me too,' I concur. 'Loathe him.'

'I was thinking of bringing him to your birthday party, actually. How's it going with the belly dancer, by the way? Have you told her you're really an old-age pensioner?'

I attempt to explain that Ruth is not a belly dancer. That she is in fact a professional academic – and that in any case, she does the classical form of Egyptian dance that belly dancing is a bastardized, vulgarized, form of – but Angela is not listening.

She is too busy hooting with amusement at her own funny line.

*　*　*

It's never entirely clear when one officially becomes part of 'an item'. I guess it may be when someone asks, 'Are you two an item yet?' and you realize that you are. Like the Mona Lisa's smile, perhaps it's one of those phenomena that can't be considered directly. Along with ageing and property price inflation, maybe it's something that happens while you're looking the other way.

Anyhow, Ruth and I are an item now. We do the things that partners in itemships do. We go to movies and the theatre; we frequent bars and restaurants; we stay home and cook for one another; and we meet one another's friends. For some reason I find it reassuring that our friends are not interchangeable. To make a sweeping generalization, my friends are outgoing characters who tend to work in newspapers, radio and television (gobshite media whores); hers tend to know several European languages – which they are worryingly liable to lapse into – and for the most part are loosely or closely connected to the world of academia (eggheads). From first contact with her people, it is clear to me – if it hadn't been already – that we inhabit very different worlds.

Yet Ruth and I 'click' in all the important areas. We find it easy to be together; there isn't that permanent low-level *buzzing noise* one suffers in relationships based on a false premise. I discover the specific words in my advert that attracted her most – apart from 'Jewish' – were the ones about seriousness and

319

frivolousness; my boast that I was equally at home in both modalities; my hope that I would meet someone of the same ilk. Although I am attracted to her seriousness – she studies *inscriptions*, for fuck's sake, on bits of old rubble – she is not someone you would label a Serious Person. And even though I can pass an amusing remark and make her laugh – and all too often my first instinct is to make a joke – she recognizes that I am not fundamentally a Frivolous Person.

She does, honestly. You can ask her if you like.

So serious and frivolous, frivolous and serious, we seem to be getting on like the proverbial flaming house. I take her to a close friend's birthday party; she is not obviously bored or horrified by all the tedious TV gossip; my mates are charmed by my lovely new girlfriend ('*so* much better than the one you brought last year'). She in turn takes me to one of the strangest events I have ever attended. In the abandoned bowels of St Pancras station, an experimental-dance performance group present a series of . . . well, the best word is *happenings* . . . around the mythical figure of Salome. Visitors are separated from their companions and sent one at a time through dusty disused corridors to encounter – and occasionally exchange dialogue with – various scantily clad incarnations of the beguiling and lethal step-daughter of Herod, all to a spooky, discordant soundtrack. I imagine it's probably got something to do with the nature of female sexuality as expressed through dance, together with the nature of male weakness as expressed through my dangling lower jawbone.

By way of retaliation, I take her to meet my parents.

My mother is utterly enchanted with Ruth. My father, who is nearly ninety and – in that charming medical phrase – demented, stares at her, puzzled. Who knows what he is thinking? – it is some years since he has been able to tell us – but I suspect he may be seeing someone he used to know in Vilnius in the Thirties. Nowadays, when he opens the front door and peers out at the quiet street in Finchley that has been his home for three decades, it is with that same puzzled expression. Where are the horses and carriages of his childhood? Where are his own mother and father? His little brother? Eventually he shrugs fatalistically – *Ah, fuck it* – and plods back to the armchair.

SCENE FROM A RELATIONSHIP

Interior: Paul's sitting room. Day. Paul and Ruth are sitting around, reading. Paul is paging through the various sections of Saturday's *Guardian*. Ruth is making notes from a well-thumbed copy of Homer's *Iliad*.

PAUL
What would you like to do this evening?

RUTH
Don't mind. What's on the telly?

PAUL
(*peruses TV guide*)
Fuck all. Shall we see a film?

321

RUTH

If you like. What's on?

PAUL

(peruses film guide)

Nothing. Actually, we don't have to do anything. We could just hang out. Spend quality time with one another. (*He pronounces it 'qualid-dee' for ironic purposes.*)

RUTH

(after a pause)

Might be nice to do *something*.

PAUL

What had you in mind?

RUTH

Maybe there's a dance thing.

PAUL

Hmm.

RUTH

There were some Moroccan trance dancers at the Barbican, but I think they've finished now.

PAUL

Hmm.

RUTH

I honestly don't mind. I'm happy to do whatever you like.

PAUL

Me too. I mean whatever *you* like. I'm totally easy. We could just go out for dinner.

RUTH
(hesitantly)
Mr Kong?

PAUL
(defensively)
Not necessarily.

RUTH

Where else is there?

PAUL

Nowhere I know of.

RUTH

I'm happy just to be with you.

PAUL

Like that bloke in the mortgage advert. (*assumes Midlands accent*) 'We want to be *together*.'

RUTH
(she hasn't seen it)
Mmm.

Time passes. Paul flicks through the travel section. Ruth
makes a few more notes.

PAUL

So, er. What *would* you like to do this evening?

RUTH

I could cook. I could cook that aubergine dish you
said you liked.

PAUL

(he has lied about the aubergine dish)

We don't *have* to go to Mr Kong. There must be other
places.

RUTH

Whatever would make you happy.

PAUL

I do *like* Mr Kong . . .

Ruth's birthday comes along about six weeks into
our relationship. I want to get it right, to make a splash
but not *too* much of a splash, if you know what I mean,
so I take her out to dinner (eight out of ten), buy her a
beautiful scarf from Liberty's in exactly the right
shades of yellow and rusty-orange (nine out of ten)
and, inexplicably, a Catatonia CD (one out of ten).

As my own birthday approaches, however, my exact
calendar age, I confess, is causing me a little anxiety.
Somehow I have never got round to correcting the

small arithmetical error in my favour in the original text of my advertisement. Ruth has never called me on it – 'Come on, mate, if you're forty-two, I'm Charlotte Church' – but neither have I found a suitable occasion to drop casually into the conversation the revelation that I erased two years from my biological CV. If, as might be argued, an error of two years against a total of more than forty hardly amounts to a major case of false accounting, why have I been so negligent in coughing up to it? Why didn't I laugh it off during the early part of our courtship? Or tell her a straight lie: *The* Guardian – *tsk, typical – they got my age wrong!* Could it be that I was afraid it might be a deal-breaker? That the admission of dishonesty would be enough to pop the balloon, even if the actual mathematics were forgivable.

In short, I am in a bit of a pickle.

I am to be forty-five. A milestone in a man's life. Not a Biggie. But still a demi-Biggie. It is a nailed-on certainty that at some point during the celebrations, a kind friend with a loud voice will remind everyone exactly how many summers have passed since my entry into this vale of tears.

I want her to hear it from me.

Lesson Fifteen:
If you're going to tell lies, remember there may come a point when you have to come clean. Be a man about it. Or develop a superior, higher-order lie within which to subsume the original lie.

One evening, some days before the Great Event, I

contrive to be sitting alongside Ruth on the yellow sofa. My arm is round her shoulders and she is leaning into me in such a manner that she cannot see my face.

I take a deep breath. The moment is here. Time, as someone in Shakespeare once advised, to screw my courage to the sticking place.

'I, er. There's a. If I, er. Do you want to see the news, at all?'

'If you like.'

'Listen. I. There's.' Heavy sigh. 'Actually, there's something I've got to tell you.'

Her head swivels. One of her eyes is looking up into mine. She can, she informs me later, hear my heart getting agitated in its cavity.

'What?'

'Something that I put in my message in the *Guardian*. Something that wasn't altogether 100 per cent accurate.'

It crosses her mind (she tells me later) that I'm about to tell her I'm married.

'I'm not really forty-two.'

'Oh.'

'I'm actually two years older than that.'

'So you're forty-four.'

'Your old maths teacher would be very proud.'

'About to be forty-five.'

'I'll make it up to you, I promise.'

'It's not important.'

'Really?'

'Of course not.'

'Are you sure?'

326

'Don't be silly.'

'I'm so sorry. I didn't know how to tell you.'

'How are you planning to make it up to me?'

'You say. Anything you want.'

She thinks about it for a moment. 'A bottle of champagne for every year you lied to me about.'

'Done.'

Afterwards, two things occur to me: a good thing and a bad thing.

The bad thing: as she didn't seem to mind very much about the misrepresentation, she probably thinks I'm so old already that another two years makes no difference.

The good thing: I got off cheap. A bottle of champagne for every year?

She should have held out for a *case*.

Morticia is benevolence itself in regard to my new girl-friend (in the past, she has been critical of my romantic selections).

'She's perfect,' she proclaims, snapping on a crudité. 'I like her very much. Exactly right for you.'

'What the fuck is that supposed to mean?'

I don't. I want to, but I don't.

'And *very* good-looking,' she adds.

'Mmm,' I purr.

'Are you going to marry her?'

'Don't be ridiculous.'

'You should. She's perfect.'

'We've only just met. Anyway, what's happening with you and Toby?'

My birthday party has lifted off. It's that point in the evening where enough guests have arrived to feel the rumble of the undercarriage retracting and that pleasant sensation of events underway. Toby is leaning against the mantelpiece, drink in hand, talking to Angela and Augustin.

'Toby,' she says, examining a floret of cauliflower from a variety of angles as though searching for blemishes, 'is an angel.'

'Really?'

Of the many words I might have picked to characterize my old friend, angel would not have been amongst them.

'Absolutely an angel.'

'What sort of angel-like activity would you cite?'

Morticia discards the floret in favour of a preferable one. 'Collecting the dry cleaning. Fixing the wonky shelf. Driving all the way to the 24-hour Tesco when we ran out of oregano and there were people coming.'

It was an impressive catalogue of achievement, although some way short of curing blindness, or enabling the lame to throw away their crutches.

'He is a dear, sweet man.'

Something about the way she spoke the last sentence worries me. It is not Toby's role in life to be a dear, sweet anything. I fear if he does not buck his ideas up he will go the same way as . . . as Morticia's last bloke, whose name I have completely wiped from my memory banks.

The one who asked if she wanted to see the racing from Monza.

Indispensable does not involve the collection of dry cleaning or the last-minute purchase of herbs and spices. He has to slay a dragon. Or at the very least twat a wasp with a rolled-up newspaper.

Malcolm, that was the bloke. In the final days, he scampered around Morticia like a terrorized spaniel.

'Did *she* buy you that?'

Morticia is referring to the shirt I am currently sporting. It is plainly too stylish and well-chosen to be anything that I would have picked out for myself.

'She did. And she bought me a book and a CD.'

'Lucky boy.'

Ruth is in a far corner of the room, talking to some of my oldest friends. I can't help feeling a little anxious at this scene, but all the facial expressions around her are positive and natural – in contrast to the frozen smiles of horror I have sometimes witnessed in similar tableaux in the past.

Angela especially was highly impressed.

'I hope you know what a good thing you've landed there, matey,' she'd told me earlier.

'You speak about her as though she were a fish.'

'Catch of the day, I'd have said.'

'What about what she's landed?' I countered. 'What am I, chopped liver?'

It was a mixed metaphor, but she took my point.

'Dunno. But if I were her, I'd chuck it back in.'

* * *

Ruth's smouldering-post dream came true. She didn't get the job. And the book she bought me for my birthday is a guide to New York City. She's going back to Princeton in the autumn.

She asked me how I thought this development would affect our flowering relationship. Displaying yet more of the sagacity and insight that I didn't know I possessed, I replied that it wouldn't: if we continued to be a going concern – as we seemed to be – I would fly out periodically to visit. After all, there was nothing resembling a proper job to detain me here in the UK. And if it all went *phut* with us – as I hoped it wouldn't – well, she would be no worse off than before.

In the meanwhile, we would enjoy the summer.

She takes me to see Eliades Ochoa, a venerable Cuban in a cowboy hat who sings of the pain and joy of the human condition. I take her to see Jackie Mason, a venerable comic in a lounge suit who jokes about the pain and joy of the Jewish condition. ('Why do Jews always answer a question with a question? Why *shouldn't* they answer a question with a question?') I drive to the south coast and watch her and her partner, a tall German woman, entertain a full house at the Portsmouth Arts Centre with a two-hour performance of Egyptian dance. Under the bright lights, in the exotic costumes and stage make-up, undulating her hips and doing exquisitely timeless things with her arms and fingers, it is hard to imagine this is the same person I'd trudged round Sainsbury's with only a few days previously. Again I am struck by the authenticity of the weird. It feels curiously *right* that she and I are so different. This is the way that the world works: *unexpectedly*.

We go to France. She has told me about the village she has visited yearly since she was a toddler, after her father bought what he calls his 'hovel' there in the Sixties. The hovel turns out to be charming and idiosyncratic; the damp a refreshing change from one's bourgeois notions of dryness and comfort, and the awesome spider population of considerable interest were one (say) an entomologist, or director of horror films. Ruth is impressively relaxed about the creepy-crawlies. 'They were here first,' is her sanguine take on the monstrous arachnids who have been allowed to throw a permanent party on the ceiling. The vistas across the river valley, however, are sublime, and the birds, butterflies and lizards that flit across the terrace a delight, being creatures that recognize they properly belong in the Great Outdoors. A French poet whom I had previously never heard of – perhaps to my shame – is buried in a nearby hamlet. The nearest town, a gem of French sleepiness, is known only to history for the arrival at the railway station in 1940 of Adolf Hitler. The Führer lingered long enough on the platform to shake hands with Marshall Petain (symbolically making France over to Nazi Germany), before re-boarding the train in time for his next appointment with the dictator of fascist Italy.

In time, I manage to overcome my middle-class distaste for bio-forms with eight or more legs, although I never quite get used to the massive emptiness and silence of the French countryside. The sheer slow pace and tranquillity is a serious culture shock after north-west London; there are *clouds* that move faster than some of the old boys on bikes here; we rocket past them in the rental car as they pedal, it seems to me, from nowhere to nowhere.

Ruth introduces me to some of those who have made their homes in the village. However, I discover that in the thirty years since I last used it, my O-level French has atrophied hideously – she, of course, can pass for a local – and aside from a few obvious nouns and verbs, the only colloquial phrases I can summon to mind are *Quel domage* and *Zut alors!* This is not nearly enough ammunition for a whole evening.

'*Je suis très désolé,*' I am obliged to tell everyone. '*Mon Français est kaput.*'

I at least manage to avoid the humiliation of a friend of mine who once – long story – contrived to inform a Spanish magistrate in all seriousness that his mother was a virgin.

We go for walks. We take car trips to nearby settlements of equal if not greater somnambulance. We eat in restaurants where we are the only customers. We sit under the stars and listen to the frogs making that spooky noise by the river bank. As we wander hand in hand through deserted lanes, I struggle to understand how a place so comatose can leave one feeling so alive.

SCENE FROM A RELATIONSHIP

Exterior: The terrace. Day. Paul and Ruth are lazing around; Paul, flicking through a three-day-old copy of the *Telegraph* and staring at the clouds as they pass slowly across the valley; Ruth, making notes from a well-thumbed edition of Homer's *Iliad*. No one has said anything for some time.

RUTH
What would you like to do this afternoon?

PAUL
Don't mind. What are the options?

RUTH
We could drive into M——. (*She names the town of stupefying dullness that Hitler dropped into in 1940.*)

PAUL
What's happening there?

RUTH
Nothing. You could get a newspaper, maybe.

PAUL
What's St ——? I saw it on a map.

RUTH
What *is* it? It's a village.

PAUL
What do they have there?

RUTH

Nothing much. A church. A bakery.

PAUL

(after a long pause)
The people that live here all the year round, yeah?
What do they do with themselves all day?

RUTH

I don't know. Visit one another. Go to market.

PAUL

They don't live longer . . . it just *seems* longer.

RUTH

What?

PAUL

Wouldn't it bore you out of your brains, living here?
It's charming now, of course. Lovely watching the
clouds and butterflies and that. But wouldn't it do
your head in . . . in November, say?

RUTH

(after a pause)
The wine's very cheap.

PAUL

Yes. I see. There would be that.

RUTH

Time is different here.

PAUL

Stationary.

RUTH

When you only have one thing to do all day,
you take all day.

PAUL

We could go to Tours tomorrow.

RUTH

Tomorrow's Monday. All the shops will be shut.

PAUL

Of course. It's obvious. First day of the working week
. . . everything shut.

RUTH

It's Napoleonic; it's so the shopkeepers can visit the
museums.

PAUL

Naturally. After a hard week behind the cheese
counter, the first thing you want to do is belt
off to a museum and stare at things in
glass cases.

RUTH

I would like to go to Tours.

PAUL

We could go Tuesday.

RUTH

On Tuesdays the museums are shut. To allow the
museum-keepers to go shopping.

PAUL

I went to Moscow once. The café in our hotel used to
close for lunch.

RUTH

When I went to Moscow, the window of my hotel
room looked into the rubbish chute. All night long
there was stuff falling past my window.

PAUL

Lizard! By the wall. There! Under that . . . oh. Well,
he's gone now.

No one says anything for the next half an hour. Finally:

PAUL

Perhaps we should go into M—— this afternoon.

When we return home ten days later, the taxi ride from
Waterloo International feels like a journey through
Hades.

'Miserable lot, the French,' says our cab-driver. 'Comes of being a defeated nation,' he opines. 'There you go, mate. That'll be a hundred and fifty quid.'

To: Toby
From: Paul Reizin
Subject: New York New York

Dear Toby
How are things? I have gradually been getting used to life in NYC. Ruth's sub-let is on 9th Avenue between 35th and 36th Streets which is south and west of the so-called Garment District and north of Chelsea. So by my reckoning that makes it SoWeGaNoChe, but I'm calling it Chelsea Borders for short, although some insist it's Hell's Kitchen. Actually it's strongly reminiscent of Camden Town. There's a 24-hour Pakistani café on the next block which has already become a favourite. Two can eat like kings for eleven bucks (closed between 11 and 1 Fridays for prayers).

Ruth's apartment, though compact, is surprisingly nice. The only ugly incident took place the other morning when I reached up to silence the 6.30 am alarm and spilled her glass of water on my head. My, how you would have laughed, although what you would have been doing in our bedroom, I don't know.

R leaves absurdly early to catch the train to Princeton (90 minutes away in New Jersey) so I am at the laptop bright and early, tapping at my novel. 49,608 words at the last count. In the afternoons, I go exploring nabes. Been to Upper West Side, Lower East Side, Chinatown, East Village, West Village, SoHo, NoHo, TriBeCa, EvEryBlooDeeWhEre.

NYC is exhilaratingly crazy. I've never been to a place where so many people talk to themselves on the street. On the assumption that they don't know they're doing it, I'm now wondering if I'm not doing it myself teapot Jesus motherfucker.

Yesterday a guy passed me a leaflet and said, very matter-of-factly, 'End of the world, comin' soon.' Couple of nights ago, walking down 34th Street, a young black man about 15 yards away lit up a huge smile, pointed a finger straight at me and cried . . . 'Fierce!'

Maybe he was dyslexic and meant Freeze.

Ruth and I have been getting on very well. We had Martinis and sashimi at the top of the World Trade Center. There's a very good view of the earth from up there. We went for smoked salmon and bagels to Barney Greengrass on the Upper West Side. Smoked-fish heaven; an institution. There's even a quote from Groucho Marx in the menu: 'Barney Greengrass may not have ruled any kingdoms or written any great symphonies, but he did a monumental job with sturgeon.'

For the first time in my life I found myself denying I was Jewish. It was some big festival involving palm fronds and a particular sort of spikey lemon – I'm sure you know the one – and I looked at this orthodox bloke on 5th Ave waving these fronds at passers-by for just a fraction too long. 'Are you Jewish?' he asked. I knew if I said I was, a half-hour demo with fronds and fruit would follow – I watched some sucker fall for this in Washington Sq – so I said No. I felt a twinge of guilt. But there are more Jews in NYC than anywhere else, so I guess if you were going to deny your heritage, here would be the place to do it. Particularly if you were in a hurry.

What's happening back in Blighty? I know about
Cherie Blair having Jeffrey Archer's baby – there was a
big piece in the *NY Post*, but what about the other stuff?
How are things with you and Beverly? And Angela and
Augustin? e me soon with news.

Love P

We are living together. On the top floor, three storeys
above a convenience store. On the same block is a
Burger King, a psychic, and a pest-control franchisee.
Our building is a modest low-rise brownstone, but just
behind us, I see in an aerial photo, rear the concrete
cliffs of Manhattan. We have a bed, an armchair, a desk
and a TV set. The aerial is broken, so all three of Dan
Rather's faces are green. The bed is a single; the pigeons
who huddle on the window-sill overlooking the light-
well have more room to turn in their sleep.

But we are living together. It's romantic and exciting; my guidebook says New York is the 'capital city of
the twentieth century'. We are both blown away by the
sheer blaring exuberance of the place. I stare endlessly
at the map of Manhattan, trying to connect the orderly
grid before me with the crashing maelstrom of people
and car horns outside.

One morning we are disturbed by movement
behind the window blinds. When I investigate, I am
astonished to discover two small Mexican men hanging
from ropes, apparently painting the front of the building. They wave at me through the glass. I wave back but
can't help noticing how old and *fuzzy* their ropes are.
Later, when we go out for breakfast, we find a man in a

collar and tie sitting on our front steps – our stoop, as I learn to call it – pouring himself a bowl of Cornflakes.

'Not like Highgate, is it?' I comment weakly to Ruth.

'Actually, there is a bit by the Archway Road . . .'

My friends are really all I miss. Ruth and I both have family in the New York area. When I meet hers in Queens – for the blow-out preceding the Yom Kippur fast which hardly anyone will observe – I realize they are every bit as peculiar, in their way, as my own family, whom we encounter the following day in South Orange, NJ, for the blow-out marking the end of the fast which hardly anyone has observed.

When she is at work, I write and roam the city. Eventually, I get the hang of the subway: a bit of a mindfuck initially, owing to the way up to four different services can run on the same tracks; and how the same station (125th Street, say) can be found in up to four different locations, sometimes miles apart. But the subway extends my range: I take it to explore Brooklyn, and one sublime afternoon, Brighton Beach, where everybody is Russian and the Atlantic Ocean rolls on to broad deserted sands.

At weekends – corny but true – we fall in love with Manhattan. With its huge energy, its heart-stopping architecture; with the vibrant theatre of its streets and avenues. We even develop a Saturday routine. Lunch at Mee Noodle in the East Village – excellent steamed chicken, if you're ever in the area – then Ruth goes to her flamenco class near Washington Square while I wander the surrounding streets, nosing in bookshops, gawping at the passing scene, and scribbling down fragments of overheard conversations for use in my novel-in-progress. (The protagonist has just found himself in Manhattan. How about that for a coincidence?) My favourite comes from a benign drunk at twilight. A rip-tide of alcoholic wonderment moves him to call out – almost poetically, it seems to me – 'New York City, man. New York *fuck-kin'* City.'

Later we might see a movie and eat supper in the Pakistani café on 9th Avenue, surrounded by taxi drivers wolfing their goat curry and reading the Arabic newspapers. We walk home alongside rivers of red brake lights.

The lack of income apart, it is an almost perfect lifestyle.

When I return home after a month, my bit of north London feels like a sleepy hamlet. And that funny noise I'm hearing everywhere, I realize, is birdsong.

The last day of 1999. We are guests of Toby's school-friend Oliver and his boyfriend Nigel in their gorgeous old pile in Suffolk. Ollie and Nige, as they are universally known, made their fortune during the Eighties in a series of almost psychically astute property deals, buying into unlikely markets ahead of the wave and selling at their peaks. Today they are largely occupied in managing their money, staving off boredom by sitting on various boards, collecting art and bottling chutney. Through Toby, I have known them on and off for years; I remember visiting Ollie and Nige's immaculate little house in the East End when the East End was merely dangerous rather than fashionable. These days their parties are either monstrous bashes – involving a flypast by the Red Arrows, or a scale model of the Hermitage in seafood – or intimate soirées. To mark the end of the twentieth century, they have gathered a select and eclectic cast of characters for what will undoubtedly be a splendid New Year's Eve dinner, followed by fireworks on the terrace at midnight.

Toby is here with Morticia; to mark his seniority in the social hierarchy, they have been given the best guest bedroom with the views down to the lake. Angela and Augustin – Augustin is going down *very* well with our hosts, I note – have been given the 'blue bedroom' (OK, but could do better). Ruth and I, befitting our membership of the outer circle, are in the eaves. Neither of us is complaining, however. We know our place.

I have just spent another month with Ruth in New York, tapping away at my novel, discovering some of the city's less obvious attractions, and seeing more movies than I normally would in a year, owing to the extreme cold. The two of us are, as they say, well up a tree. My life seems to have changed radically from its loveless, purposeless condition at the opening of 1999.

Over drinks in Ollie and Nige's exquisitely ordered sitting room, Ollie tells me I'm looking exceptionally well. 'For you, I mean,' he can't help adding.

'You are, actually,' agrees Nige. 'You look a bit . . . fuller. Fuller in a good way.'

'It's lurve,' says Angela.

Ruth, who is on a sofa flicking carelessly through *Country Life*, pulls a suitably embarrassed-but-not-really expression.

'I noticed it too,' says Toby. 'There's a gleam in your eye. Instead of the usual dead fish on a slab.'

Interesting that Toby should have put it like this, because he too has undergone some kind of personal conversion. He's exhibiting a new confidence and ease around Morticia – and for her part, she's displaying an acceptance, even the suggestion of a sweet demure quality that is *so* unlike her – that earlier I was forced to get him on his own and ask him straight out.

'What happened?'

'Not with you, old chap.'

'You and Beverly. You seem different.'

Toby tapped the side of his nose.

'You've had a nose job?'

He goes *tsk*. 'I've mastered the crisis. Slayed the dragon.'

'Fantastic. What was it? Spider in the bath?'

Toby shook his head. 'Freddie.'

'*Freddie?* What, Freddie the ridiculous cunt?'

'The ridiculous cunt.'

'Tell me everything.'

Well. Apparently it was the ridiculous cunt's birthday and he – the RC – had booked a private room at a pointlessly expensive restaurant where his friends were expected to turn up, swig champagne, shower him with gifts, listen to his balls-aching swivel-eyed foppery all evening and then have their credit cards savagely rubbed to the tune of something truly horrible (I paraphrase).

'It was more than flesh could stand,' said Toby. 'I baulked.'

'You baulked.'

'It wasn't even the money.'

'No.'

'It was the thought of having to be pleasant to the ridiculous cunt.'

'Absolutely understandable.'

'I was very polite. I said that if it was all the same to her, I'd rather not come. That I found Freddie somewhat tiresome.'

'Fuck. King. Hell. What did she . . . ?'

'She lost it big time. How could I say such a thing? Freddie was priceless. Freddie had been very good to her when she was low. Sometimes she thought Freddie was the only real friend she had. She actually blubbed.'

'Christ.'

'I know. Anyhow, through gritted fucking teeth, I say OK, OK. If it's what you want, I'll come. I'll come for *you*, not for him, and I'll even pretend to enjoy myself and be civil to the ridiculous cunt, although I didn't call him that.'

'No.'

'And that's what happened. *Torture* would be the best way of describing the evening. But I was charm personified. I even shook his sweaty little hand and laughed at his bons mots, such as there were. And then the funny thing. All through this tedious dinner, she was a bit downbeat and thoughtful. But then when we got home, she was all over me, romantically speaking.

And the next morning . . . well, let's just say she was especially grateful.'

'Ah.'

'And then, OK? Here's the killer. Over the boiled egg and toast she said that I was right. That Freddie *was* rather irritating. And when I pushed her – Oh come on, he's far worse than that – she giggled and agreed he was a prat. She said she'd seen him anew through my eyes. And she admired me both for my honesty in telling the truth, as I saw it, and for my strength in enduring what must have been a horrible evening.'

'Blood. Dee. Hell.'

'I know. And ever since . . . well, something's happened. Things are different between us.'

'I can see that.'

'Honesty, mate. It's the best policy.'

'Who would have guessed?'

A huge log fire spits in the grate in Ollie and Nige's gothic dining room. Down the long table, faces flick in and out of the shadows cast by the melting candles. Electric lighting has been eschewed for the occasion, and everyone looks a good deal more glamorous as a result. In keeping with the momentous nature of the evening, Ollie wants each of us in turn to say a few words: specifically about our achievements in the outgoing century, and what we hope to achieve in the incoming one.

There are howls of protest.

'That's silly,' says Nige.

'What if we haven't achieved anything?' choruses Angela.

'All *right*,' says Ollie, a tad irritably. 'Just say *something*. Something about the last century and something about the next.'

'Too vague,' chirps Nige.

'OK. Tell us something – anything – you did in the last century, and something – anything – you'd like to do in the next. I mean, it's not rocket science, honestly.'

There are some facetious replies (one involved certain members of the Queens Park Rangers first team), some quite heartfelt. Ollie says that in the twentieth century he concentrated on material rewards and in the twenty-first he wants to develop his spiritual side. Nige says he would echo Ollie, but would replace spiritual side with chutney-making side. I am feeling faintly paralysed as it gets closer and closer to my turn. Morticia says something interesting about the worth of people and discovering who your true friends are. Angela says something rather foolish about there being a great big wide old world out there and how she wants to be less insular and more global (I interpret this as a desire to go on holiday with Augustin).

'In the last century,' I find myself saying, 'the best thing that happened to me was meeting Ruth.' There are spontaneous outbreaks of *ooh* and *aah*. 'And in the next century my ambition is to see more of Ruth.' Light applause greets the second part of my statement.

Perhaps it's the wine – Ollie has treated us to something rather special from his cellar – but I believe I understand it all too clearly now. Beyond the physical desire, what I like so much about Ruth: it's the fact that we *accept* one another. That we acknowledge we're not perfect – I *know*, it's a shock, just let me run with this here – but there's a tolerance, a recognition, an acceptance of the other. As Rilke put it, we are *two solitudes bordering, protecting and saluting one another*. In the paradigm, we are not the lovers holding hands and staring into each other's eyes (although we have done this). Rather we are the lovers holding hands and staring side by side at the world.

At midnight, we listen to the chimes of Big Ben and toast the hopeful new century. In every direction there are flashes of light behind the clouds, like heavy bombing seen from a distance.

Some time during the next hour, Angela finds me alone.

'That was lovely, that thing you said at dinner,' she says. 'And *so* not like you.'

'I was insane with drink,' I jest.

'I hope you realize what you've landed there, matey.'

They were the same words she'd spoken to me once before. But this time, for some reason, I felt the movement of inner tectonic plates.

On Sunday 2 January, a queasy grey day in London, Ruth and I take a walk on Hampstead Heath. Twice I suggest we stop to sit on a bench and admire the view – and twice I fail to find the right words.

It is only when we return to my flat, and we are on my yellow sofa, my arm round her shoulders and she leaning into me in such a manner that she cannot see my face, that I – deep breath – *just fucking say it, man* – I unbottle the genie.

'There's something I've been meaning to ask you,' I croak.

She twists her head round towards me. One eye peers up curiously. Later she will tell me she can hear my heart hammering in its cavity. I find I have to clear my throat to continue.

'I was wondering if – er – you would like to marry me, at all?'

She cries a little, I think. It is difficult to tell because my own vision has become rather blurry.

A Sunday in August.

I am as nervous as a kitten. Actually, a kitten would appear a model of calm by contrast. A friend tells me later that when she comes up and asks me, 'Can I do anything?' my reply is almost perfectly incoherent.

It's not panic, although since proposing, I have had several 'wobbles' of the *Oh my God, what have I done* variety. But these – although considered normal, I was relieved to read – declined in both power and frequency before disappearing altogether.

So this isn't one of those. This is more the panic the producer of the live show suffers when it's ten minutes to on-air and the star hasn't shown up yet. I know I'm going to feel a lot better about life when Ruth appears.

When I do finally clap eyes on her backstage in all her finery surrounded by her retinue, I find a big lump in my throat.

'You look wonderful,' I croak.

Now, beneath the wooden beams of a house in

Highgate built by Charles II for Nell Gwynn, the bridal party makes its formal entrance. A klezmer group plays medieval music as Ruth and her father advance between the assembled rows of our friends and family, preceded by two small children scattering rose petals. From where I am standing under the wedding canopy with the (young female) rabbi, I feel I am watching something very ancient. In the words of Sylvia Plath – she was talking about losing her virginity, but the words hold good – I feel part of a great tradition. Not a religious or a Jewish tradition, more a *human* tradition. The idea of a man and a woman coming before their loved ones in a public union.

The ceremony that is about to unfold, the rabbi, Ruth and I have negotiated almost line by line. I guess I'm not the first atheist to be married 'in the sight of God' – certainly His name will be coming up at several points in the proceedings – but there are some things I am not prepared to say, particularly the ones in Hebrew. Happily, the rabbi is prepared to make a deal. If I agree to say *this* bit, she'll cut me some slack over *that* bit. From her point of view as a religious officer, the only non-negotiable words in the service she allows me to speak in English.

Various blessings are offered; seven in total, including one which suggests that developing wisdom may make us God-like. (*May*. Love that *may*.) My view is this: it surely doesn't matter whether or not I believe in God. The only thing that really counts is whether He believes in me.

Ruth's uncle reads from Plato, a passage from the

349

Symposium that he has to fight back tears to complete.

> *Once human beings were spherical creatures with two faces, four arms and four legs each. They could walk, like modern humans, or roll themselves along the ground like balls. Some were male, some female, and some were a mixture of male and female.*

(I know this to be true. I have worked at the BBC.)

> *But they became too ambitious and threatened the gods, who decided to weaken them by cutting them in half, making humans as we know them today. All the halves went around searching for each other and clung to their lost half when they found it.*
>
> *It is the same, with humans today: When someone meets their other half they are overwhelmed by the affection, warmth and love they feel. The reason is that we want to become what we were originally: whole beings. The name we give to the desire and pursuit of wholeness is Love. Love guides us towards our other halves and holds out the assurance that he will restore us to our original nature, healed, and blessed with perfect happiness.*

The sight of a man in his seventies so visibly moved by words written around 380 BC is itself powerfully moving.

But there is levity when it comes to the bit where I have to say 'I do.' I think it may have come out a bit too Jewish ('I *do*?') and I am conscious of laughter in a section of the audience where some of my friends are sitting.

Then I stamp on the glass wrapped in the tea towel and we are man and wife. Ruth and I make our way towards a private room within which we must symbolically consummate our union. In the old days, it would have been bad form to emerge without the bloody sheet waved aloft in triumph. Instead we sip champagne from the bottle I have thoughtfully secreted, and when sufficient time has passed, we join our guests in the party zone.

We have planned the reception like an old-fashioned variety bill. Ruth's Aunt Vicki, a former trooper from the Catskills and still a singer of considerable power, has agreed to perform 'a couple of numbers'. In the event, she constructs a mini-musical of the story of our marriage, adapting various compositions to the needs of the narrative. Thus Sondheim's 'Not While I'm Around' from *Sweeney Todd* becomes 'Not While Paul's Around', which is simultaneously absurd, hilarious and touching.

Two old friends, Nicola and Tina, sing their party piece, 'Diamonds Are A Girl's Best Friend'. It is hard to convey just how comic a performance this is, and despite having done it hundreds of times before, they still manage to forget the words halfway through. Or perhaps it's just schtick.

The best man, Martin Kelner, provides the stand-up routine. With permission, I reproduce part of his script:

351

Paul wasn't sure which was the right newspaper for his advert. He thought about the Telegraph, but he didn't really want to meet a retired colonel. He tried Exchange and Mart, and that worked out quite well . . . he picked up a nice Sierra with less than 20,000 miles on the clock. And then he plumped for the Guardian, hoping to meet a pinko softie like himself. Because Paul has always been very much of the soft left, believing in capital punishment only for child murderers and anyone who orders anything in sweet and sour sauce at Mr Kong.

Mr Kong, I should explain for our overseas visitors, is London's finest Chinese restaurant and Paul is very particular about what to order. The reason he won't let us order what we want goes back to the night when we were in there – a whole crowd of us – and we all ordered different things. Well, the waiter did what waiters do when they don't want to mix up the orders: they put down 'blue shirt' – Singapore Noodles; 'blonde girl' – Vegetable Chow Mein, and so on. But this night the waiter came back with his little pad, scratching his head and saying, 'Sorry, who ordered sad bald man?'

He then describes how I met Ruth.

Their first crisis came when they'd been going out about six weeks and Paul confessed to Ruth that he'd lied in his advert.

What on earth could he have lied about, thought Ruth? 'What? He's not Jewish? He's not intellectual?'

Turns out he's knocked two years off his age. Well,
their relationship survived that little lie . . . and again
two weeks later when he confessed he'd also been lying
when he said he had a full head of hair.

Later, Martin reminds me how he met his own wife.
He was working as a DJ on a Leeds radio station at the
time. One night, at a promotion the radio station had
organized in a city nightclub, a woman breaks into
conversation with him.

'Are you on the radio, then?' she asks.

'Yes. I am, actually,' he replies.

There is the deadliest of pauses. 'Well, I can see why
you're not on the telly.'

Martin and Janet now have four children.

As Ruth and her dance partner Juliana shimmer and
sway to a piece of music that speaks strongly of
minarets and souks, again I am struck by how reassur-
ingly *odd* all this is; a strangeness that contains the
peculiar quality of family life. Perhaps it's something to
do with my own family; with my parents, who were
born in Poland and who transplanted themselves to the
UK after the war. Their own new life in a foreign
country must have felt pretty strange to them – it
certainly felt strange to me by the time I was old
enough to understand what had happened to them.

At some point I make a short, mostly serious, speech
containing the usual thank-yous. My only joke is a reference to the rabbi, who, I note for the benefit of those who
are interested in these things, cost less than the cake.

We segue into the disco-inferno portion of the

evening. Barry from Young's Mobile Discotheques and Equipment Hire has been supplied with a list of favoured tracks which we believe will fill the dance floor. Toby and Morticia chuck themselves around gratifyingly to 'Love Shack' by the B52s (one of mine); Angela and Augustin are seen getting into 'Dimelo' by Marc Antony (one of Ruth's).

'Fucking *great* wedding,' roars Toby. Morticia, lurching out of her heels, clamps on to his arm with both hands and smiles in an unfocused sort of fashion (she's pissed as a rattlesnake).

'I'm glad you could come,' I roar back.

'We bought you a bowl,' yells Toby. 'You can never have too many bowls,' he insists. 'They're useful for putting things in.'

'Thanks. I'll try to remember that.'

Ruth and I dance the slow one at the end, 'Perfect Day' by Lou Reed; corny, but look at it this way: it could have been 'Lady in Red'.

'So do you like being Mrs Reizin, then?' I inquire.

'Is it too late to change my mind?'

I am conscious of the photographer using up the rest of her film on us as I struggle not to topple on to my new bride.

'How do you think it went?' I mumble.

'Brilliantly.'

'What was your favourite bit?'

She thinks about it for a moment. 'This bit.'

'Who was that bloke with the grey hair? Who was groping your friend from Italy. Toby said he was coked off his head.'

'She got talking to him on the plane. She's always meeting men like that.'

We fall silent and twirl with the other twirling couples for a while.

'I love this,' I say eventually. 'I love *you*.'

She squeezes me back, by way of a reply.

'Toby says he and Morticia have bought us a bowl. He says you can never have too many bowls. They're useful for putting things in, apparently.'

But it turns out Toby is wrong about the bowls thing. When Ruth and I finally get home – exhausted, exhilarated – and open our presents, it appears we have been given no fewer than eleven bowls.

In the days that follow, when I am asked, 'So, what's it like being married, then?' I inevitably reply, 'Oh, very much like it was before; only with more bowls.'

Epilogue

IT'S NUTS.

Nuts how chancy it all was.

If my advert hadn't run that Saturday. If she hadn't bought the *Guardian* that Saturday. And then all the bigger and wider ifs leading up to those specific ifs. If my last relationship hadn't ended when it did but had lasted another month, say. Or if I'd continued working at the BBC and, instead of searching for love, had thrown myself into my next factual-entertainment project (no, please).

And then if one attempts to factor-in all *her* ifs?

We could so easily have missed each other.

In a parallel universe, this may be what happened. In a parallel universe, Ruth is going out with **Sincere Doctor**, or possibly **Caring and Romantic**. Given an infinite number of parallel universes, logic demands there must even be one in which she's with **Bored in Peterborough**.

In one of those universes, one in which there is no floppy-haired Logan to obsess and frustrate her, perhaps I am with dreamy (and suddenly available) Julia. Or Alice, the angry comedian, who, in another universe – where there is no Ray to steal her albums, flood her bathroom and shag her best mate – isn't quite so annoyed about everything. Or with Miriam, the Easter Island Statue who became impossibly exotic after four vodka Martinis. Or Gemma, the scary nurse. Or Diana, who I might have ended up going out with in *this* universe, if I hadn't met Ruth.

Perhaps this is an interesting way to consider these failed encounters: that in alternative worlds, there are versions where they succeed. This, by the way, isn't an entirely fanciful notion. Scientists speculate about the so-called *dark matter* in the cosmos, the invisible substance whose gravity is so important in keeping the galaxies from flying apart. Some believe the matter may actually be located in parallel universes less than a millimetre away from our own in a different dimension. Because we are only attuned to our three dimensions of space and one of time, runs the argument, we cannot see these other worlds, but we can feel their gravity because they are so close by. I must confront the possibility that in one of these universes, things may have taken an altogether different turn in a café in Peckham . . .

Oddly enough, one evening a few weeks after we are married, there is a message on the answerphone when Ruth and I return from dinner at Mr Kong. The voice is enough to chill my blood.

'Look. This is Annie. OK. Well. How to explain this? There are some poems of mine that have gone missing that I'm trying to locate and. OK. Well. I'm

357

kind of going through some old numbers that I've come across. (Long pause) No, that didn't really sound like you, at all. OK. Well. Thanks anyway.'

'Don't even ask,' I reply to Ruth's quizzical gaze.

Another evening, around nine months later, we make a tape. The contractions are coming a little more powerfully and frequently now, but it's still not obvious that this is the moment to break out for the Royal Free.

So I make a tape. As Ruth paces round the sitting room, breathing and exhaling deeply, I am dubbing on to a cassette all the suitably relaxing material I can find in our joint CD collection. Mahler's more sublime adagios. Some Mozart. Even a little moody Wagner in there as well. Fine music to come into the world to, I'm thinking.

But four days later, we are still waiting. Even dripped full of the chemicals that induce the process, insufficient progress is being made. My right foot is a slave to the rhythm of the foetal-heart monitor.

Bo-boom, bo-boom, bo-boom, bo-boom, bo-boom, bo-boom . . .

The doctor – impossibly young, reeking of fag smoke – shines a bright light and delicately takes a scratch of blood from the baby's head to analyse for distress.

'I'll tell you one thing,' he says cheerfully. 'She won't have red hair.'

The baby is fine in there, but it's agreed the mother has had enough. Within minutes we are in an operating theatre. Someone switches on Capital Gold – I have completely forgotten about the birthing tape – and what happens next happens so casually, so breezily, that it's clear that pop music is what you need here, not some endlessly uncoiling third movement. Indeed Barry White has only just begun to self-diagnose his trouble (he ain't nothing without his baby, apparently) when he starts competing with what sounds very like a hairdryer. And then crying; big lusty wails from the other side of the green screen that separates Ruth's head – and all of me – from the action.

A midwife-style person raises her face over the top. 'You can come and see, if you like.'

Carefully avoiding catching sight of what is happening to Ruth, I am led to a clear plastic tank where a bawling female infant – that's what it says on the tag round her ankle, like a cigar label, *female infant* – is being generally smartened up for life on earth.

Spared the rigours of passage through the birth canal, she is perfect.

The midwife wraps her and carries her back to be introduced to Ruth; anaesthetized to the elbows, she is now the only member of the immediate family not to be blubbing freely. Somehow I manage to take a picture.

Only later do we realize that the doctor was wrong. Perhaps he had been working for ninety-six hours without a break and was out of his mind with fatigue; perhaps these things look different in artificial light. Perhaps it was a slip of the tongue.

But she *does* have red hair.

It is – was – my red hair and now it's hers.

It is wonderful to see it again

Afterword

THIS IS A TRUE STORY. However, aside from a specific individual who features in the final chapters, I have gone to great lengths to protect the identities of the women mentioned in these pages. They never expected – and I never imagined – that one day we would end up in print together. Therefore, names have been changed, physical characteristics altered, locations mucked about with, radical career makeovers engineered. No one should recognize herself or anyone else in this account. If they believe they do, they are mistaken.

Cracking the Lonely Hearts Code:
A Complete A-Z Guide

A is for **Attractive**. A key female buzzword. As a woman, you are either attractive (or even beautiful) or you are caring, creative, loving, warm, tactile, self-aware, or multi-faceted. Many men won't answer ads that don't specify the a-word, leading to widespread overuse. The most powerful buzzword employed by male advertisers is **Professional**. This can mean anything from chief executive of a FTSE company to pizza delivery operative. *Never* admit you're jobless. You're either 'juggling' or 'between contracts' or 'weighing various options.'

B is for **Bubbly**. The Footballers Wives of adjectives. Loud, big hair, drinks too much. Men are never 'bubbly'; the closest would be arsehole.

C is for **Caring**. At best, has teddies on the pillow; draws smileys in her lower loops. At worst, the Kathy Bates character in *Misery*. This advertiser will not be impressed by cheesy chat-up lines. Under no circumstances lick your finger, dab it on her sleeve, then your own sleeve, then suggest, 'Why don't we slip out of these wet clothes into something more comfortable.'

D is for **Down to earth**. Lively. Life and soul of the party type. After eight pints of snakebite, has been known to light his/her own farts. D is also for **discreet**. Think: married.

E is for **Eating out/Eating in**. Displays either a well-balanced approach to life or a crushing conventionality. You decide. Warning: in a romantic situation, food can be a minefield. Spaghetti may splatter your shirt. Anything involving chopsticks and baby button mushrooms is inviting derision. Do not be tempted to attack a tower of seafood with metal implements; the crab claw will either fail to crack (wimp) or explode (idiot). Stick to fishcakes.

F is for **Feisty**. We're talking bubbly with attitude. Only women are 'feisty'. A feisty male would be called a prick. On a date, this advertiser may well turn up late without an apology. A fashionable ten to fifteen minutes late is acceptable. After more than an hour, the law says she must offer to sleep with you by way of reparation.

G is for **GSOH**. Good sense of humour. Funny, you never see BSOH, do you? But why single out humour? Why not GSOD (direction)? Or GSOB (balance). Both are important in relationships. Advice: never express your GSOH through your choice of wardrobe. Leave the Pocahontas tie on the rail.

H is for **Home-loving**. Obliged to wear an electronic tag.

I is for **Interesting**. Usually claimed by male advertisers. Liable to tell you, apropos of nothing, that humans share 35% of their genetic material with the daffodil.

Or that scientists reckon there could be parallel universes less than half an inch away from our own, but in another dimension. Better than being 'interesting' is to ask questions. It's flattering. Inquire about her job, her hobbies, where she grew up (never about who won the FA Cup in 1958 or what colour her underwear is).

J is for **Jazz**. Only men cite Jazz as an interest. Just as only women mention dance. Both are wasted words; women are indifferent to jazz and men dislike dancing unless they are pissed or gay.

K is for **Knight**. As in shining armour. The metal-clad swordsman still has a mythical appeal for women, even if he turns out to be a balding cost-controller from Esher. On a first date, men should transmit an impression of masculine inner fortitude even if the biggest dragon faced all day was the photocopier.

L is for **Log Fires**. Frequently mentioned in connection with good food, red wine, and sometimes Coldplay. The subliminal image is of abandoned lovemaking before the naked flames. Sex of course is what this whole exercise is leading towards. If at any point she angles her knees towards you, plays with her hair or touches your arm, the chances look good. (This is only what I read in a newspaper once, so don't sue me if it all goes wrong, okay?)

M is for extended **Metaphors**. You know the sort of thing: Vintage gent seeks considerate lady driver. Must have nice upholstery and good bodywork. This is tedious and open to satire (e.g. is his big end gone?). M is also for **Movies**, the single best topic to test compatibility around. If her favourite is *L'Annee Derniere a Marienbad* and yours is *Porkies Two*, you might want to cancel that second drink.

N is for **Not unattractive**. False modesty? Or low self-esteem? Their voice message may yield clues. Top tip for recording your own message: listen to the competition. Don't they sound like a bunch of losers? Be upbeat and conversational. Never say, 'Hi girls.' Or '*Hello*' like Leslie Phillips. The key is sincerity. If you can fake that, you've cracked it.

O is for **Optimistic**. Sad. Disappointed. Possibly borderline-tragic. Will have a catalogue of broken romances. Important: never discuss former lovers. Don't talk about yours; don't ask her about hers. If it all comes out anyway, try not to laugh at the bit where he floods the bathroom and shags her best friend.

P is for **Personal growth**. May mean a quest for spiritual enlightenment; or the advertiser has put on six pounds over Christmas.

Q is for **quirky**. Annoying personality. Again this is a female-specific term. The nearest male equivalent is wanker.

R is for **Red wine**. Often associated with log fires and

candlelit dinners. Oddly, no-one ever mentions white wine. The only beverage cited as frequently is real ale.

S is for **Soul mate**. Someone who doesn't irritate the tits off you. S is also for **sensitive**. May be as nervous as a kitten on a first date, so you may need to remind them that the first time for anything's a little ticklish. Like the first day at school, or the first time the doctor slips on the rubber glove and says, 'Relax.'

T is for **Theatre**. Once received a free ticket for *Jailhouse Rock*.

U is for **Up for a laugh**. Will howl uproariously at your terrible jokes. But caution: women generally don't really like jokes. They prefer joined-up conversation. Only tell jokes if absolutely desperate (and never the one about the couple playing golf for fifty pounds a hole)

V is for **Vibrant**. Only the elderly describe themselves in this way. Rough translation: still breathing.

W is for Country **Walks**. Implies fit and healthy lifestyle; means they recently crossed Shepherds Bush Green to visit the off-licence.

X is for **Ex**. Ex-pole dancer. Ex-city trader. Defining oneself in terms of one's past. Think: unemployed.

Y is for **Young**. As in young 60. Or 72-years-young. As

in old. Age is another lonely hearts minefield and many – okay, most – lie about it. However lying is an art. Yes, by all means say you're 42 if you're really 44. But don't claim you're 6'2 if you're only 5'6. There's a chance you could get found out.

Z is for **Zany**. Engagingly madcap or carpet-chewing bonkers. A sneaky glimpse inside her handbag can determine which. Bad signs include: uncapped biros, grape stalks, shrunken human heads.

A SELECTED LIST OF NON-FICTION TITLES AVAILABLE FROM TRANSWORLD PUBLISHERS

81523 7	THE MAN WHO MARRIED A MOUNTAIN	*Rosemary Bailey*	£7.99
81442 7	A POUND A PAPER	*John Baxter*	£7.99
99600 9	NOTES FROM A SMALL ISLAND	*Bill Bryson*	£8.99
77160 0	PECKED TO DEATH BY DUCKS	*Tim Cahill*	£7.99
77296 8	A YEAR IN THE MERDE	*Stephen Clarke*	£6.99
15077 0	THE 8.55 TO BAGHDAD	*Andrew Eames*	£7.99
15146 7	HOTEL BABYLON	*Anonymous and Imogen Edwards-Jones*	£7.99
81557 1	KIWIS MIGHT FLY	*Polly Evans*	£6.99
81479 6	FRENCH SPIRITS	*Jeffrey Greene*	£6.99
81725 6	LOST IN TRANSMISSION	*Jonathan Harley*	£7.99
14595 5	BETWEEN EXTREMES	*Brian Keenan and John McCarthy*	£7.99
81620 9	TWO STEPS BACKWARDS	*Susie Kelly*	£7.99
81601 2	HOLY COW!	*Sarah Macdonald*	£7.99
50667 6	UNDER THE TUSCAN SUN	*Frances Mayes*	£6.99
81655 1	THE FUNNY FARM	*Jackie Moffat*	£7.99
81637 3	VROOM WITH A VIEW	*Peter Moore*	£7.99
81460 5	THE WAR AND UNCLE WALTER	*Walter Musto*	£7.99
81635 7	MONSOON DIARY	*Shoba Narayan*	£7.99
81448 6	TAKE ME WITH YOU	*Brad Newsham*	£6.99
81551 2	THE BIG YEAR	*Mark Obmascik*	£6.99
81550 4	FOUR CORNERS	*Kira Salak*	£6.99
81566 0	FROM HERE, YOU CAN'T SEE PARIS	*Michael Sanders*	£7.99
81528 8	NOBODY IN PARTICULAR	*Cherry Simmonds*	£6.99
81656 X	EDUCATING ALICE	*Alice Steinbach*	£7.99
81668 3	THE BONE MAN OF BENARES	*Terry Tarnoff*	£6.99
81532 6	CUBA DIARIES	*Isadora Tattlin*	£6.99
81476 1	HALFWAY HOME	*Ronan Tynan*	£6.99
81555 5	AN EMBARRASSMENT OF MANGOES	*Ann Vanderhoof*	£7.99